The Bible

in Cross-Cultural Perspective

BY THE SAME AUTHOR

The Bible

in Cross-Cultural Perspective

Jacob A. Loewen

William Carey Library
Pasadena, California

The Bible in Cross-Cultural Perspective

Cover design by Kathleen G. Walker

Published by
William Carey Library
P.O. Box 40129
Pasadena, California 91114
(626) 798-0819
E-mail: orders@wclbooks.com

Printed in the United States of America

Library of Congress Cataloging-in-Publication Data

Loewen, Jacob A. (Jacob Abram). 1922-
  The Bible in cross-cultural perspective
Jacob A. Loewen

    p. cm.

  Includes bibliographical references and index.
  ISBN 0-87808-266-2

  1. Bible—Hermeneutics—Cross-cultural studies. 2. Ethnology in the Bible.
  3. Christianity and culture. 4. Christianity and other religions. 5. Ethnology—
  Religious aspects—Christianity. 6. Missions—Theory. 7. Loewen, Jacob A.
  (Jacob Abram). 1922-   I. Title.
BS476.L62 1996
220.6'7—dc20   96-3432

*This book is dedicated to the memory of those faithful
indigenous translators, speaking many of the languages of
the world, in whose work I was privileged to participate.
They were patient in teaching me about their ways of
looking at the world and opened my eyes to many of the
worldview issues in the Bible. I am deeply indebted to them.*

Contents

Part V. Some Implications of Cross-Cultural Perspective

Appendixes

Bibliography

Indexes

Biography of Author

Figures and Tables

Figures

Tables

Publisher's Foreword

It is both a blessing and an astonishment to note how many fields of study Dr. Loewen has been able to draw together for the benefit of the reader of this book.

Many scholars have known Loewen and valued his writings. Several have read this work in manuscript. Indeed, hardly any mission scholar has had as large or avid a following over the years as Jacob Loewen. His articles in *Practical Anthropology* during the two decades of its publication (up until 1972) provided for thousands of readers all over the world a continuing sparkle and insight that readily eclipses the work of any other contributor.

This book, he feels, is his final book. It brings together a radical bouquet of meaningful, even electrifying thoughts. With time running out, Dr. Loewen has simply been unable to refine certain dimensions. He is the first to recognize the value there would be in pursuing further, for example, the virtual explosion of biblical scholarship in recent years bearing on some of its themes.

Publishers usually take lots of time to work with creative minds to enable what might in some ways be a more polished product. But on other occasions it is understandable that those lengthy processes must be laid aside. It is some comfort to know that Jacob Loewen has many followers who will be nourished and blessed by his final testimony and will try to carry forward the remarkable ministry his life has generously provided. We publish, confident that his friends and younger followers will be able to make their own contributions which, along with his, will give an even richer picture.

At the same time, as he has done, we wish here to note the selfless endeavors of that other person without whom this book could not have appeared at all—William A. Smalley. That is another story. He has already gone on. His unexpected death prevented his final assistance in this book, but did not damage the many helpful contributions he had already made. Bill, we salute you! Jake, we are deeply indebted to you! Standing behind both of these men in many ways, of course, is Eugene A. Nida, whose coworkers and followers both of them were for many years. He can be especially proud of their major contributions.

Ralph D. Winter
Pasadena, California
November 3, 1999

Foreword

On June 4, 1993, Jacob A. Loewen was incapacitated by a severe stroke. After months of hospitalization and therapy, and with a medical prognosis estimating three more years of sufficient mental capacity, he returned to the three partially-finished books which he felt God wanted him to complete while he was able. One of the three dealt with his growing awareness of and extensive research on worldview issues related to the Bible in cross-cultural perspective.

But as Loewen turned back to the lectures, the research notes, the draft papers on various topics which composed the substance of his many years of work in this area, he realized that he no longer had the physical capacity to do the weeding, consolidating, integrating, editing, and polishing which would be required. He had no use of his writing hand, and had been otherwise weakened. But he could still participate; he could read, could react to what someone else did, and could dictate tapes which his secretary would keyboard into the computer. In addition to sensing his physical limitations, he knew he could not finish all three books if he spent too much time on any one. So he offered me the opportunity to help.

I have had contact with Jake Loewen since 1961, when he submitted his first article to the little journal *Practical Anthropology*, which I was then editing, primarily for missionaries. By 1964 his articles were flooding in, and for six years his prolific writing became the backbone of the periodical. These writings based on field experience showed unusual insight both into culture and into its implications for the missionary task. And they were fun to read, because they were usually triggered by a challenging, often humorous, event or startling encounter with another culture, from which he drew fascinating conclusions. After *Practical Anthropology* was merged with *Missiology: An International Review*, I collected most of these articles for publication in a single volume (Loewen 1975).

In time, we knew each other in other ways, also, because we were both translation consultants, first for the American Bible Society and then under the United Bible Societies. We met occasionally at various translation staff consultations, but did not see each other often as we worked in different parts of the world.

In considering Jake's request for help, I read through the various materials which he supplied and immediately realized that the substance and insight revealed there must be published. So we worked together, he in British

xiii

Columbia and I in Connecticut. I made thousands of suggestions; he accepted most of them. When he disagreed we did it his way, of course. He wrote more chapters and filled in other lacunae at my suggestion. I tried to integrate everything, seeking coherence and providing transitions.

The cross-cultural perspectives of this work form two dimensions. On the "horizontal," or synchronic dimension, people of different contemporary cultures see the same biblical events in contrasting or complementary ways. And contemporary cultures different from our own sometimes throw light on biblical events and concepts, of which our knowledge is constricted by assumptions arising from the Western and classical cultures of which we do know something.

On the "vertical," or diachronic dimension, the very time depth within the Bible itself involves contrasting cultures. The culture of Solomon's kingdom was significantly different from that of the early Canaanite period, which was not the same as the desert culture. People of such varying cultures sometimes saw God differently, saw themselves differently, saw covenant differently. So as we in our time and our location look at the Bible, we see a set of writings which themselves are a panorama of cross-cultural viewpoints, both horizontal and vertical.

Some of Loewen's chapters are largely horizontal in perspective, others vertical. The selection of topics is necessarily limited, but rises out of Loewen's own experience as a missionary, a translator, a translation consultant, and a Christian no longer fully at home in his own national and denominational cultures. The result is intensely personal in its expression but also powerfully general in its implications. It is a refreshing, illuminating look into a vast area where our worldview blinders are constricting, and where our gift of sight is selective.

The Bible in Cross-Cultural Perspective is fascinating, provocative, and challenging, but may also be disturbing. However, I suggest that Loewen's data, ideas, and insights rate thoughtful and prayerful reading. There is a fresh wind blowing through these pages.

William A. Smalley
Formerly Regional Translations Coordinator
Asia-Pacific Region, United Bible Societies
Former Professor of Linguistics, Bethel College (MN)

Acknowledgments

I want to thank ...

... Ralph Winter for the immediate inspiration behind this book. Ralph asked a question: "How much anthropology does a person have to know to read the Bible intelligently?" I responded, "I don't think a person needs to know any anthropology, but the reader does need to be aware of culture." Ralph then asked me to write down some of my thoughts so that he could read and digest them. I started writing, and before I knew it I had written 150 pages of material which led to this book.

... William Smalley for his patient editing of the material. Bill gave months of his time to form it into intelligible, readable shape. The process has been a great learning experience for me.

... Carole Springthorpe, my secretary, who has been with me since I retired in 1984. She has patiently typed and corrected these chapters many times, even when they sometimes ran counter to her own beliefs. Her dedication and faithfulness have kept me productive even after I suffered a stroke.

Part I

The Bible
in Cross-Cultural Perspective

Introduction

This book is about discovering more of the message of the Bible than we see through the eyes of our own culture. Africans, for example, have great interest in the genealogies of the Bible, and find them significant. I first noticed this when I observed committees of African translators working on the Gospel According to Matthew, with its genealogy of Jesus' ancestry. Matthew lists fourteen generations from Abraham to David, another fourteen from David to the exile in Babylon, and a final fourteen to the birth of Jesus (Mt[1] 1:1–17).

When one group of African translators read the three sets of fourteen generations listed there, they held a long discussion, speculating about why the people in the Bible remembered only fourteen generations, when African people like themselves remembered sixteen. Did that imply inferior memories, or what?

I was intrigued because for me biblical genealogies were totally uninteresting and of no significance. "What do you do when you reach the seventeenth generation?" I asked.

"Oh," they said, "we consider sixteen to be the maximum that a non-literate person can remember, so when the seventeenth king dies, the elders of the tribe review the sixteen. If one of them is not considered important, but the king who has just died accomplished a great deal, they eliminate the unimportant one from the genealogy and add the deceased king. If the recent king is not very important, they don't count him."

A short time later, in a closely related language, I watched how carefully the translators went through the births and deaths in Genesis. When they got to chapters four and five, they suddenly stopped and had a lengthy discussion about the genealogies there (Table 1).

They recognized immediately that the two seemingly different genealogies listed the same people.

---

[1]Abbreviations and acronyms are explained in Appendix A.

3

TABLE 1

GENEALOGIES IN GENESIS 4 AND 5

GENESIS 4:17-25	GENESIS 5:3-29
Adam	Adam
Cain (Kain)	
Seth	Seth
Enoch	Enosh
Irad	Kenan (Cainan)
Mehujael	Mahalalel
	Jared
	Enoch
Methuselah	Methushael
Lamech	Lamech
	Noah

Cain/Kain occurs in both lists (in the form of Kenan/Cainan in the second).[2] Enoch/Enosh appear as grandchildren of Adam in each of the lists. Enoch, however, also appears in the seventh place in the second list. Mahalalel corresponds with Mehujael, Methuselah with Methushael, and Jared with Irad. When I pointed out to the Africans how important position seven was in Israel, they decided that Enoch must have been a very important person indeed to occur in the same genealogy two times and especially to occupy position seven.

When the Africans asked me the significance of these two lists, I had no idea what to say. It was the first time I realized that the same genealogy came in two partially different orders, and sometimes with slightly divergent spellings.

The Africans then enlightened me. "This is a very common occurrence in our societies," they said. "When a tribe gets big, it develops sub-tribes and these sub-tribes often do not have the same loyalties. Very often one part of the tribe will remember someone as worthwhile, while the other sub-tribe considers that same person unimportant. As a result, differences in the genealogies develop."

---

[2]Kain and Kenan are closer transliterations of the Hebrew than Cain (the traditional English spelling) and Cainan (the spelling in the King James Version).

They also said that sometimes an exceedingly important person is moved into a position of greater importance, just as had happened in chapter 5, with Enoch in position seven. Again, when a person had done some nasty things, but was still worth keeping in the list, he was sometimes made grandson rather than remaining as the grandfather, as in the case of Cain/Cainan in chapter 5.

1

Cross-Cultural Perspective

Normally we look at the cultures of the Bible through the lens of our own culture, modified to some degree by our education, which introduces a minimal amount of cross-cultural information. We read, for example, that the patriarchs lived in tents, but how we imagine those tents depends on many factors, including Sunday school pictures. If we have no other information, we are likely to think of them as being like the ones we see in any modern campground.

Some of the peoples through whose eyes we look at the Bible have cultures more similar to those of the Bible than our own are. They can therefore sometimes understand aspects of biblical cultures more clearly than we do. Likewise, we can look at various major cultures of the Bible through the eyes of people of other cultures within the Bible, and thus examine the similarities and differences in the worldviews of the people of God. We can try to understand the variation in their perception of God and of their relationship to God.

Culture enables us to know how to live. Human beings do not have proportionately as many of the instincts which enable animals to do what is necessary for survival, but must learn most of the processes through a long childhood and adolescence. In fact, we never stop learning. By observation, mimicry, experimentation, education, and other forms of learning, adults are able to live much as the people around them in their own society. Our culture shapes how we think, reason, evaluate, and behave. It provides us with our religion and much of our sense of right and wrong.

In a complex society like ours, of course, culture is not uniform but has many variations, many subcultures. Yet underlying similarities also exist among them. North American culture in general differs from Chinese culture in spite of wide variations within each.

One important function of the culture we learn is to provide us with a feeling of belonging, comfort, and security. We are used to it, normally feel at home in it, depend on it to guide our thinking and behavior. This "at home" feeling, the feeling that our culture is "right," persists even when we meet people of another culture and observe what they do. Where they differ from us, we often feel that their behavior is incongruous or even wrong. The at-home feeling also often makes us inclined to resist change.

When we were missionaries in Noanama, Colombia, my wife Anne got out our wedding picture one day and displayed it. The young woman who had already been working in our home for several years was shaken when she saw it. She said, "But you can't be married!" When Anne insisted that we were, Delia continued, "But married people fight! Husbands beat their wives, but you and your husband don't fight. I have never seen him strike you!"

In this village of forty couples, none were legally married to their partners. The people informed us quite confidently that common law was the only way to live because it assured that partners maintained mutual respect. "Once married," they said, "the husband always assumes that he is the absolute boss. Then the union is no longer peaceful or violence-free." The Noanama people did not feel comfortable with our way, nor we with theirs.

On my first trip to British Guiana, now Guyana, I arrived at the airport in Georgetown close to midnight and took a taxi. En route to the hotel I "died many deaths" as the taxi sped along the left side of the road, passing oncoming traffic on its right. Later, when I was stationed in East Africa, I myself drove on the left side of the road for almost a decade, but I still had to be careful on country roads, especially at night, when I would unthinkingly drift to the right. In ten years of driving on the left, I was never able to become fully at home with it.

But culture does change, and our feeling of what is right may also change. When I was growing up in a Mennonite community, men habitually shared a kiss of brotherhood with each other when they met, especially after an absence, or at a religious service. When I returned home on retirement, however, there were no more brotherly kisses. Even the Latin American bear hug between men was almost frowned upon. The handshake was now the standard form of greeting between men.

One area in which exposure to another culture has changed my sense of right and wrong is my attitude toward giving and receiving something with my left hand. After living in cultures where the left hand is considered unclean and where to give or to receive something with the left hand is insulting, I have come to feel an inward repulsion about receiving or giving anything with that hand. My recent stroke, which wiped out the use of my right hand, has seriously complicated this matter for me. My left hand is now my only functional one, leaving me with inward withdrawal from giving or receiving.

Much culture change results from culture contact, when people from different cultures interact with each other. Much of that change is superficial, like learning to drive on the "wrong" side of the road. The world of urban young people mimics the clothing and mannerisms of an entertainment star. Television antennas rise above the roofs of remote villages. Thai restaurants proliferate in North American cities.

In cases like these, culture changes by outright borrowing, but usually the process of really significant change is more subtle. When people from one culture get to understand another culture's view, they may subtly begin to modify their previous views, especially in those aspects of the new culture that make good sense within their own culture.

And sometimes culture change is radical and profound. Eastern block countries have taken steps toward more democratic government and Western-style capitalism. South Africa voted down apartheid. A village of people in Central America is converted to a new relationship with God.

My Culture History

This book reflects my experience, and as a whole this study is the testimony to people of my own culture, of my faith in God's word, so I need to describe how my cross-cultural perspective was formed. I have lived among people of many cultures, sometimes having been forced to do so, sometimes willingly.

Russian Mennonite Cultural Experience

I was born in 1922, in Russia, when that country was already in the throes of the Bolshevik revolution after World War I. My family lived in an isolated and relatively closed German Mennonite colony near the Ural Mountains. Up to then, the colony had enjoyed its own local government and its own German schools; it had taken care of all its own affairs. But now everything was in flux. A succession of revolutionary governments was turning everything upside down. The latest crisis had even put an atheist teacher, teaching in Russian, into the local Mennonite school. That was the last straw for my mother and my stepfather, so they kept me out of school and began preparing to leave Russia.

I never knew my real father, Jacob Isaak. He had returned from alternative service at the end of the war and had married my mother, but by the time I was born, he was seriously ill, probably of typhoid fever. He died before I reached my third month.

I was born allergic to milk, even mother's milk, and almost immediately became eczematous. Untreated, I became an oozing mass of seeping ulcerations. My mother speaks of picking me up and pulling off part of my scalp where my hair had dried to the bedding.

The pious neighbors began praying for my demise, kindly asking God to relieve this poor widow of her hopeless, festering burden. Such prayers were daggers in my young mother's heart, as the baby was all she had. In desperation, one night she threw herself across my wooden cradle and harangued her Maker in prayer, "Lord, if you cannot heal him, then take him right now. But if you can heal him, I will take care of him as long as you see fit to afflict him. I dedicate him to your service." The knowledge that this event took place lies deep in my psyche, helping form my own personal culture, even though it occurred when I was so young that I cannot remember it.

When my family arrived in Moscow, the city was clogged with some 25,000 Mennonite refugees desperately wanting to leave the country, although the government wasn't issuing exit permits. The German government finally extracted a promise from the Russians that any German-speaking person who would be in Moscow on November 25, 1929, would be given an exit permit. So the Russians systematically filled up trains of cattle cars with Mennonites and shipped them to concentration camps far from Moscow, in the Siberian Arctic.

In Moscow, the home in which my family found lodging had eight rooms. A Russian caretaker lived in one, a Mennonite family in each of the others. Each family had to pay rent for the whole house, and do so for six months in advance. During the five months that my family was there, the secret police visited nearly every night, rounding up Mennonites to send to a concentration camp. The owner of the house must have been adept at bribery, as any family which had enough money to pay the exorbitant rent was not taken. When money ran out, the family was picked up by the police.

I still remember those terror-filled moments, night after night, when the secret police came, gun butts banging on the door or on the floor, angry stentorian commands, mothers rousing the children to kneel and cry to God for deliverance, while fathers presented our papers to the police. The fear of armed men has never fully left me.

Finally, only the six families remaining in our house were still left in our whole area. On November 25, 1929, we were still in Moscow, together with some 1,500 other Mennonites who had escaped the forced exodus. We received the promised permission to emigrate to Canada.

Subsequent Cultural Experience

The religious climate in which I grew up was highly evangelical, fervently revivalistic and tending towards fundamentalism. Even in Canada, the communities in which I lived were solidly Mennonite. The pressures of church and community for conformity to the accepted religious mores were strong. I grew up in a church in which conversion was defined as the once-and-for-all transaction that transformed sinners into children of God. A favorite sermon text was, "Therefore if any man *be* in Christ, *he* is a new creature: old things are passed away; behold all things are become new" (2 Cor 5:17 KJV). I underwent a crisis conversion at ten years of age, and spent the succeeding years in intense inner conflict over the difference between the actuality of my experience and the ideal proclaimed from the pulpit.

The church ordained me as a minister in 1943, after I began preparing for missionary service. I was considered too young to preach on Sunday mornings, so was restricted to evenings. Even so, time and again on Monday morning the church elders would inform me that what I had said might well be true, but that I was too young to say it.

However, in spite of the strength of this core Mennonite culture, when World War II began in 1939, the closed community was torn wide open by high-paying jobs in urban centers, and intense tensions began to develop within it. Soon beckoning economic opportunities caused many traditional Mennonite values to wither. Piety and thrift were replaced by education, accumulation of wealth, and conspicuous consumption. Our minority culture was changing in various parts and to varying degrees toward the dominant culture.

My missionary preparation involved five winters of Bible school, one year at a missionary medical school, two summers at the Summer Institute of Linguistics, and a four-year college degree, in that order. My wife Anne and I were then sent to Colombia, to the Waunana Indians, to develop a writing system for their language and to translate the Scriptures into it. I arrived convinced that I knew the truth, the whole truth, and nothing but the truth, but quickly became aware that the truth is not easy to communicate cross-culturally.

The most common complaint I heard from the Waunana was that they were suffering from fever spirits, an illness which I was usually able to diagnose as malaria. So I enlightened them with the true cause of their illness, showing them what malarial parasites looked like through a microscope.

When the Waunana saw the blue-stained parasites on a glass slide, they were amazed. "We always knew that fever spirits had blue noses," they said, "but we didn't know that they were all blue and that they were so small." I was ready to tear out my hair because instead of communicating the "truth" to them, I was reinforcing their "error."

Later, after the Choco church[1] was organized in Panama, the church leader's wife became ill with pneumonia at a time when no sulfa drugs or antibiotics were available. The Christian people prayed for her and she was fully healed. But they did not invite me into the circle because they realized that my culture, with its emphasis on the material, was preventing me from removing evil spirits literally (chap. 5). I vowed then and there to get adequate cultural preparations. I wanted to be a good missionary. I would study anthropology.

When I was accepted by the University of Washington, I was overjoyed. However, that enthusiasm was dampened somewhat when the head of the department informed me, "We accepted you because we have never had a missionary in the department, and we want to see how good a department we are. If we are as good as we think, we should be able to get rid of your faith in one year."

At the university I was never tempted to ditch my faith, but I struggled over choosing between a church whose truth was canned and not growing, and a university in which people were constantly discovering new truth. The analogy that gave me hope in my dilemma was the piano keyboard. I saw one church was playing high C, and the other middle C, and a third low C. They all felt they had found the perfect note, but there was a whole keyboard there to be used, even some black keys. I became determined to be open to the full range of God's truth, which meant, of course, that I had to be ready and willing to examine everything, including every sacred cow.

After I received my Ph.D., I could not get another mission assignment so I taught at a Mennonite church college for several years. There I encountered the awful distress under which many Christian young people lived, having grown up with a revivalistic philosophy and early conversion in Sunday school, but now doubting the reality of their childhood experiences. I realized that the once-and-for-all conversion which the church was teaching did not work for most people.

In these ways, and in many others, the culture in which I grew up had become uncomfortable, even painful for me. It seemed seriously wrong. I needed to develop a partially different culture for myself.

Then a rather pleasant chapter opened up for me. The United Bible Societies invited me to become a translation consultant. I was to train native speakers of third-world languages to translate the Bible into their own languages. This opportunity exposed me to all churches and to many cultures. Trying to be sympathetic and to look at truth from their individual points of view, I came to appreciate subtle nuances of different cultures, and the

---

[1]The Waunana of Colombia moved to Panama, where they joined the Empera, another tribe of the Choco linguistic family.

vicissitudes of culture change. My experience up to this point had prepared me to seek perspectives which were new to me, as people of those cultures examined the Bible while translating it. My cross-cultural perspective gained new lenses.

Inevitably, when I retired and came back to my childhood environment, I found that it was no longer fully my culture. The church I grew up in was now concerned about whether or not to cushion its pews, while I was concerned about millions of people in the third world who did not have basic necessities. Churches were spending increasingly more money on themselves, until many no longer had funds to do anything outside of themselves.

Probably what disturbed me most was that the church was still reading the Bible through the same monocultural glasses I had used before I went abroad. People were unaware of how much their own culture had changed in the forty years since I had left the community. They were also unaware of the culture changes that took place in the two thousand years of Bible history. They were unaware as well of the powerful force of biblical cultures in shaping the message of the Bible, and of the cultures through which I now looked at the Bible, cultures much more like Bible cultures than any they knew.

When I tried to express my concern about reading the word of God with cultural awareness, I found church leadership unimpressed. Some people did find my multicultural reading interesting, but the majority were disturbed instead. A few exceptional individual believers spurred me on in my approach to the Scriptures, and this book is a result of their encouragement.

The Nature of Worldviews

Some parts of all cultures are relatively superficial and may easily change. Others lie deep within us, providing the foundations for our thinking and behavior, the assumptions (often unconscious) on the basis of which we live. Our culture, for example, provides us with models of reality. It tells us whether our world runs like a machine, or whether spirit forces operate as well. It tells us whether or not women and men should be equal. It tells us what constitutes success and failure in life and by what criteria we should evaluate ourselves. It tells us the role of our country in the world. It tells us why some people are poor, and explains why we have illness and suffering.

Some aspects of our culture are learned in the very earliest years of our life. We learn whom to trust and whom to mistrust, who are friends and who are enemies, what to think of strangers and how to treat them. We learn who we are, whether the people of our culture are leaders or servants, urban or rural, White or Black, Mennonites or "them," and how to behave accordingly.

We do not normally question the assumptions of our culture unless we are forced to do so because we notice that some of them are mutually contradictory, or because we see other models of reality—other cultures which make more sense at some point or other. Even then we may not see the contradictions in our culture or the "more sense" in another because our culture blinds us to them. It is that level of normally unquestioned cultural assumptions that I am primarily concerned with in this book, although parts of it deal with more superficial levels of culture as well. That deep level of our fundamental assumptions is called worldview.

Deep-seated as worldview is, it can change at least in part, as I have already mentioned. We should remember that radical conversions like that of the Apostle Paul on the road to Damascus involve profound changes in worldview. Paul's thinking, some of his most fundamental assumptions about God and his faith, were radically modified. In Paul's case the change began with one remarkable experience (Acts 9:1–22), but evolved over a considerable period of time (Gal 1:17–18).

When the Empera people mentioned above (fn. 1) were converted, parts of their worldview likewise became radically altered, though not necessarily in the ways I expected. In other respects their new faith was integrated into their old worldview. That is why it was easy for them to believe that the woman would be healed when they prayed in obedience to words from the Bible. Their belief in the power of spirits was already in place.

For worldviews to change, however, people must be ready in some way. Some years ago, stymied missionaries in Central America asked Don Jacobs, an Eastern Mennonite anthropologist, and me for anthropological help. The tribe in which they were trying to establish their work was said to have once had a thriving group of Christians as a result of earlier work by Wycliffe Bible Translators. But that organization specialized in Bible translation, and did not focus on establishing churches, so the translators moved on after the New Testament was completed. All the former believers had backslidden by the time the new mission took over. In fact, the new missionaries found absolutely no interest in the gospel, as if the people had been immunized against it. The missionaries were therefore desperate to find a new opening, and asked for our help.

In Central America, the aboriginal worldview of many peoples includes a number of cataclysmic destructions of the world, usually divine punishment for rapid increases in human wickedness. For some of the tribes, two of these judgments are believed to have already passed, the one by water (flood) and the one by wind. The flood of the Bible and local flood accounts attest to the first, and some of the destructive hurricanes that have hit Latin America in known history are examples of the second. Two other judgments, however, are still pending—destructions by darkness and by fire.

We inquired, and learned that this tribe expected that the next destruction of the world would be by darkness. When asked whether there were any signs that such a destruction might be imminent, the people readily agreed that the wickedness had greatly increased and that it was likely that such a judgment would come soon.

We knew that in about a year an eclipse of the sun was to occur in Central America. We therefore suggested to the missionaries that they get all the information they could from the various meteorological services, both national and American, and that they begin to call meetings of the tribal medicinemen to brief them about the coming eclipse. As the date approached, they should stress the point that this darkness was not the end of the world, but that it would last only a specified amount of time. When the eclipse did occur, and the darkness lasted only for the specified time, the people of the tribe were deeply impressed.

Some time later a delegation came to the missionary's house. Solemnly they said, "We have been impressed by how much you knew about the darkness that came and that it was not the end of the world. We now have another question. There is this matter about the gospel of Jesus Christ. We wonder whether you can tell us how much there is to that message. Should it be taken seriously?" The missionaries had found the opening that they had been seeking.

If we compare this tribal reaction to an eclipse to that of North Americans, the marked difference is due to their respective worldviews. Americans may want to know how long the eclipse will last and enjoy the unusual experience but place no major significance on it. They are not fearful that it portends the end of the world. However, an eclipse creates enormous panic in a Latin American tribe that anticipates destruction by darkness. At the same time, demonstration that their own worldview led to false conclusions created an opening for them to wonder if the Christian worldview of salvation might also be true.

On a more abstract level, the worldview of a people provides it with its values. A number of outside observers have pointed out that money is one of the highest values in North American culture, something I learned myself in one of my early mission experiences.

After fellow missionary David Wirsche and I arrived in Noanama, Colombia, at the height of the dry season, we were anxious to make a trip to visit some tribal homes up river. We were told, however, that the trip was usually made by canoe, but that now the river was too dry.

When we inquired about going overland, we sensed strong hesitation because these people always traveled by water. But eventually one Waunana man agreed to guide us on a one-day overland trip to some of the nearest Indian houses up river.

When the arranged-for day arrived, however, he did not show up, and we were deeply disappointed. The next day he came towards evening, and told us that someone in his family was ill, and it would be another day or so before he could make the trip with us.

To make very sure that he would come on the new date we set, I offered him double the amount of money that we had originally agreed upon. He turned to me with a pained expression, and said, "I know that money is very important for you, but it is not for me. I am going with you because I am your friend, not because you're giving me a pile of money."

For most North Americans the accumulation of wealth is believed to be the product of hard work and thrift. Some North American evangelicals see accumulation of wealth as a sign of God's blessing on Christians of their group, rewarding its particular kind of orthodoxy. However, in no case do North Americans interpret disparity of wealth as due to evil spirits.

In much of Africa, however, such disparity is immediately understood as a spiritual phenomenon. In most cases, Africans suspect soul-stealing at once when someone becomes more prosperous than the others of the village. According to their worldview, the more wealthy person has stolen other people's souls, either doing it by himself or with the help of a shaman. The accumulated soul-power has enabled him or her to amass wealth more rapidly than anyone else.

In 1960, when the Belgian Congo (recently Zaïre, now the Democratic Republic of Congo) was in turmoil over independence, a group of Mennonite missionaries headed out of the country for safety, but were met at the border by angry church members. These Christians from their own missions demanded that the missionaries turn over all the church records to them. They were certain that the missionaries who baptized them and wrote down their names had harnessed their soul-power. That was why the Christians were not getting wealthy—their soul-power had been tied up. They wanted to make sure that the missionaries did not get out of the country with this stolen soul-power.

More recently in Central East Africa, the rapid spread of AIDS is often interpreted not as a disease that is transmitted through sexual activity, but rather as the result of soul-stealing by unscrupulous Westerners.

Evaluation of Worldviews

Is there no absolute truth? Yes, there is, but it does not lie in one worldview, any worldview, or even all worldviews together. Our minds are finite, not able to comprehend absolute truth. We do have God's revelation to lead us toward the truth, but the worldviews of the Bible are not able to contain absolute truth any more than are other worldviews.

I hope that this study will help make a few readers deeply aware of what culture-bound creatures we human beings are. We need to remember that "now we see through a glass darkly" and that our knowledge of things, at best, is partial (1 Cor 13:12 KJV). We need to look for the perspectives illumined by other cultures and to remember that people of other cultures also hold that what they believe is truth. We also need to listen patiently to people whose way of looking at things is radically different from our own, and to hear them in humility.

A missionary to a tribe in Bolivia was once asked by the tribal people whether or not he had ever seen God. His answer was "No." Had his father seen God? "No, of course not!"

Some time later, the missionary received word that his father was seriously ill and might die. When he made plans to go to his father, people of the tribe hurriedly carved a figurine from balsa wood, painted and decorated it, and brought it to him, saying, "We are sad that neither you nor your father has ever seen God, and since your father is about to die, we want to send this god with you so that he may see one before he dies. No man should have to die before he has seen God!"

The test of a missionary in such a situation as this is the thankfulness, grace, humility, and love with which he or she responds. Such traits get reflected in openness to understand as fully as possible the view of the native peoples.

2

Biblical Cultures and the Bible

The Bible itself is multicultural, with various worldviews among different groups of the people of God at various times and places. Cultures change over time, as we have seen, parts of them faster than other parts. They change a lot over a long period of time. The Bible spans two thousand years, which means great culture change, and seeing that pattern of change—the trajectory of change—helps us to understand the Bible. To see the Bible in cross-cultural perspective means, in part, to see parts of it in the perspective of other parts.

One reason for culture change is culture contact, as we have seen. People interact with peoples of other cultures, and learn from them, for good or ill. That is how much of my own personal culture has changed, both in contact with cultures around the world and in contact with the ancient cultures of the Bible. Changing situations, new locations, new challenges sustained over a long period of time can also bring culture change. Such reasons for change are to be found in the cultural history of Israel.

Biblical Worldview Changes

When we read the Bible we are exposed to multiple cultures, even multiple worldviews, and thus contrasts not only between the descendants of Abraham and the people around them, but also among the Israelites themselves and between successive Israelite generations. To help the reader understand my perspective in this book as I look at the Bible and its message, I will here sketch briefly my understanding of some of the major cultural periods in Israel's history. Some of these points made in passing will be developed more fully in later chapters where I will also add biblical references. Of course, my thoughts expressed here are not the only ways in which scholars have looked at these events.

The Patriarchal Period

Abraham, Isaac, and Jacob, the great founding ancestors of the people of Israel, were pastoral nomads. They lived in tents moving slowly from season to season, with their herds of camels, donkeys, goats, and sheep to find new pasture lands and water. As such their culture was fairly typical of pastoral cultures elsewhere in Asia and Africa, even today.

Abram (later Abraham), the first of the patriarchs, migrated from Ur of the Chaldees (in modern Iraq, near Kuwait) to Canaan (modern Israel and Palestine) via Haran (in modern Turkey). This was not a highly unusual move for peoples of his times. He traveled with his wife, herds, servants, slaves, and some relatives (including his nephew Lot who also had servants and slaves).

In the account, Yahweh[1] appeared in Haran as Abram's personal God. Yahweh called Abram to move, and made a personal contract with him. As Abram's personal God, the God of an individual, Yahweh was a special type of deity in the culture of Abram's people. In time, Yahweh became successively the God of Abraham's son, Isaac, and then his grandson Jacob. He was later frequently referred to as "the God of Abraham, Isaac, and Jacob," and eventually increasingly understood as the God of all peoples.

At this point, however, Yahweh was probably perceived by most people in strongly anthropomorphic, human-like terms. He was male; he walked with and talked to people; he ate with and visited with them. The interactions between him and human beings were like normal human activity except that he was the all-powerful sovereign.

Under pastoral conditions in many cultures, the loyalty of a wife to the head of the family is exceedingly important. She is therefore often a close relative or a slave. Abram married his half-sister; Isaac married his own niece; and Jacob married two cousins. For an additional wife alongside his close-relative mate, Abram also had her slave, Hagar; Jacob likewise had several slaves of his wives as additional wives.

In this pastoral period of Israel's history, death was not understood as the soul leaving the body and surviving in the beyond, but as the body being deprived of its animation when someone died. Animation, the breath of God, went to Sheol (also called the grave), a dark place, far from God, a place where people did not praise their Creator. In this period, Sheol made no separation between the just and the unjust, not even between human beings and animals.

---

[1]God's personal name in the Old Testament is Yahweh, translated as LORD (with small capitals) in most English translations. On the origin of the divine name, see chap. 15 and references there (Gottwald 1985b:212–13; Moberly 1992:91–93).

The Egypt Period

The Bible recounts only the beginning and the end of the Egypt period, the stories of Joseph and Moses, respectively. After Joseph's family moved into Egypt to avoid famine, they remained there for a time as a separate people, and continued their herding lifestyle. However, shifting from nomadic to sedentary pastoralism greatly increased their population so that when the government of Egypt changed, and Joseph was no longer remembered, the new rulers saw them as a national threat, and enslaved them. As a result, the descendants of the fractious brothers (sons of Jacob from four wives) were blended together in the crucible of suffering in Egypt to form the people of Israel (Ascham 1918:47–53).

The period of slavery also changed the lives of the people. No longer independent herders, they were now drafted into all kinds of work by the government of Egypt, learning new trades and specialties as a result.

Egyptian religion also suggested novel ideas to the Israelites. They learned Egyptian views of the survival of the soul—the spiritual dimension of the person—and the possibility of ultimate reward and punishment. Thus began to emerge their awareness that human beings consisted of both a body and a soul.

Despite some hints in the Pentateuch of God's concern with the entire world, the patriarchs conceived of God largely as a personal God. Thus in Egypt the people thought in terms of the God of the last patriarch, Jacob. When God was revealed to Moses as the God of Israel and of the whole earth,[2] most of Israel got its first inkling of the development of a tribal, national, or universal God rather than a personal one.

The Desert Period

The focal event of the years of wandering in the desert was the covenant that Jacob's God, Yahweh, made with the whole nation of Israel at Mount Sinai. Yahweh revealed the divine name to Moses, and Israel swore allegiance to the God of the patriarchs as their tribal God.

> Then Moses went up to God; the LORD called to him from the mountain, saying, "Thus you shall say to the house of Jacob, and tell the Israelites: You have seen what I did to the Egyptians, and how I bore you on eagles' wings and brought you to myself. Now therefore, if you obey my voice and keep my covenant, you shall be my treasured possession out of all the peoples. Indeed, the whole earth is mine, but you shall be for me a priestly kingdom and a holy nation. . . ."

---

[2]See quotation from Ex 19 below.

So Moses came, summoned the elders of the people, and set before them all these words that the LORD had commanded them. The people all answered as one: "Everything that the LORD has spoken we will do" (Ex 19:3–8 NRSV).

The feeling of peoplehood which had developed in Egypt was now forged into a national entity in the desert. In order to resist the enemies they encountered, Israel also built an army and developed a national government. God gave the Israelites the law, including many aspects of civil life beyond the religious. The law included a different marriage code from the pastoral one, one that prohibited marriages like those of the patriarchs.

In the desert also, the presence of God with the people was accentuated by the tent of the tabernacle, containing the ark of the covenant and "the place of God's residence." God lived in a tent—the tabernacle—but did not make public appearances on a daily basis. God was treated somewhat less anthropomorphically, becoming more transcendent. There were exceptions, though, as when seventy elders, the new government of Israel, met with Moses and God on the mountain to have a picnic.

During this period, increasingly, life in the beyond is pictured as involving a separation—the just and the unjust in different places.

The Conquest Period

When Israel settled in Canaan and took on a more agricultural existence, it quickly became uncertain about where God should be located and worshiped. The tent of the tabernacle could be pitched at only one place at a time, and Israel had not yet established a central place of worship. Since people had become used to living with the presence of God in their midst, and since each of the tribes now had its separate area of residence, much of the group's religious practice was transferred away from the nation, back to the family or the local tribe. The teraphim, family gods, were revived, similar to the time of the patriarchs. A whole host of local family shrines were erected.

The Israelites were also strongly influenced by the people already living in the land, with their territorial gods, the *baal* (male gods) and the *ashtaroth* (female gods). While they may have begun with the worship of Yahweh, they quickly adopted these other deities of a more regional kind as well, together with the custom of worshiping them in high places. Yahweh was still recognized as the greatest of the gods, but for most of Israel Yahweh was distant, and various other, more immediate gods were often worshiped more fervently than Yahweh.

Another reason for adopting other deities was that Israel's covenant with Yahweh was made in the desert. This God of the desert could provide manna and quail when the people needed food, but once Israel settled as an agricultural society in Canaan, many people never had confidence that Yahweh really knew much about crops and fertility. Exceptional individuals, however, kept calling Israel back to Yahweh and the desert covenant.

The Period of the Monarchy

The model of God as king, which was weakly established after Israel's occupation of Canaan, was eventually converted into a literal human kingdom in the pattern of other kingdoms around Israel. With the kingdom came centralized worship, and eventually a temple in Jerusalem as the place of God's residence. Especially under David, and later under Solomon, an attempt was made to strengthen Yahweh worship and to reduce the number of polytheistic shrines.

With the kingdom also came a shift in the covenant, which had first been that of a personal God with Abraham and his descendants, then that of a tribal God with Israel as a people. Under the monarchy, the covenant was established with the king. God promised that King David and his descendants would rule forever. Zion (the mountain on which Jerusalem was built) was also promised as God's eternal dwelling place.

When the kingdom split after Solomon's death, each of the kingdoms attempted to maintain Yahweh worship, but separately. In the north, the kingdom of Israel, which established one shrine for Yahweh worship on its southern border and another on its northern border, the absence of the temple and especially of the ark of the covenant opened the way for more polytheistic worship. In the south, the kingdom of Judah attempted to maintain Yahweh worship in Jerusalem, and the emerging prophets, who served an extremely important function in the development of Israelite worldview, urged even stricter monotheism. Yahweh challenged the kings, through the prophets, to follow Yahweh more closely.

One of the developments against which the prophets spoke was the increasing place of Ashtoreth, goddess of fertility, who came to be known as the queen of heaven (Jer 7:18; 44:15–30). Women were specially dedicated to her worship (Hastings 1902 4:181).

The Periods of Captivity and Restoration

Two new captivities, one of Israel beginning in 721 BC and the other of Judah beginning in 587 BC, had a profound effect upon Israel's religion and culture. The Israelite worldview which had been developed during the monarchy was radically challenged as people brooded in a foreign land. What had happened to the Davidic covenant? In it, God had promised that David's descendants would rule forever. And how could people worship Yahweh where they were? Yahweh was conceived of as territorial, located in

Jerusalem, living in the desecrated temple. When the king was defeated, the temple destroyed, and the land promised by Yahweh lost, the concept of a national God was profoundly challenged.

But while the Hebrews were captives in a foreign land, some of them began to realize that their concept of Yahweh was much too limited. A few began to sense that the God of the tribe, or the God of the king, or the territorial God, must really be the God of the world. Perceptions of the transcendence of God increased rapidly. God was less anthropomorphic, no longer as near, except as some Israelites began to locate God in the law, the Torah (Eliade 1982:274–75). During this time they began the process of canonization, of deciding which books were inspired by God.

As the Jews were rethinking God, they also rethought a lot of other religious issues. Since the later captivity came at the height of Zoroastrianism, the influence of that religion became strong (Eliade 1978:302). Zoroastrianism made a sharp distinction between good and evil, with a god of light and a god of darkness. Since these deities were conceived of as royalty, it also meant that God and Satan had retinues. For God, a host of angels and archangels developed, and for the devil, a host of evil spirits and other followers was postulated (Berquist 1995:181–83).

The greater awareness of evil also caused a sharper division in the place of the dead. Paradise now became the place of those who were on God's side when they died. Sheol remained as the resting place of those who were on the side of evil. With the Zoroastrian emphasis on fire, the fire of hell now became part of Israel's thinking (Ascham 1920:209–19). The concept of a savior, final triumph of good in the future, and resurrection of the body were also Zoroastrian influences on Judaism (Eliade 1978:302–33).[3]

In this same period came the perspective manifested in Isaiah 40, and beyond. In the earlier part of the book, in a pre-exilic context, the author still proclaimed what the other prophets had said. Even though he was beginning to see God as the God of the world, it still was as the God who punishes the heathen for their evil and their idolatry. But beginning with Isaiah 40, in an exilic context, the Gentiles can become part of God's kingdom, if they will keep God's law, be circumcised, and follow Sabbath rules. Then in chapter 60, in a post-exilic context, a new vision emerges, a vision of people from all nations coming to Jerusalem, with some of them being made God's priests and Levites.

Many of the Hebrews, especially women, had worshiped the goddess Ashtoreth/Astarte, consort of the Canaanite god Baal, during the periods of conquest and monarchy (Hanson 1986:326–27). She was a goddess of

---

[3]Not all scholars agree. See chapter 6, fn. 1.

fertility, common to many agricultural peoples. But in captivity the Hebrews were also exposed to the Babylonian goddess Ishtar, the queen of heaven, and as they became dissatisfied with the concept of an entirely male god, allegiance to the queen of heaven grew on the foundation already gained in the monarchy (Hanson 1986:327–28).

In the northern kingdom, after many of the Hebrew people were taken away, other peoples were brought in to intermingle with the remainder. A syncretized version of Hebrew worship developed. The descendants of these people were the Samaritans whom observant Jews religiously avoided in Jesus' day.

In the south, some people were eventually allowed to return from captivity, tried to rebuild the kingdom of Judah (with its capital in Jerusalem), constructed a new temple, and reconstituted Yahweh worship. But it never was the same, as the power and glory were gone. At the popular level, the queen of heaven now played an even greater role. The process of locating Yahweh in the Torah was strengthened, and the quest for the canonization of Scripture grew until the Old Testament canon was finally completed in three sections. The name of the people changed from Israelites to Jews because the people who returned from captivity were all from the Judean area.

The Intertestamental Period

Most Christians proceed from Malachi 4 (end of the Old Testament) to Matthew 1 (beginning of the New Testament) with only the title page intervening, and assume that the cultural history of the Old Testament carries over directly into the New Testament. Others, more aware of the intertestamental period, have nevertheless called it the "silent centuries," as if no ongoing revelation had continued. But the intertestamental period is one of great religious ferment and many new religious ideas penetrated Judaism. The last two centuries before Christ produced some major worldview shifts which carry over into the New Testament.

We learn of this period through two types of literature written at the time. One type, the deutero-canonical or "apocryphal"[4] books, was accepted as part of the Old Testament by some Jews, but not by others. The Jewish community in Palestine proper, which continued to use the Old Testament Scriptures in Hebrew, did not accept them, but the Jews of Egypt, especially, did include them in their canon and in their Septuagint—their Greek translation of the Old Testament.

---

[4]The word *apocrypha* means "hidden." That is, the books were not brought to light to the extent that the Old Testament and the New Testament books were. In modern usage, *apocryphal* has also picked up a connotation of not being authentic.

The Septuagint translation takes on special significance for Christians because it was the Bible of the Greek-speaking early Church. The writers of the New Testament, therefore, knew the Apocrypha as part of their Bible, and today some Protestants and all Roman Catholics accept at least some of the apocryphal books as part of their canon, although in a secondary position. But whether or not Protestants consider them canonical, they do shed light on the development of Jewish history and worldview leading up to the New Testament.

The religious writings of intertestamental times did not end with the Apocrypha, however. From 400 BC until late in the first millennium after Christ—from after the return of Ezra and Nehemiah to Judah until well into the Christian era—many other writings now known as the pseudepigrapha[5] were circulating in Jewish and later in Christian communities. Mostly written in Hebrew, Aramaic, or Greek, they were a continuation of Old Testament Jewish thought, while in the later centuries some of them contained notable Christian elements (Appendix B).

Some of these books were considered candidates for inclusion in the Christian canon in an early period. Jude and 2 Peter reflect two sides of the struggle over whether or not to include them. Jude, for example, quotes from 1 Enoch as authentic prophecy.

> And Enoch also, the seventh from Adam, prophesied of these, saying, Behold, the Lord cometh with ten thousands of his saints, to execute judgment upon all, and to convince all that are ungodly among them of all their ungodly deeds which they have ungodly committed, and of all their hard speeches which ungodly sinners have spoken against him (Jude 14, 15 KJV).

The source reads as follows:

> Behold he will arrive with ten million of the holy ones in order to execute judgment upon all. He will destroy the wicked ones and censure all flesh on account of everything that they have done, that which the sinners and the wicked ones committed against him (1 En 1:9).

Jude also refers to the Assumption of Moses, another pseudepigraphic book, when he mentions Michael the archangel contending with the devil over the body of Moses (Jude 9; Priestly 1983:923).

Jude thus represents that branch of the church which considered at least some books of the pseudepigrapha to be of inspired quality. Second Peter, on the other hand, takes the other point of view. It repeats many of the ideas

---

[5]These writings as a whole were called pseudepigrapha because many of them were written by others than the people who were claimed by the title to have written them. The word pseudepigrapha means 'of fictitious title or superscription.'

mentioned by Jude, and uses wording that is reminiscent of quotations from the pseudepigrapha, but includes no references to the pseudepigrapha (2 Pet 2:4,11).

Eventually the view of 2 Peter prevailed in the early Christian church, and the pseudepigrapha fell into disrepute. But with the discovery of the Dead Sea scrolls, interest in the pseudepigrapha has revived because these scrolls are elucidated by information contained in the pseudepigraphic books.

The pseudepigraphic books, along with the Apocrypha, thus help to fill in a crucial part of the development in Jewish culture and worldview which leads into Christianity and the early church. Jesus' own environment was not that of the New Testament books (which were written some time after he died), nor of the church (which came into being after his resurrection), but of the Jewish intertestamental period. Half of the New Testament (the gospels) was lived in intertestamental times, in intertestamental culture, with inter-testamental worldviews. In the pseudepigrapha, for example, the former three-tiered heaven gave way to the Greek view of a seven-tiered heaven. Some of the books contain lengthy discussions of the origin of evil, the development of Satan and his followers, and the work of angels and archangels. Understanding of the resurrection of the dead grew in this period.

Events of the Intertestamental Period. The last defeat and captivity of the Jews by Chaldea in 587 BC brought them into the area where the Persian empire was soon to gain ascendancy, and from 400 to 330 BC the whole Middle-Eastern world was under Persian domination. Many Jews continued to live outside of Judah even after the end of the Babylonian exile, though some did return to Judea.

The Persian period was followed by the Greek period. Alexander the Great conquered most of the Middle-Eastern world, ruling briefly from 330 to 323 BC. When he died suddenly, his empire was broken up into four parts, each under one of his four generals. Israel, or more aptly Judea, was subject to either the Ptolemies of Egypt or the Seleucids of Syria. This lasted from 323 to 166 BC, during which time Greek language and thought exerted strong influence. One of the influences of Greek religion was the concept of incarnation. While the Greeks were not the only ones who had gods that were born as human beings, their thinking helped prepare for Christian understanding.

Eventually, two of Alexander's successors, the Ptolemies in Egypt and the Seleucids in Syria, became dominant, competing with each other for control of the Middle East. Under Antiochus Epiphanes, one of the Syrian rulers, the Jews suffered outrage. He defiled their temple, which they had rebuilt after their return from captivity, by erecting a statue of Jupiter in the most holy part, and by ordering that pigs be sacrificed. All this plus his brutality finally led to the Maccabean revolt in 166 BC.

In spite of events like these, the years 323 to 166 BC were years of relative Jewish independence, although most Jews were either in the area under Syrian control or under the Ptolemies in Egypt. In Palestine proper, Judaism split into a number of significant divisions, most of which carried over into the New Testament (Hanson 1986:347–64).

First were the conservative Sadducees. They accepted only the five books of Moses as canonical and believed only in God, not in angels, spirits, or an afterlife.

The second group consisted of the Pharisees, 'separated ones,' who were diligent in studying not only the Torah but also the prophets and the writings. They wrote commentaries and codified many of the rules that are mentioned as characteristic of them in the New Testament. They accepted such newer beliefs as the immortality of the soul, the resurrection of the body, and future judgment, all of which are important in Christianity. Their cosmology was heavily influenced by the Greek view of the universe.

The third group which developed in intertestamental times consisted of the Essenes, an ascetic community which believed that living the righteous life and abstaining from all worldly indulgence preserved one's spiritual and physical health. When the Dead Sea scrolls began to be discovered in 1947, they shed enormous light on the Essene community from which they came. Josephus, the Jewish historian, also gave a detailed account of Essene initiation and cultic life (Josephus n.d.:394, 544, 690–91). Many scholars believe that John the Baptist was an Essene and that he baptized in the Jordan near the Essene community at Qumran.

The fourth group consisted of the Zealots. Simon the Zealot, one of the twelve apostles (Lk 6:15; Acts 1:13), probably belonged to this party. Paul speaks about himself as having been a religious zealot (Acts 21:20; 22:3; Gal 1:14), but we do not know whether or not this means that he actually had ties to the Zealot party. Josephus describes the Zealots as the "fourth philosophy" among the Jews.

Eventually the Zealots became revolutionaries, and especially when Antiochus IV of Syria tried to suppress the Jewish religion, beginning about 165 BC, the Zealots formed the core of the Maccabean rebellion against him. The last Zealot stronghold was the fort at Masada, captured by the Romans in AD 73.

Judea became subject to Rome in 63 BC when the Romans conquered Syria, and was under Roman rule throughout the New Testament period, as was the rest of the New Testament world. Under Rome, Judea was ruled by the Herods, a corrupt family of nominal Jews, formerly from Idumaea (Edom). Important as it was politically and in the life of the early church, the Roman period did not have much effect on New Testament worldviews, as Greek thinking dominated at the time, even in Rome itself.

The last major significant event in this intertestamental period was the building of Herod's temple in Jerusalem in 19 BC, the temple frequently mentioned in the gospels and Acts.

The New Testament Period

Christians are on more familiar ground with the New Testament. After the death and resurrection of Jesus, at first the faith in this messiah was a continuation of Judaism, but significant differences in worldview also arose. In the Old Testament, Jewish understanding of Israel's captivity in God's design tended toward exclusivism. But before long in the New Testament this was challenged when, especially under Paul, the church included Gentiles.

In the Old Testament, direct divine rule had given way to a human Israelite kingdom which was finally abandoned altogether, whereas in the New Testament, the kingdom of God was reinterpreted spiritually as people everywhere submitting to God's rule. The central focus of Old Testament Hebrew religion was on atonement for sin, which gave way to the New Testament emphasis on the forgiveness of sin. Some modifications in cosmology also appeared.

The New Testament picked up from or fulfilled points from various epochs of the Old Testament. Jesus was the son of King David, heir to the throne of David and to the kingly covenant of the period of monarchy. God is the God of the whole world, a concept which struggled to be born all through the Old Testament. Salvation in the New Testament was modeled on the captivity in Egypt, the rescue from there, and the desert experience.

Some exilic and intertestamental concepts were fundamental to New Testament faith. Jesus was the incarnation of God and was resurrected from death, as his followers also will be. After the judgment the righteous will live with God forever and the unrighteous will be consigned to hell.

Culture Change and the Trajectory of Divine Purpose

If the Bible is God's revelation, how can the worldviews it reflects change so much? A God who was first a personal God, then a tribal/national and territorial God, then a God especially related to the kings, followed by a God dimly becoming the God of the whole world, and finally established as a changing God seems hard to reconcile with the changeless God which Christians proclaim, as does the Bible also, sometimes. How are we to understand revelation if God is conceived of in so many different ways?

As a boy, I grew up on Bible stories. Listening to them was a favorite pastime for winter evenings in Manitoba. Of course, the story of Joseph stood high in the list—Joseph sold by his brothers, which led to Israel's moving to Egypt as an extended family during a famine and taking up long-term residence there. Eventually, with a change of Egypt's rulers, the Israelites became slaves of the Egyptians, living in that country for 400 years until God delivered them.

Later in life, I realized that my boyhood teaching about Israel in Egypt wasn't very enlightening. Nobody asked why Israel had to stay there for over 400 years. Why did they not go back when the famine was over, or why not stay permanently? Why 400 years?

During my years as translation consultant for the Bible Societies, I worked with the Bible in many languages and became exposed to the religious views of people from many cultures. I watched them as they grappled with the meaning of the word of God and with the best way to translate it accurately into their respective languages. In the course of this I came to see a reason for Israel needing to spend centuries in Egypt.

Captivity in Egypt began Israel's slow shift toward understanding the nature of the afterlife. God may have brought Israel to Egypt to expose the nation to the Egyptian conception of an afterlife for Pharaohs. It took many years to absorb this lesson, but that this exposure had an effect on them is without doubt; bit by bit statements in the Hebrew Scriptures begin to suggest a growing awareness.

Revelation does not come to an empty mind but to one which already has a deeply established worldview. Additional revelation may modify the worldview, or add to it, or clarify it, but does not entirely replace it. New revelation therefore has to be incremental, to some degree. Thus, at each stage along the way, revelation had to come to Israel in terms it could understand. Revelation brought new information, of course, but that new information was framed at least partly in terms of the existing cultural matrix. As history moved on and culture changed, as Israelites were exposed to the ideas of other peoples, opportunities for revelation in a different form or the revelation of new information became more possible. God's revelation was therefore dynamic, moving, developing, not static, and as we look back at it, we see that it forms a trajectory of growth (Hanson 1986:522, 525–46; Moltmann 1977) as Israel's (and later Christians') knowledge of God grew.

In order for New Testament revelation to take place, worldviews held by the early Hebrews had to be modified over time. For example, Sheol, the place of the dead, originally received the souls of all human beings who died, good or bad. Such a worldview did not provide much of a foundation for the New Testament conception of an afterlife with reward and punishment.

Captivity in Egypt began the shift; the Assyrian and Babylonian captivities enlarged it, as Zoroastrianism had a fully developed belief in the afterlife for both the good and the bad. During this captivity, Sheol and Paradise became the final homes of unrighteous and righteous dead, respectively. Both of these ideas were later critical for Christianity.

Zoroastrian concepts of the god of light and the god of darkness served as a foundation for ones which we find prevalent in the Dead Sea scrolls and in the New Testament. In these later sources light refers to that which is of God and darkness to the Satanic.

So, human understanding of divine revelation grows slowly but at every stage it does bring something new to existing worldviews. At every stage God uses people's experience to question, mold, and alter existing assumptions. At every stage God gives a few especially insightful people the gift of seeing a little bit beyond the confines of their worldviews and of opening the minds of their contemporaries to changes which accumulate over time. At every stage God continues to speak, a fact from which we sometimes cut ourselves off because the canon is closed.

Part II

The Universe:
Physical and Metaphysical

Introduction

Until the mid-1960s, when space exploration was getting well under way, and pictures of the earth were being recorded in outer space and shown on television around the world, a small group of people in Great Britain and the United States belonged to the Flat Earth Society. They believed that contrary to the standard modern Western conception of the earth and the universe, the earth is flat. The purpose of their society was to promote the truth of a flat earth and to stand against the prevailing view that the earth is a sphere. Their cosmology, their understanding of the structure of the universe, was based in good part on the Bible.

Cosmologies vary widely in time and place. Drawings in the tombs of the Valley of the Kings in ancient Egypt (2200–1500 BC) show the earth as the center of the universe. Above the earth, the god of air holds up the dome which contains the heavenly bodies. During the day, the sun god Ra rides his canoe through the heavens and at night rides back on the waters underneath the earth, preparing to begin the next day's journey through the sky again.

Later, the Greeks also thought of the earth as located at the center of the universe. Plato (427–347 BC), for example, described it as rotating underneath a spherical dome which housed the moving heavenly bodies. Beyond the dome was ether or nothingness (Boorstin 1983:294–304).

The cosmology of the early Christian church was based upon the Greek one, and the church made this geocentric universe critical to parts of its theology, and it remained unchallenged for centuries. Then Copernicus (1473–1543), a Polish astronomer, realized that a heliocentric (sun as the center) universe made more sense, although he had no scientific evidence on which to base such a claim. However, even this proposal made the Protestant reformer Martin Luther attack him as "an upstart astronomer who seeks to challenge God."

Not until the telescope was developed and Galileo (1564–1652) made astronomical observations through it was the concept of a geocentric universe severely challenged. Galileo first examined the moon, with its mountains and craters, unlike the shiny smooth sphere that theology claimed it was. Even more disturbing than that, he realized that the moon was not a light in and of itself, but only reflected the light of the sun. This was a direct challenge to theology's fourth day of creation (Russell 1961:19–48).

Next Galileo studied the four moons revolving around Jupiter, concluding that our moon is likewise revolving around the earth, and inferring that the earth is revolving around the sun. These observations raised the anger of Protestants and Catholics alike.

Martin Luther said, "Joshua commanded the sun to stand still, not the earth" (Josh 10:12–13).

His fellow reformer, Ulrich Zwingli, said, "God fixed the earth and it cannot be moved" (Ps 93:1).

The Roman Catholic Inquisition said,

> The first proposition, that the sun is the center and does not revolve around the earth is foolish, absurd, false in theology and heretical, because it is expressly contrary to Holy Scripture. . . . The second proposition, that the earth is not the center but revolves around the sun, is absurd, false in philosophy, and, from a theological point of view, at least, opposed to the true faith (Russell 1961:37).

Galileo himself tried not to contradict the church's theology. In his *Dialogue on the Two Chief World Systems*, he proposed to consider the two views as two different ways of expressing the same truth:

> Both the Holy Scriptures and nature proceed from the divine Word, the former as the saying of the Holy Spirit and the latter as the most observant executrix of God's orders . . . (Boorstin 1983:22).

However, such writings did not pacify the Catholic Church, and in 1633 the Inquisition found Galileo guilty of heresy, forcing him to recant. It then commuted his death sentence to house imprisonment (Boorstin 1983: 294–327).

Cosmologies are foundational in worldviews. They define our universe and our place in it. The Flat Earth Society may no longer exist, but contemporary conflict over creation and evolution is in great part a conflict about cosmology, about who we are, about how we define ourselves.

The shape of the earth and its relation to the universe is only one part of a people's cosmology, and a people's cosmology is only one part of its worldview, as we shall see. Cosmologies, furthermore, may not only differ radically from each other, but may also be quite difficult to translate into each other's categories, even when the latter are overtly recognized. Furthermore, people are not fully aware of the extent to which their cosmologies color, shape, and limit their mental, linguistic, and even overt behavior.

3

The Heavens and the Earth

While Aureliano, Empera tribesperson from Panama, was visiting my wife and me in Hillsboro, Kansas, we did some Bible translating together and came to this passage:

> And then shall he send his angels, and shall gather together his elect from the four winds, from the uttermost part of the earth to the uttermost part of heaven (Mk 13:27 KJV).

Aureliano insisted on translating "to the uttermost part of the earth" as 'to the last earth.' I wondered if he could possibly be thinking that there was more than one earth, but the idea seemed so preposterous that I dismissed it out of hand.

I was also afraid that the expression which he was using might somehow tie into the Empera view that the universe has three tiers. In this view, the bottom tier consists of an underworld which is both older and lower than the current earth. Above it lies this present earth, and above that there is to be another, future earth. I let the question drop, but decided to do a better job of exegesis the next time around.

The next translation project we tackled was the book of Acts where we soon came again to "unto the uttermost part of the earth" (Acts 1:8 KJV). I first explained the geography of the verse and then made a detailed statement of the philosophy of world evangelism. I explained the passage both in Empera and in Spanish, which Aureliano spoke fluently.

But in spite of all that explanation, Aureliano again rendered "to the uttermost part of the earth" as 'to the last earth.' So I reprimanded him: "Why don't you translate the way it says in the text 'to the uttermost part of the earth,' which is like saying, 'to the most distant shore of the earth'?"

Aureliano then countered, "But what about the long explanation you

gave? And what about the people who live on the other side of the bank?"
Clearly, we were talking past each other, but where?

"Do you know that the world is round?" I asked Aureliano, to which he
answered with a condescending affirmative. So the flat earth seemingly wasn't
what was causing the difficulty. I tried every imaginable way to solve the
impasse, but to no avail.

Finally, on a sudden inspiration, I wheeled a large globe into the room. I
located Panama, the United States, and Russia, and showed Aureliano the
course of his flight from Panama to Hillsboro, via Portland, Oregon. Then we
traced his return route to Panama via Havana, Cuba. Aureliano was deeply
fascinated, sitting as if glued to the globe, so that further work became
impossible.

Suddenly he blurted out, "So it isn't true?"

"What is not true?"

"That the world has seven seas?"

"We generally speak of five oceans, but you can have as many as you
please by giving different names to different sections of the water."

"That is not what I mean. The earth is really one sea and a number of
islands."

"Do you see that the blue of the water has different shades? This light blue
here means shallow water. This dark blue here means deep water. There is a
'land' bottom under the whole sea."

Aureliano continued turning the globe and asking questions. Finally he
went to the blackboard and said, "I always knew that the world was round,
but I thought it was like this." He drew a circle, placing Panama and the
United States in the center. Then he drew additional concentric rings of land
and water for seven lands and seven seas (Figure 1).

So different were our understandings of the shape of the earth that only
when Aureliano saw the representation of my spherical world did he
understand what I was talking about. And only when I saw his drawing did I
understand what he was talking about. The two visual models "translated" our
respective views of the earth for each other.

Aureliano then countered with a statement of his own predicament: "Of
course, I knew that 'to the last earth' was nonsense because the last two
earths are frozen to the sky, and absolutely no people live there. But since you
didn't know any better, I had to say such nonsense." When Aureliano returned
to Panama, he took a globe with him because "I will never be able to explain
God's word to the people correctly if I can't show them what the round world
is really like."

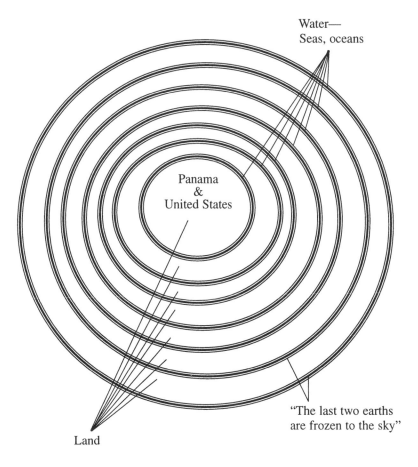

Water—
Seas, oceans

Panama
&
United States

"The last two earths
are frozen to the sky"

Land

Figure 1: *An Empera's View of the World with Seven Seas*

The Early Hebrew Cosmology

The cosmology reflected in the Bible, however, is different from both mine and Aureliano's, and Aureliano's globe would not help him or his people understand any of the biblical cosmologies. Something of the difference between the biblical cosmology and ours may even be seen in the phrase 'the uttermost part of the earth,' which gave Aureliano so much trouble. For us it is a figurative expression, but it reflects the biblical picture of a flat earth with an edge.

When I became a translation consultant in East Central Africa and began dealing with translations of the Old Testament, I discovered that awareness of Hebrew cosmology was essential for African translators (Figure 2 on page 41). And Westerners, with a cosmology as different from those of the Bible as mine was from Aureliano's, can be as unconsciously misled by biblical cosmologies as I was by his.

In the biblical view of the universe, the flat earth stands as God created it on two massive pillars which hold it just above the ocean water on all sides (Fosdick 1941:46–47; Gottwald 1985b:476). Beneath the earth lies the hideaway of darkness, to which God at creation banished the darkness, a kind of spiritual monster. Here it abides during the daytime, but at night, when the sun goes beyond the firmament, it comes out again.

Toward the bottom, between these two pillars, lies Sheol, the place of the dead—a place for both the good and the wicked, and even for animals (Ecc 3:19–21). The whole area around the pillars is often referred to in the Scriptures as the 'deep' or the 'pit.' Below all this lie the waters of the deep, and finally the foundation on which everything rests. (See Figure 2.)

Above the earth lie the heaven of the birds and the heaven of the heavenly lights, including the daytime sun. All this is capped by the firmament which also holds up the upper waters. Finally, above these waters lies the third heaven, the abode of God.

By day, the sun lights the world by crossing below the firmament, but during the night it returns invisibly above the firmament to reappear again in the morning and banish the darkness to its lair beneath the earth once more. The stars are permanently fixed in the firmament, as are windows that can be opened to let water through. When all of them are open simultaneously, floods occur (Gen 7:11). The waters above the firmament, divided at creation from the waters below, are kept in chambers to provide rain, hail, and snow.

Unless North Americans are aware of this early Hebrew view of light and darkness, we do not understand why the first account of the creation story has a series of expressions like "And there was evening and there was morning, the first day" (Gen 1:5,8,13,19,23,31 NRSV). Our day begins with the morning and ends with night.

But for the Hebrews, the cycle of night and day was a re-enactment of creation, a daily reaffirmation that the creator was still active in controlling and operating the universe. As the sun disappeared in the evening, darkness emerged from between the pillars of the earth, blanketing the earth once more as it had done in the primordial, pre-creation state of chaos. But in the morning, when the sun came out of its hidden nighttime trajectory, daylight appeared as if light had been created anew. As in creation, therefore, night preceded morning, another day.

Numbers in the figure refer to the corresponding numbers in Table 2.

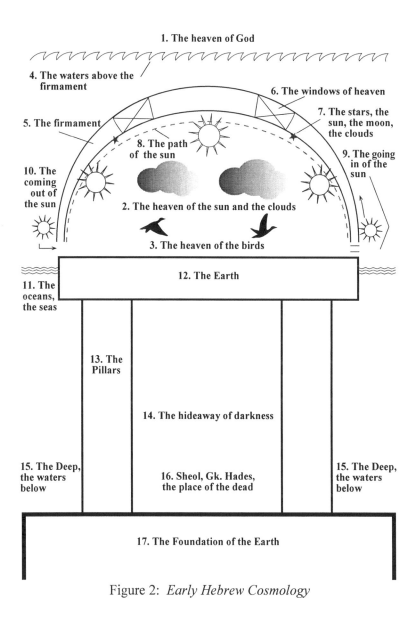

Figure 2: *Early Hebrew Cosmology*

TABLE 2

<small>SAMPLE SCRIPTURE REFERENCES FOR THE
LABELED PARTS OF FIGURE 2</small>

FIGURE 2	REFERENCES
1. The heaven of God	Deut 4:39; Job 22:14
2. The heaven of the sun and clouds	Gen 1:14–15; Ps 89:36–37
3. The heaven of the birds	Gen 1:20; Is 13:10
4. The waters above the firmament	Gen 1:7; 7:11; 8:2; Is 51:16
5. The firmament	Gen 1:6
6. The open/closed windows of heaven	Gen 7:17, 8:2; Is 24:18; Mal 3:10
7. The stars, sun, moon, and clouds	Gen 1:14–15
8. The path of the sun	Ps 19:5-6
9. The going in of the sun (sunset)	Gen 15:12; Dan 6:14
10. The coming out of the sun (sunrise)	Gen 19:23; Num 2:3
11. The oceans, the seas	Neh 9:6; Is 11:9; Jon 2:3
12. The (flat) earth	Deut 13:7; Is 5:26; Jer 25:31–33
13. The pillars of the earth/heaven	1 Sam 2:8; Job 26:11
14. The hideaway of darkness	1 Sam 2:9; Ps 88:6
15. The deep, the waters below	Gen 7:11; Neh 9:11; Ps 69:15
16. Sheol, the place of the dead	Deut 32:22; Job 26:6; Jon 2:3
17. The foundation of the world	2 Sam 22:16; Ps 104:5

Change in the View of the Heavens

This early Hebrew cosmology did not remain fixed or static over the whole two thousand years spanned by the writing of the books of the Bible. However, changes are particularly noteworthy in concepts of the heavens, some of them being changes of function (particular levels of heavens changing to serve different purposes), others involving increases in the number of heavens. Many of the changes show most clearly in the pseudepigraphic books (chap. 2), and then culminate in the views of the heavens hinted at in the New Testament.[1]

---

[1]Sheol (the place of the dead) and varying understandings of life after death will be discussed in chapter 4.

Three Heavens

Figure 2 showed the heavens of the early Hebrews in three tiers: the heaven of the birds, the heaven of the sun and clouds, and, above the firmament, the heaven of God. But in the Testament of the Twelve Patriarchs,[2]Figurewritten about 200 BC, the three heavens are not the same as the early Hebrew ones. In ascending order they are the heaven of water, the heaven of light, and the heaven of God's dwelling (Kee 1983:779).

> [The LORD said,] "Levi, Levi, enter!" And I entered the first heaven and saw there much water suspended. And again I saw a second heaven much brighter and more lustrous, for there was a measureless height in it. And I said to the angel, "Why are these things thus?" And the angel said to me, "Do not be amazed concerning this, for you shall see another heaven, more lustrous and beyond compare. And when you have mounted there, you shall stand near the LORD" (TLevi 2:7–10).

This quotation raises questions like "what happened to the heaven of the birds and the heaven of the clouds of the earlier cosmology?" But such questions are impossible to answer.

The same book goes on to say,

> Listen therefore, concerning the heavens which have been shown to you. The lowest is dark for this reason: It sees all the injustices of humankind and contains fire, snow, and ice, ready for the day determined by God's righteous judgment. In it are all the spirits of those dispatched to achieve the punishment of mankind. In the second are the armies arrayed for the day of judgment to work vengeance on the spirits of error and of Beliar. Above them are the Holy Ones. In the uppermost heaven of all dwells the Great Glory in the Holy of Holies superior to all holiness. There with him are the archangels, who serve and offer propitiatory sacrifices to the Lord in behalf of all the sins of ignorance of the righteous ones. They present to the Lord a pleasing odor, a rational and bloodless oblation. In the heaven below them are the messengers who carry the responses to the angels of the Lord's presence. There with him are thrones and authorities; there praises to God are offered eternally (TLevi 3:1–5).

Is "fire, snow, and ice" in the second quotation an elaboration on "water" in the first? We do not know. The pseudepigrapha do not present material very logically and are often quite contradictory. However, behind the inconsistencies, the changes in function from the earlier biblical view of the heavens are clear.

---

[2]For brief sketches of pseudepigraphic books mentioned, see Appendix B.

More than Three Heavens

The Greek Apocalypse of 3 Baruch, written after the time of Christ, is unusual among pseudepigraphic books in that it describes five heavens. The book recounts Baruch's experience as God's angel takes him through these heavens.

First heaven	a plain (3 Bar 2:2–3)
Second heaven	a prison for strange creatures (3 Bar 3:1–8)
Third heaven	Hades, gloomy and unclean (3 Bar 4:3)
Fourth heaven	the path of the sun (3 Bar 7:2)
Fifth heaven	where the good works of the righteous are kept; angels serve people (3 Bar 12:1–5)

Much more common in this late period, however, were seven heavens, which developed as Greek culture impinged upon the Jews. The seven-heaven view of the universe may have come into later Greek mythology from the Middle East. In Zoroastrianism, a religion which began in Persia in the sixth century BC, the universe had seven heavens, a number associated with perfection (Hastings 1902 2:322).

In the pseudepigraphic book, Questions of Ezra (date unknown), the lower heavens are negative, the upper ones positive (Stone 1983b:593). Hades, the Greek counterpart of Hebrew Sheol, is located on the third level, where it is icy cold. The souls of the righteous are led through all these levels until they reach the seventh heaven, the presence of God.

First heaven	bad and wondrous
Second heaven	fearsome and indescribable
Third heaven	icy cold Hades
Fourth heaven	quarrels and wars
Fifth heaven	investigation of just and sinners
Sixth heaven	the souls of the righteous sparkle like the sun
Seventh heaven	the throne of God (QuesEzra variant A 1:19–21)

God is seated in the highest heavens, but his face is invisible to all, even to his heavenly hosts. His throne is opposite paradise (QuesEzra variant A 1:21–26).

2 Enoch (first century AD) describes how the angels take Enoch up through a still different set of seven heavens. This book implies no association between the heavenly bodies and the forces of evil.

First heaven	place of 200 angels who govern the stars and the heavenly constellations (2 En 3:1–4:2)
Second heaven	great darkness; prisoners under guard awaiting judgment, weeping all day long (2 En 7:1–2)

Third heaven	paradise, inconceivably pleasant (2 En 8:1–8)
Fourth heaven	various tracks of the sun and moon (2 En 11:1–5)
Fifth heaven	myriad fallen angels imprisoned with Satanail, their leader (2 En 18:1–3)
Sixth heaven	various groups of glorious angels (2 En 19:1–5)
Seventh heaven	location of God (2 En 20:1–4).

God's throne is so massive that it reaches up from the seventh heaven into the tenth heaven (2 En 22:1), where God's face is located, and where human beings cannot look at it. This was a figurative way of referring to the transcendence or the greatness of God. God's throne, while it is in the seventh heaven, is so great that it extends, as it were, up three more heavens.

Presumably Paul was operating in a seven-heaven worldview when he said that in his out-of-the-body experience he was taken to the third heaven, where he heard unrepeatable words (2 Cor 12:1–4 NEB).

Implications

What are we to make of this jumble of pre-scientific cosmologies? What are we to make of our own cosmology in light of them? Clearly, we have more physical evidence for ours than the ancients (or the Empera) had for theirs, with images from our giant telescopes and our spaceships. But that physical evidence does not make our cosmology "true" and theirs "false," for ours, too, will seem amateurish, primitive, and amusing to people two thousand years from now.

The point is not to compare worldviews or to decide which of these temporary ones is the truth, for all are partial. The purpose is to see that God is revealed through different worldviews at different times and places, and to see some of the presuppositions underlying the wording of the Bible, presuppositions which are the bases for its logic and its imagery.

The pseudepigrapha, from which we get our understanding of the development of the cosmology of the Jews in intertestamental and New Testament times, obviously contain contradictions and inconsistencies, especially of detail. But the detail is not the important part for us. We need to realize that the universe was geocentric, and that by New Testament times people believed it had seven heavens, the topmost one of which was God's dwelling place. Multiple heavens and God's location in the highest one are consistent views throughout the Bible and are part of the ideological framework through which God's nature and God's relationship to us is revealed in the Bible.

To look honestly at biblical cosmologies through our own eyes, or through the eyes of the Empera, and to attempt to translate them into forms intelligible to us is to look at them cross-culturally. But without having seen the outlines of biblical cosmologies, we cannot really look at them more deeply. Then we read the Bible much as though its cosmologies are the same as ours, which is to read it monoculturally, and to read it monoculturally is to read it wrong.

4

The Afterlife

When I was growing up in a Mennonite community, the only concern about afterlife I remember hearing discussed was whether people were saved or not when they died, which decided whether they would go to heaven or to hell. Once people died, their link with the living was irreparably broken. We might grieve the loss of a loved one, but just as Paradise and Hades were separated by a bottomless pit that could not be crossed (Lk 16:26), we were also cut off from the dead. No communication was possible.

I carried such presuppositions with me to our first mission assignment in Colombia where the rains were heavier than usual in 1952, and flood waters rose twenty-five feet above the usual flood stage. The Waunana Indians, among whom we were working, began to express concern.

One day we heard that a woman we knew had been in her plantation when she saw a cute little white puppy. She picked it up, but it scratched her so badly that she dropped it, and when she tried to catch it again, it ran into the forest.

As she followed the puppy, the woman suddenly found herself face to face with her deceased father, who said, "Daughter, I have come back to warn all the people that Ewandama ['God'] is upset about the wickedness of the people and is once more considering destruction of the world and its people, just like with the first flood. People must revive our old 'beseeching' ceremony to plead for mercy from God." When I heard the story, I listened with interest and sympathy but attributed the appearance of the deceased father to his daughter's over-active imagination, stimulated by the flood.

Later, after I had been working in Africa for almost ten years, a number of Christian African graduate students in an American university came to me with a question, "When our mothers or our grandmothers say that an ancestor

47

appeared to them and gave them a message, that is just a figment of their imagination, isn't it?"

By that time, my perception had changed. "I know that your mothers are more sensitive to the spirit world than I am because my culture has made me insensitive. Your mothers may have had a vision or seen an actual appearance. The Bible says that 'we are surrounded by . . . a cloud of witnesses' (Heb 12:1 NRSV), and those witnesses may be our deceased ancestors." Having heard testimony after testimony of African communication between the living and dead and knowing that the Bible recounts an appearance of dead Samuel to King Saul (1 Sam 28:7–14), I can no longer discount messages from the dead.

Old Testament Conceptions of the Afterlife

The cosmologies of the Bible have more dimensions to them than the physical one highlighted in the last chapter. In them at least one of the heavens is also the abode of God, and Sheol is the location of the souls-of-the-dead. Separating the physical from the metaphysical is always difficult, but now I want to focus on some aspects of biblical cosmology which relate to life after death.

In the parts of the Old Testament which were written earliest, or are based on the earliest oral traditions, the soul went to Sheol when human life ended. Sometimes wicked people were subject to an early death—like Er and Onan, the sons of Judah (Gen 38:2–10), or like the band of Korah, which revolted against Moses (Num 16:26–35)—but good or bad behavior made no difference of destination in the beyond. No final reward or punishment was anticipated. The early Old Testament, furthermore, gives little description of the afterlife, except that Sheol is pictured as dark and silent (Ecc 9:10; 1 Sam 2:6).

Human beings had been created by the breath of the immortal God (Gen 2:7) and, since God was eternal, the divine breath of life in human beings was also eternal. Everything else that had breath also went to Sheol, although the Scriptures do not specify how animals qualify (Ecc 3:19–22). Thus, their view was that there was a general existence of souls in the afterlife, but not a continued personal existence. Although Sheol was not a place of punishment, existence there was not happy since it was removed from God (Ps 6:5; 30:9; Hastings 1902 4:222–37).

The early Old Testament does not contain references to the resurrection of the dead, either. Sheol is described as "the abode of the dead" and not of those who live again after death. And at this stage, also, the Old Testament offers no clear conception of the origin of evil. While the fall of humankind is recorded, the account gives no indication of how the snake became evil and got the idea or the impetus to tempt Adam and Eve to disobey God (Gen 3:1–19).

Later Changes. The Hebrews were first exposed to the idea of an afterlife with reward and punishment when they lived in Egypt (chap. 2), later meeting it again through the Canaanite worldview. When they went into captivity in Chaldea, they came under Zoroastrian influence, which again stressed reward and punishment in the afterlife. So the Hebrews increasingly conceptualized a future in which the righteous would not be separated from God, and the unrighteous would go to a place of punishment (Hastings 1902 4:222–37). Sheol was no longer a neutral place.[1]

> Thy pomp is brought to the grave, *and* the noise of thy viols: the worm is spread underneath thee and the worms cover thee (Is 14:11 KJV).
>
> Behold, for peace I had great bitterness: but thou hast in love to my soul *delivered it* from the pit of corruption: for thou hast cast all my sins behind thy back. For the grave cannot praise thee, death can *not* celebrate thee; they that go down into the pit cannot hope for thy truth (Is 38:17–18 KJV).
>
> For he seeth *that* wise men die, likewise the fool and the brutish person perish, and they leave their wealth to others . . . Like sheep they are laid in the grave; death shall feed on them; . . . and their beauty shall consume in the grave from their dwelling (Ps 49:10,14 KJV).

At this time Sheol was still located underneath the earth:

> For the wise the path of life leads upward, in order to avoid Sheol below (Prov 15:24 NRSV).
>
> But you are brought down to Sheol, to the depths of the Pit (Is 14:15 NRSV).
>
> I cast it down to Sheol with those who go down to the Pit. . . . They also went down to Sheol with it (Ezek 31:16–17 NRSV).

As punishment became associated with Sheol, English translators sometimes translated Sheol as "hell" (2 Sam 22:6 KJV; Ps 9:17 KJV; Prov 15:11 KJV).

Intertestamental Conceptions of the Afterlife

The Greeks believed in the immortality of the soul and in reward and retribution for good and bad behavior. Under this Greek influence, the Hebrews finally arrived at more satisfactory answers concerning the afterlife. The apocryphal Wisdom of Solomon (first century BC) elucidates the Greek

---

[1] In the following passages, Sheol is translated variously as 'grave' or 'pit.'

point of view, there re-expressed as a Hebrew point of view. The first chapters show how the wicked will reap the consequences of their wicked life (Nicklesburg 1972).

> Perverse thoughts separate men from God, and when his power is tested, it convicts the foolish (WisSol 1:3 RSV).
>
> Inquiry will be made into the counsels of an ungodly man . . . to convict him of his lawless deeds (WisSol 1:9 RSV).
>
> The ungodly will be punished as their reasoning deserves, who disregarded the righteous man and rebelled against the Lord (WisSol 3:10 RSV).
>
> They will come with dread when their sins are reckoned up, and their lawless deeds will convict them to their face (WisSol 4:20 RSV).

On the other hand,

> The souls of the righteous are in the hands of God, and no torment will ever touch them (WisSol 3:1 RSV).
>
> For God created man for incorruption, and made him in the image of his own eternity, but through the devil's envy death entered the world, and those who belong to his party experience it (WisSol 2:23 RSV).

The Second Book of Maccabees (first century BC), furthermore, assumes that the future life is not restricted to the soul, but that the person will live again (Hastings 1902 4:222–37).

> You dismiss us from this present life, but the King of the universe will raise us up to an everlasting renewal of life, because we have died for his laws (2 Mac 7:9 RSV).

Thus, the changes which began in the later Old Testament period continued and accelerated in intertestamental times. Here I will mention only some of those which lead to or parallel New Testament views of the afterlife.

Separation of the Just and the Unjust

Separation of the righteous from the unrighteous dead becomes stronger in the pseudepigraphic books of the intertestamental period (Coenen, Beyreuther, and Bietenhard, eds. 1979 1:711, 2:997, 998; Ausubel 1964:173). For example,

> At that moment, I raised a question regarding him [the angel] and regarding the judgment of all, "For what reason is one separated from the other?" And he replied and said to me, "These three have all been made in order that the spirits of the dead might be separated. And in the manner in which the souls of the righteous are separated (by) this spring of water with light upon it, in like manner, the sinners are set apart when they die and are buried in the

earth and the judgment has not been executed upon them in their lifetime, upon this great pain, until the great day of judgment (1 En 22:8–11).

In another account, the souls of the righteous ascend to God's throne after death and enjoy God's presence there (3 En 43:2). However, this source allows also for some intermediate souls who are first sent to the purgatorial fires of Sheol and then presumably are allowed to join the righteous after they have been purified. The wicked, however, are consigned immediately to the flames of Ge-Hinnom[2] (3 En 44:3; Alexander 1983:245).

The Apocalypse of Elijah also contains the idea of separation between good and evil. The righteous obey the law and therefore come under the covenant. Sinners disobey it, are cut off from the covenant, and fall under God's wrath (Wintermute 1983:731).

Others describe conditions for the unrighteous in Hades:[3]

> And I saw there the [punishment] of the air and the blowing of the winds and the storehouses of ice and the eternal punishments. And I saw there a man hanging by his skull. And they said to me, "This one transferred boundaries." And there I saw great judgments and said to the Lord, "O Lord, Lord, which of men, having been born, did not sin?" And they led me farther down in Tartarus and I saw all the sinners lamenting and weeping and evil mourning. And I too wept, seeing the race of men punished thus (GkApEzra 5:23-28).

When the angel led Enoch on his second journey, he saw the great fire burning and he saw a cleavage that "extended to the last sea." Flowing out of it were "great pillars of fire." This, said the guardian angel, was the prisonhouse of the fallen angels who are detained there forever (1 En 21:7–10).

The Hebrews also changed their view of Sheol's location. By the time of the Maccabees (150 BC), Sheol was no longer in the deep between the pillars on which the earth rested (chap. 3, Figure 2). It had been moved to be level with the earth, but outside the bounds of the created earth. It was described as the place of the pit with no heavenly firmament above it, nor earthly foundation under it, a desolate and terrible place. The angel who guided Enoch told him that it was the prisonhouse of the stars, that is, of the fallen angels (1 En 18:12–15).

The biblical view of Paradise, on the other hand, begins with the Garden of Eden, located in the east.

---

[2]A term for hell. See below.

[3]Many of the intertestamental books were written in Greek, so use the Greek term Hades, which corresponds to Sheol in Hebrew. Hades is also used in the New Testament.

> And the LORD God planted a garden eastward in Eden and there he put the man whom he had formed (Gen 2:8 KJV).

This was obviously not then a place for the dead, but later, as the Jews were exposed to foreign ideas about the afterlife, it became identified with the home of the righteous dead.

Many pseudepigrapha contain picturesque images of Paradise, sometimes with conflicting ideas. Paradise is sometimes placed in the third heaven (2 En variant A 8:1–6; ApMos 37:5, 40:1) and sometimes on the earth (1 En 30–32; ApMos 38:5). It is depicted as either without inhabitants (1 En 32; 2 En variant A 8:1–8; 4 Ezra 8:52) or with inhabitants (PssSol 14; 2 En variant A 42:3; ApAb 21; OdesSol 11:18–23).

In one account God, the Father, seeing Abraham meeting his end, ordered angels to take the patriarch's soul into Paradise where there are "tents for my righteous ones and mansions for my holy ones" (TAb 20:14–15). Elsewhere, the archangel Michael put Abraham on a cloud and transported him into Paradise (TAb version B 10:3).

When Ezra asked, "Lord, reveal to me the punishment and Paradise," the angel led him east, where he saw the tree of life. He also saw Enoch, Elijah, Moses, Peter, Paul, Luke, Matthew,[4] all the righteous, and the patriarchs (GkApEz 5:20–23).

Enoch also reported,

> While looking toward the northeast over the mountains . . . far toward the east of the earth . . . I came to the garden of righteousness [Paradise] (1 En 32:1–3).

Elsewhere, Paradise is located east of the sun beyond the earth, in the area where the sun rises. It seems to be on the same level with the earth at one end, but its far end reaches up into the third heaven (2 En 42:3–4). Then again, Enoch goes westward to find Paradise, to the extremities of the sky.

In keeping with Genesis 3:8, where "God walked in the garden," the Jews often associated Paradise with the heaven where God dwells, called "the garden of God" (Ezek 28:13). Elsewhere, while one end of Paradise extends to the third heaven, the other exit leads to the earth. So Paradise is located somewhere between the corruptible earth and the incorruptible heaven (2 En 8:4–6).

---

[4]The Greek Apocalypse of Ezra was written late in the first millennium of the Christian era, which accounts for the New Testament names.

Resurrection

Although few explicit references to resurrection from the dead are found in the Old Testament, some pseudepigrapha written in New Testament times or later do discuss it. The author of 2 Baruch, for example, devotes a whole section to the description of the resurrected body (2 Bar 49–52; Charlesworth, ed. 1985:33; Hare 1985:379–400; Isaac 1983:33). In Lives of the Prophets, the resurrection of the dead is assumed without argument or polemic (LivPro 2:15; Hare 1985:382).

The first and longest fragment of the Apocryphon of Ezekiel contains an eloquent statement about the resurrection.

> God will unite the body and the spirit in the future at the time of the final judgment, handing out reward or punishment (Mueller and Robbins 1983:489).

New Testament Concepts of the Afterlife

In the New Testament, much of the variation of the intertestamental period has jelled into a common Christian view with which we are more familiar because it is incorporated in Western Christian theology and imagery. For example, Jesus' story of the rich man and Lazarus (Lk 16:22–26) pictures Paradise as the final home of the righteous dead and Hades as the final place of the unrighteous dead. Both are at the same level but are divided. The rich man who lands in Hades, looking across the impassable gulf that separates the two, sees Lazarus resting in Abraham's bosom in Paradise. The deep, where Sheol had formerly been located, has now been interposed between Paradise and the place of the unrighteous dead.

Once the separation between Paradise and Hades had been made, the idea of Hades as a place of punishment developed, changing into hell with its fires of punishment introduced into Hebrew thought by Zoroastrian influence (Mt 5:22; 18:9; Mk 9:47; 2 Pet 2:4; Ascham 1918:209–19). A model for these fires lay just outside of Jerusalem, which was surrounded by a wall, the south-western corner of which looked down on Ge-Hinnom, 'the valley of Hinnom' (Greek: Gehenna). Here the inhabitants threw their refuse over the wall into fires which burned perpetually. In the following passages, 'hell' is a translation of Gehenna.

> Whoever calls his brother a worthless fool will be in danger of the fire of hell (Mt 5:22 GNB).

> It is better for you to enter life with only one eye than to keep both eyes and be thrown into the fire of hell (Mt 18:9 GNB).

> Fear God, who, after killing, has the authority to throw you into hell (Lk 12:50 GNB).

> The tongue . . . sets on fire the entire course of our existence with the fire that comes to it from hell itself (Jas 3:6 GNB).

Resurrection of the Dead

A strong non-resurrection view was carried over into New Testament times by the Sadducees, the traditionalist conservatives who believed only what they found in the books of the Law. Opposing them, the Pharisees accepted those religious ideas from Greek and Persian sources that fitted into their existing belief system. They differed from the Sadducees especially as they believed in the soul's resurrection and its afterlife (Coenen, Beyreuther, and Bietenhard, eds. 1979 2:1002).

Jesus, of course, not only manifested the resurrection worldview, but ultimately demonstrated resurrection, an event which is at the very heart of the Christian worldview. The New Testament is unequivocal about resurrection:

> This is the will of him that sent me, that everyone that seeth the Son, and believeth on him, may have everlasting life; and I will raise him up at the last day (Jn 6:40 KJV).

> The Lord himself will descend from heaven with a shout, and with the voice of the archangel, and with the trump of God: and the dead in Christ shall rise first (1 Thes 4:16 KJV).

> Have hope toward God, . . . that there shall be a resurrection of the dead, both the just and the unjust (Acts 24:15 KJV).

In the New Testament, furthermore, resurrection is associated with a final judgment for all (Mt 25:31–46).

> We must all appear before the judgment seat of Christ; that every one may receive the things *done* in *his* body, according to that he hath done, whether *it be* good or bad (2 Cor 5:10 KJV).

> Behold, the Lord cometh with ten thousands of his saints, to execute judgment upon all, and to convince all that are ungodly among them of all their ungodly deeds which they have ungodly committed, and of all their hard *speeches* which ungodly sinners have spoken against him (Jude 14–15 KJV).

> I saw the dead, small and great, stand before God; and the books were opened: and another book was opened, which is *the book* of life: And the dead were judged out of those things which were written in the books, according to their works (Rev 20:12 KJV).

The existing heavens and the heavenly powers will also be shaken at the end of time, just before the arrival of the returning Christ and the appearance of the new world and the new heaven (Mk 13:25; Lk 21:26). The elements that make up this present earth will melt in great heat (2 Pet 3:10) to produce a new heaven and a new earth (Rev 21:1).

Purgatory

When Christianity came along it added to the Jewish separation of Paradise and Hades the fact that Jesus conquered death and Hades. Eventually, the Apostles' Creed declared, "He descended into hell," where he preached to the inhabitants (1 Pet 3:18–20; 4:6). The saints could not be held by death and Hades, and there was some possibility of redemption from the nether world.

Paradise was for those who were clearly on God's side. Likewise, those who were irredeemably lost went to hell. But others who were possibly redeemable also went to hell. So by the first and second centuries AD, both the rabbis and the Christians were in agreement that Hades was not necessarily final. It would have to give up its dead eventually (Rev 20:13). Cleansing fire was therefore invented for purgatory (Coenen, Beyreuther and Bietenhard, eds. 1979 1:712–3). The Catholic Church finally accepted purgatory as an official doctrine at the councils of Florence (1431) and Trent (1545–1563) (Ferm 1945:276, 793 respectively).

Closely related to the concept of purgatory was prayer for the dead. It first appeared in Jewish writing of the first century BC (2 Mac 12:42–45) and was eventually appropriated by Christians, including practices of being baptized on behalf of the dead (1 Cor 15:29) or praying for the dead (2 Tim 1:16–18, in the interpretation of the early church fathers). The early church fathers often included prayers for the dead, and the catacombs have prayers for the dead inscribed on some of the walls. The Protestant Reformation, however, largely rejected prayer for the dead, although the Anglican Church did not (Ferm 1945:603). (See Table 3 on the following page.)

TABLE 3
DEVELOPMENT OF BIBLICAL WORLDVIEWS CONCERNING THE AFTERLIFE
(Parentheses enclose ideas which may not have reached worldview significance, but which lead into New Testament worldview.)

INFLUENCES		WORLDVIEWS
		Early Old Testament immortal souls Sheol, the place of all dead three heavens, God in the highest
Egyptian afterlife: reward and punishment	→	
Canaanite afterlife: reward and punishment	→	
Mesopotamian afterlife: reward and punishment by fire	→	
		Later Old Testament (changes only) punishment of the wicked dead in Sheol hell fire reward of the righteous dead
		Intertestamental
Greek purgatory separation of righteous and unrighteous dead final judgment resurrection	→	
		3-7 heavens (purgatory for purification) varied locations of Sheol (Ge-Hinnom, place of fire) (paradise for righteous dead) (resurrection) (final judgment)
		New Testament paradise/heaven for righteous dead purgatory fiery hell resurrection final judgment new heaven and new earth

The Afterlife in Worldview

This brief overview of the 2,000-year Judeo-Christian development of concepts of heaven, hell, and the afterlife is confusing in its variety of conflicting detail, especially in the intertestamental period. Lest changing biblical worldviews have been lost among the many manifestations in these last two chapters, Table 3 provides a summary. Certainly many of the manifestations represent speculative attempts to give the worldview reality, concreteness. A more fundamental and more pervasive series of worldviews lies behind these imaginative embellishments.

It is as though scholars two thousand years from now should study the worldview of twentieth-century Christians, and should read C. S. Lewis' (1946) masterpiece, *The Great Divorce*. If they considered this work alone, they might think that we believed hell to be a vast, gloomy city where rain drizzles constantly and where houses do not keep it out. A bus goes regularly from hell to heaven, and travelers from hell can stay in heaven if they want to but most prefer to return.

Of course, the scholars would be wrong if they concluded that Lewis described our view. We know that Lewis' picture is, rather, an attempt to interpret the significance of hell and heaven. But we also know that behind his portrayal lies a worldview which is common to many Christians, a belief in the eternal punishment of those people who have refused God's salvation and a heaven in the presence of God.

In many cultures expectations of afterlife are related to beliefs about the spirit world, and this is notably so in some of the cultural periods of the Bible. Biblical cosmologies and views of the afterlife are also intertwined with views of the spirit world, to which we turn in the next chapter.

5

The Old Testament Spirit World

The missionaries and the young church among the Choco of Panama faced some urgent spirit world concerns when Nata, the pastor's wife, fell ill. My one year of missionary medical training made me aware that she was suffering from pneumonia, but we had no antibiotics in the church at the time, and none were available in town.

Day by day, everyone was deeply worried as Nata's condition worsened. I was especially troubled because I happened to be studying the book of James for my devotions at the time, and when I came to the fifth chapter, I didn't know what to do.

> Is any sick among you? let him call for the elders of the church; and let them pray over him, anointing him with oil in the name of the Lord: and the prayer of faith shall save the sick, and the Lord shall raise him up (Jas 5:14–15 KJV).

I was sure that if the believers knew of the passage, they would do exactly what it said, but my Western worldview made it difficult for me to say anything. I knew pneumococci! I knew their medical antidote! But how does the spirit of God destroy pneumococci?

On the other hand, a voice within me kept asking, "If you don't tell the church about this passage, and Nata dies, won't she be on your conscience?" Finally, I wrote out a translation for the pastor, and went off into the forest to pray, continuing my struggle alone.

When I returned after an hour and a half or so, the pastor was frantic. "Where were you so long?"

"I was praying."

"Well you don't usually pray that long. Why were you praying so long today? We need to know what kind of oil we should use. We have three

59

kinds: castor oil, motor oil, and a small vial of olive oil left here by a doctor on a previous visit." I opted for the olive oil.

The elders of the church had already been called. The pastor organized a circle with them and the two missionaries. We joined hands, and the two people at the ends put their hands on Nata's body. Then we all prayed.

When we finished, Nata was not fully healed, but was visibly relieved. I congratulated myself. So far, so good! At least it had not been a flop.

By the next morning, however, Nata had suffered a relapse, and her condition was more serious than ever. I noticed that messengers were sent and the elders were called again. The Indians gathered in a circle once more and prayed over her but did not invite me or my missionary colleague to join them. The woman was healed!

Later that afternoon while Nata was preparing a meal and her husband was repairing a canoe outside, I sat down beside him. "Look at Nata!" I said. "She is up and well and making supper."

"Yes," he said, "the Lord is good. God's spirit is very powerful indeed. When his spirit gives a boot to the fever spirits, they just skedaddle, and they don't come back." He was deeply moved, overjoyed.

I pressed on, "I realize that you prayed for your wife once more this morning, but that this time you did not invite the missionaries into the circle."

The pastor put his arm on my shoulder sympathetically and said in a sad voice, "Jake, we're awfully sorry we couldn't invite you. You and your partner don't believe, and if unbelievers are in the circle, prayer will not heal the sick."

These words, though spoken in love, still cut me to the quick. My culture, with its complete separation between the material and the spiritual, was robbing me of the capacity to believe. Suddenly I was painfully aware of how important it was for me to take my own worldview seriously in relation to those of the Bible and of the peoples among whom I worked. In matters of faith it doesn't work to play make-believe. I had prided myself that I believed in faith-healing, but I realized now that when the chips were down, my faith was not genuine (Loewen 1967:19–20).

I became increasingly aware of the centrality of the spirit of God in the process of healing in the Choco church. Church meetings usually lasted several days, with the healing part occupying as much as a day or two. As soon as the people began arriving, the children were given worm medicine. People with fever were given the appropriate medicines. Open wounds were dressed, sores treated, skin rashes medicated.[1] When a new medicine bottle

---

[1]Medicines were provided by Christian doctors serving with the Panama Canal Company and the US Southern command in the Canal Zone.

was opened, it was blessed and strengthened by prayer. Before each administration of medical care, the patient was individually prayed for. And in the evening, when the people gathered, their prayers repeatedly emphasized that since the spirit of God was in their midst, all the evil spirits had been banished.

Years later, when I spoke to an African colleague about the way my culture limited my faith, he nodded seriously, and said, "Yes, yes, no Westerners believe when it comes to spirits. But missionaries are a sad case indeed. They try to fool themselves that they believe, but it's impossible."

People whose worldview clashes strongly with the worldview of Scripture operate in their own worldview, not in that of the Scriptures. Beyond that, if missionaries with a materialistic worldview teach the gospel through that worldview, they create severe dilemmas for local Christians whose tribal or national worldview is more like that of the New Testament.

This is not to say that worldviews do not change, or that people cannot be converted from one worldview to another. But whether changed or not, thoughtful Christians must be honestly aware of both their own worldview with regard to spirits, and that of the Bible. In this chapter and the next, therefore, we continue our exploration of biblical worldviews, now in respect to the spirit world.

God

When most Western Christians try to verbalize how they view God, their intellectual ideal is:

> God is spirit, and those who worship him must worship in spirit and truth (Jn 4:24 RSV).

In the Old Testament, however, we search in vain for a comparable statement about God's spirit nature.

The images by which God is portrayed in the Old Testament are widely varied. For one thing, God is totally different from humanity:

> I am God, and no mortal, the holy one in your midst (Hos 11:9 NRSV).

> O Lord, our Sovereign, how majestic is your name in all the earth! (Ps 8:1 NRSV).

Or, God is above and greater than all other gods.

> O LORD God, . . . what god in heaven or on earth can perform deeds and mighty acts like yours! (Deut 3:24 NRSV).

> What god is so great as our God? (Ps 77:13 NRSV).

> Who is like the LORD our God, who is seated on high, who looks far down on the heavens and the earth? (Ps 113:5–6 NRSV).

> I know that the LORD is great; our Lord is above all gods (Ps 135:5 NRSV).

The Old Testament also stresses that God is exalted in God's own right.

> Yours, O LORD, are the greatness, the power, the glory, the victory, and the majesty; for all that is in the heavens and on the earth is yours; yours is the kingdom, O LORD, and you are exalted as head above all (1 Chr 29:11 NRSV).

> More majestic than the thunders of mighty waters, more majestic than the waves of the sea, majestic on high is the LORD! (Ps 93:4 NRSV).

> O LORD my God, you are very great. You are clothed with honor and majesty, wrapped in light as with a garment (Ps 104:1–2 NRSV).

> For thus says the high and lofty one who inhabits eternity, whose name is Holy: . . . (Is 57:15 NRSV).

God's holiness is emphasized.[2]

> Who is like you, O LORD, among the gods? Who is like you, majestic in holiness? (Ex 15:11 NRSV).

> Who is able to stand before the LORD, this holy God? (1 Sam 6:20 NRSV).

The Old Testament God is perfect.

> The Rock, his work is perfect (Deut 32:4 NRSV).

> This God—his way is perfect (Ps 18:30 NRSV).

Divine transcendence, God's otherness, continues and grows in the intertestamental period. The writers of that time place God in the highest heavens, far removed from the earth and humankind (1 En 71:5–11). In most of the apocrypha and pseudepigrapha, God is described as majestic and transcendent (2 Mac 3:39; 3 Mac 2:15; 1 En 71:5–11; Charlesworth 1983:xxxi).

But nobody called God "spirit," perhaps because nobody had ever challenged the assumption that God is spirit.

Early Old Testament Anthropomorphism

God, without doubt, is the primordial spirit even in the Old Testament, transcendent over humanity. But in spite of that, early depictions often seem quite human, quite anthropomorphic.

---

[2]On holiness, see chapter 13.

In the act of creating human beings, God *formed* the human body out of clay and *breathed* life into it (Gen 2:7). In the creation of woman, God *opened* Adam's side and *took out* a rib (Gen 2:21–22). In the cool of the evening God *walked* and *talked* with Adam and Eve in the garden (Gen 3:8). God *saw* human wickedness and *repented* of making human beings (Gen 6:5–6). God *remembered* Noah (Gen 8:1), and *smelled* the pleasing odor of his sacrifice (Gen 8:21). God *realized* what human beings were planning to do at Babel, and so *came down* and *mixed up* human language (Gen 11:6–9 GNB).

Such anthropomorphism continued in later parts of Genesis, but in increasingly subdued form. The LORD and two angels appeared as three men at Abraham's tent. Later, the men (angels) left to go to Sodom, and Abraham grappled with the LORD, face to face, to save Sodom. In Sodom, the two men are first called angels, but are later spoken of as men again. Finally, the angels took Lot, his wife, and their two daughters by the hand and dragged them from the city (Gen 18:2–19:16).

God appeared to Jacob in the form of a man, and the two wrestled together. After the struggle, Jacob said, "I have seen God face to face and my life is preserved" (Gen 32:22–32 NRSV).[3]

In the form of a flame out of a bush, the LORD met Moses (Ex 3:2–6), but later tried in person to kill Moses (Ex 4:24). In another anthropomorphic scene, God had a picnic on Mount Sinai with Moses, Aaron, and the seventy elders of Israel (Ex 24:9–11). God eventually buried Moses in the land of Moab (Deut 34:6).

Anthropomorphism in the representation of God in later parts of the Old Testament is especially notable in the many occasions on which God spoke to people, called them, chose one or more of them, and revealed something to them.

Angel of the LORD

Increasingly, in the early part of the Old Testament, purely anthropomorphic depictions of God are replaced by ones which imply spirit as well, namely "the angel of God" and "the angel of the LORD." The angel of the LORD has the appearance of a human being and continues to function in human ways (speaks, calls, sends, fights, blesses), but is classified as angel—as supernatural—rather than as human being. When Hagar ran away from her mistress Sarah, God appeared to her as "the angel of the LORD" (Gen 16:7–11). The angel of God called to Hagar when Hagar's child was

---

[3]See discussion of the taboo against seeing God in chapter 13.

dying of thirst, comforted her, and showed her a source of water (Gen 21:17–19).

When God ordered Abraham to sacrifice Isaac, the angel of the LORD stopped the patriarch from killing his son (Gen 22:11–14). The angel of God also appeared to Jacob when he was getting ready to flee from his father-in-law, Laban. That time, the identity of the angel of the LORD as God was made explicit: "I am the God who appeared to you at Bethel" (Gen 31:11, 13). The angel of the LORD appeared to Moses in the flame of the burning bush, but God talked to him out of the bush (Ex 3:2–6). In a speech to Israel, the angel of the LORD spoke as God:

> The angel of the LORD went from Gilead to Bochim, and said to the Israelites, "I took you out of Egypt and brought you into the land that I promised your ancestors" (Judg 2:1 GNB).

When Gideon was called to lead the army of Israel, the angel of the LORD visited him, and in the interchange God is sometimes referred to as the LORD and sometimes the angel of the LORD:

> The angel of the LORD came and sat under the oak at Ophrah, which belonged to Joash . . . as his son Gideon was beating out wheat. . . . The angel of the LORD appeared to him and said to him, "The LORD is with you . . ."
>
> Gideon answered him, "But sir, if the LORD is with us, why then has all this happened to us? . . . The LORD has cast us off. . . .
>
> Then the LORD turned to him and said, . . .
>
> The LORD said to him, . . .
>
> The angel of the LORD said to him, . . .
>
> Then the angel of the LORD reached out the tip of the staff . . . and the angel of the LORD vanished from his sight.
>
> Then Gideon perceived that it was the angel of the LORD; and Gideon said, "Help me Lord GOD! For I have seen the angel of the LORD face to face." But the LORD said to him, ". . . do not fear, you shall not die" (Judg 6:11–23 NRSV).

The angel of the LORD appeared to Manoah's wife to announce the birth of Samson. When she reported this welcome news to her husband, he prayed that the LORD also would let him see the angel. The angel of the LORD then reappeared, but Manoah was hard to please, even asking for the angel's name. While the angel did not give his name, he put flames to the offering Manoah had placed on the altar, and Manoah said to his wife, "We shall surely die, for we have seen God" (Judg 13:2–22 NRSV).

Spirit of God

Although not explicitly described in the Old Testament as being spirit, God is frequently mentioned as having spirit or having a spirit. This spirit works in and through people.

In light of human sin, God said, "My spirit will not always strive with man" (Gen 6:3 KJV). When Balaam, who had been hired by Balak to curse Israel, was warned by God and decided to bless them instead, God's spirit came upon him (Num 24:2). Joshua was called "a man in whom the spirit is" (Num 27:18). The spirit of the LORD was upon Othniel, Caleb's younger brother (Judg 3:10). When Gideon attacked the Midianites and the Amalakites, the spirit of the LORD took possession of him (Judg 6:34), as it also did at other times of Jephthah (Judg 11:29) and Samson (Judg 13:25). Samson performed all his feats of strength in the power of the spirit of the LORD (Judg 14:6,19; 15:14).

When Samuel anointed Saul, the spirit of God empowered Saul (1 Sam 10:6, 0; 11:6). David had the same experience when he was anointed to be the king (1 Sam 16:13). In a rather strange occurrence, when Saul sent soldiers to take David prisoner in order to dispose of him, they were seized by the spirit of God and began to prophesy (1 Sam 19:20–21 KJV). Then when Saul went in person, he was himself likewise seized by the spirit (1 Sam 19:23–24).

The spirit of God spoke through David (2 Sam 23:2). The spirit of God came upon Azariah as he went out to comfort the King of Israel (2 Chr 15:1). When Judah was invaded during the reign of King Jehoshaphat, the king repented before God, and "The spirit of the LORD came into the midst of the congregation" (2 Chr 20:14). Later when King Joash began to worship idols, the spirit of God took possession of the prophet Zechariah who warned the people about their wrong-doing (2 Chr 24:20). Isaiah, speaking of the coming Messiah, said, "The spirit of the LORD shall rest upon him" (Is 11:2).

The first mention of God's spirit in some translations of the Old Testament is "The Spirit of God moved upon the face of the waters" (Gen 1:2 KJV), but this translation is dubious. The Hebrew word *ruach* can mean 'spirit' when used figuratively, but literally it means 'breath' or 'wind.'[4]

Other Spirits

God and God's spirit are not the only spirits in the Old Testament. In a number of instances God said, "Let us . . . ," which is probably a reflection of a heavenly council (Gen 1:26). Spirits of various kinds are also mentioned in some more direct references to the council:

---

[4]See the footnotes in some modern translations.

I saw the LORD sitting on his throne, with all the host of heaven standing beside him to the right and to the left of him. And the LORD said, "Who will entice Ahab?" . . . Then one said one thing, and another another, until a spirit came forward and stood before the LORD, saying, "I will entice him" (1 Kgs 22:19–22 NRSV).

God has taken his place in the divine council; in the midst of the gods[5] he holds judgment (Ps 82:1 NRSV).

One day the heavenly beings came to present themselves before the LORD, and Satan also came among them. The LORD said to Satan, "Where have you come from?" Satan answered the LORD . . . (Job 1:6–7 NRSV; see also Job 2:1–2).

Angels

Angels are not the same as the angel of the LORD, for they are not appearances of God but are messengers or intermediaries who serve God (Zech 1:9,14–17; 2:3–4). On the whole, the Old Testament has relatively few references to angels proper (cherubim, specialized guardian angels appear in Gen 3:24), who did not play an important role until the exile and after (Coenen, Beyreuther, and Bietenhard, eds. 1979 2:226–7). Their spirit nature is normally not stressed either, in the passages in which they do occur.

The first recorded appearance of angels in Scripture has already been mentioned. Two angels, appearing as men, visited Abraham along with the LORD and then went on to Sodom (Gen 19:1,15).

The fleeing Jacob had a vision of angels ascending and descending a ladder from heaven to earth. Such a multitude of angels is often referred to as the host/army of heaven or of the LORD (Josh 5:14–16; 2 Chr 18:18; Neh 9:6). In one of God's praise names, "the LORD of hosts," "hosts" is a reference to angels (1 Sam 1:3; 2 Sam 5:10; 1 Kgs 18:15; Ps 24:10). In other passages, angels are listed as witnesses of the creation (Job 38:7). God not only uses them to bring punishment (Ps 78:49) and even death (2 Sam 24:15–17), but also to provide protection (Ps 91:11). They are not always perfect beings (Job 4:18). Some appear war-like (Ex 12:23 GNB).

Not all heavenly beings are called angels, but some are referred to by names such as "heroes" (Gen 6:4) and "sons of God" (Gen 6:2; Job 1:6; 38:7 KJV). A less misleading translation of the latter would be "heavenly beings," as in some modern translations.

The growth in importance of angels in Jewish worldview was stimulated by Israel's neighbors. Only after the exile did angel beings become prominent in the religion of Israel, although angels were present earlier. In the

---

[5] "In the midst of the gods" could be translated "in the midst of the mighty ones."

intertestamental period, the pseudepigraphic book Jubilees (probably second century BC) pictures a host of angels who are called God's servants. These angels are structured in ranks, the highest two of which are the "angels of the presence" and the "angels of sanctification." They are said to have been born circumcised (Jub 15:27).

One of the prominent classes of angels was the watchers, originally intended to instruct people in deeds of righteousness (Jub 4:15). But they eventually corrupted themselves by having sexual intercourse with human women, thereby producing various kinds of offspring, including giants (Jub 7:21–25; see also Gen 6:1–4). These angel watchers of the nations are shown as punishing King Nebuchadnezzar for his arrogance (Dan 4:17), apparently reflecting the Babylonian view of the universe. Daniel himself, however, attributes these same events as carried out on the command of the Most High himself (Dan 4:24). Only when the Babylonian ruler finally acknowledges the sovereignty of the Almighty is his sanity and his royal dignity restored (Hammer 1976:56).

Jubilees also stresses that angelic spirits control the forces of nature in this world (Jub 2:2), and good angels teach skills to people (Jub 3:15). Angels inform people of God's will (Jub 12:22), test them (Jub 19:3), report their sins to God (Jub 4:6), announce future events (Jub 16:1–4), reveal cosmic laws (Jub 4:21), bind evil spirits (Jub 10:7–9), and assist those who are attacked by evil spirits (Jub 48:4,13).

The same source also speaks of various kinds of angels whom God created to serve him: angels of the spirit of fire, angels of the spirit of winds, angels of the spirit of the clouds and darkness, snow, hail, and frost, angels of thunder and lightning, angels of the spirit of cold and heat and winter and springtime, angels of the summer, and "all the spirits of his creatures which are in heaven and on earth" (Jub 2:2).

Evil Spirits

The Old Testament does not shed much light on the origin of evil spirits. Some people have suggested that they were lesser deities (demons) from a polytheistic past (Coenen, Beyreuther, and Bietenhard, eds. 1979 1:482); but more likely they are God's creation.

Evil spirits in the Old Testament are not as diametrically opposite from God as they are in the New. They even serve occasionally as God's messengers:

> God sent an evil spirit . . . (Judg 9:23 KJV).
> An evil spirit from the LORD troubled [Saul] (1 Sam 16:14 KJV).

As we have already seen, the LORD sent a lying spirit to Ahab's prophets.

God also sent an evil spirit to trouble Abimelech and the people of Shechem (Judg 9:23).

Only once in the Old Testament are evil spirits referred to as "unclean spirits," which is the favorite label for them in the New Testament (Zech 13:2).

The Old Testament shows some variation in depicting Satan, who became the chief of evil spirits by New Testament times. When the first recorded temptation of a human being occurred, a snake served as tempter, with no reference to Satan (Gen 3:1–5).

The Hebrew word *satan*, furthermore, means 'adversary' or 'opponent,' as when the Philistine army leaders accuse David of being a satan, a fifth column in their midst to undermine their war effort against Israel (1 Sam 29:4). Rezon, an Edomite, became a satan of the Israelite king, and remained a satan of Israel even during Solomon's days (1 Kgs 11:23–25).

Even the angel of the LORD (the term used of God, as described above) is called a satan:

> God's anger was kindled because [Balaam] went: and the angel of the LORD stood in the way for a satan against him" (Num 22:22 KJV adapted).
> The angel of the LORD said unto him, . . . "I went out to satan thee" (Num 22:32 adapted).

Satan is listed with "the sons of God" (Job 1:6; 2:1–6), and also appeared before God in the role of a heavenly prosecuting attorney, accusing or drawing attention to the weaknesses and foibles of human beings (Zech 3:1).

Satan never appears in the Old Testament as the ultimate anti-God principal, the root of all evil, as in the New Testament. The Septuagint—the translation of the Old Testament into Greek, which appeared shortly before the birth of Christ—still did not usually translate satan as 'devil.' Satan as the source of evil developed in intertestamental times, to be discussed in the next chapter.

Various Spirits

Familiar spirits, spirits with whom people establish working partnerships, are mentioned infrequently in the Scriptures, and are treated negatively. The witch at Endor, for example, called Samuel's soul (spirit) from Sheol (1 Sam 28:7–20). Her own words were, "I saw *elohim* [literally 'God' or 'gods'] ascending" (1 Sam 28:13 KJV). The Good News Bible here says "a spirit." Sometimes non-personal negative forces are pictured at work (chap. 13):

> Thou shalt not be afraid for the terror by night; *nor* for the arrow *that* flieth by day; *nor* for the pestilence that walketh in darkness; *nor* for the destruction that wasteth at noonday (Ps 91:5–6 KJV).

Evil spirit forces are occasionally represented as animal spirits:

> But wild animals will lie down there, and its houses will be full of howling creatures; there ostriches will live, and there goat-demons will dance (Is 13:21 NRSV).

> Wildcats shall meet with hyenas, goat-demons shall call to each other; there too Lilith shall repose, and find a place to rest (Is 34:14 NRSV).

The goat-demon is otherwise known in mythology as the satyr, or "night hag" (Duling 1983:947). Lilith is thought to be a female demon who lived in desolate places.

Some expositors interpret the dragons or other monster animals mentioned in the Scriptures as representing evil spirits. Such are Rahab and the Leviathan (Isaac 1983:40). Some intertestamental sources picture the abyss as the infernal home of these monster-spirits. Rahab is a female monster who stands for 'chaos' and 'evil.'

> God's anger is constant. He crushed his enemies who helped Rahab, the sea monster, oppose him (Job 9:13 GNB).

> You crushed the monster Rahab and killed it; with your mighty strength you defeated your enemies (Ps 89:10 GNB).

> It was you that cut the sea monster Rahab to pieces (Is 51:9 GNB).

In some cases Rahab is not referred to by name but by 'sea monster.' The meaning is the same.

> If they hide on the top of Mount Carmel, I will search for them and catch them. If they hide from me at the bottom of the sea, I will command the sea monster to bite them (Amos 9:3 GNB).

Leviathan was another sea monster. It was used as the basis for a major figure of speech:

> Can you draw out Leviathan with a fishhook, or press down its tongue with a cord? Can you put a rope in its nose, or pierce its jaw with a hook? (Job 41:1–34 RSV. The passage continues in the same vein.)

Modern readers of Scripture find mythical or mythological references in the Bible to be strange. We overlook them because our worldview does not recognize them, but they were an integral part of the Hebrew worldview.

The history of the Jews does not break at the end of the Old Testament, of course. The story continues in the next chapter.

6

The New Testament Spirit World

One afternoon when I was working with a translation team in Surinam, we came to a passage which contained the word 'devil,' for which the translators had used *tepïlï*, which I recognized immediately as a transliteration from English. When I asked the missionary about it, he said that they had tried to find an indigenous word, but had not been able to do so, which seemed strange to me because I had never before met a shortage of names for the devil in South American languages. When I checked with the native speaker who was assisting in the translation, I drew a total blank, but came away feeling that he was not being truthful.

That evening, the informant suddenly left the room he shared with the missionary, coming back agitated. He pressed a piece of paper into the missionary's hand and hurriedly left again for about half an hour. When he returned, the missionary did not pronounce what was written on the paper, but asked, "So that's his name?" The Indian nodded vigorously.

"Why didn't you tell us this afternoon?"

"I couldn't. If someone pronounces this name it will kill him and his family. It is taboo! I was too much afraid."

This believer's worldview was limiting his experience of the gospel, and the worldview-insensitive missionary had not been aware of the fact.

Developments in Intertestamental Times

Between the time of the Old Testament and that of the New, the Hebrew spirit world continued to become more elaborate. Influences[1] from the

---

[1]A contrary view is held by scholars who see enough evidence in the Old Testament itself

Assyrian, Babylonian, and later Persian captivities continued to fuel new beliefs about Satan, demons, angels, and especially final judgment, resurrection, fiery punishment, heaven, and hell (Boyce 1982 2:xii, 44–47, 1979:76–77; Hultgard 1979:516–17; Winston 1966:210–13).

God's Heavenly Court

In intertestamental times God's heavenly court, alluded to occasionally in the Old Testament (chap. 5), was developed into the celestial equivalent of the earthly Sanhedrin, the governing assembly of the Jews. It was described as made up of seventy-two princes of the kingdoms of the world with Satan (the prince of the world), and Satan's two representatives, Sammael, the prince of Rome, and Dubbi'el, the prince of Persia, as the accusers in this court (2 En 26:12). Beyond them were all the angels who served God (3 En 18:19–24, 26:1–12; 28:8; 30:1–33).

This parallels the thinking of the Greeks who held that demons or lesser deities were in charge of each nation in the world (Hammer 1976:51). The apocalyptic writings of 3 Enoch (30:1–2) refer to these angel authorities of nations as "seventy shepherds" and also speak about a God-appointed ruler for every nation. In Deuteronomy 32:8–9 (NEB): "When the Most High parceled out the nations, . . . he laid down the boundaries of every people according to the number of the sons of God," with "sons of God" here referring to angel authorities (cf. Dan 10:13,21; 12:1). Some commentaries attribute the development of these views as a counterpoise in response to an increasing emphasis upon the transcendence of God (Nicklesburg 1977).

Angels

As angels proliferated in the intertestamental period, different writers described them in different ways. In the Testament of Job (between first century BC and first century AD), for example, good angels appear in bright light (TJob 3:1; 4:1). The Testament of Solomon describes thwarting angels which are paired with evil spirits to stop their evil work (TSol 2:4, 6:8). The daughters of Job spoke in ecstatic languages, which were identified as the languages of the angels (TJob 48:3).

The angels in the Testament of the Twelve Patriarchs (second century BC) are active in the first heaven, helping to punish the wicked. Beliar, who

---

to account for the later beliefs (Eichrodt 1961 2:517; Alfrink 1959:369; Yamauchi 1990). Gottwald (1985:587) considers the view I propose questionable in part because of problems with the dating of Zoroastrian texts. However, the timing of the proliferation of Hebrew discussion of such phenomena after the captivity and exposure to Zoroastrianism is incontrovertible (Hanson 1987:340–81).

operates in the second heaven, is the head of the evil spirit world. The third heaven is the home of the archangels (TLevi 3:2–6).

Angels are sometimes ranked in a hierarchy of orders. In one source, for example, the hierarchy consists of angels, archons, and cherubim (TJob 48:3; 49:2; 50:2). Other unidentified heavenly creatures carry Job's soul to Paradise at his death (TJob 52:6–10; 47:11; Spittler 1983:835).

Angels also play a big role after the Christian era began. One book depicts six orders of angels. The lowest order consists of ordinary angels. One guardian angel accompanies each human being in the world to protect and serve him or her. Above the guardian angels are the archangels who manage creation according to God's design, care for the world, and guide it. Archons are in charge of things atmospheric, like rain, snow, dust, and hail. They also produce thunder and lightning. Authorities administer the sun, moon, and stars. Powers keep the demons from destroying God's creation. Dominions rule over the kingdoms, and have a hand in their victories and defeats (TAdam 4:1–7).[2] In the Greek Apocalypse of Ezra, one of their chief functions is to interpret for Ezra. Some of the many angels are mentioned by name, like Michael the archangel, Raphael, and Gabriel (GkApEzra 1:3, 4:7). Seven angels from Tartarus, the place where fallen angels were being punished (2 Pet 2:4), led Ezra on a tour of the domains (VisEzra 1:2). Later Michael and Gabriel lead him to heaven (VisEzra 1:56).

The names of the archangels, both good and bad, probably came from the time of Jewish captivity in Assyria and Babylonia. In the Scriptures, only Gabriel (Dan 8:16; Lk 1:19,26) and Michael (Dan 10:13,21; 12:1; Jude 9; Rev 12:7) are mentioned as archangels, but in the pseudepigrapha, one source names Michael (the prince of Israel), Raphael (the prince of healing), Oriel (the prince of light), Duma (the prince of Gehenna), Ridiah (the prince of rain), Lailah (the prince of the night) (Ausubel 1964:3).

In 1 Enoch, on the other hand, some of the leading archangels are Suru'el, Raphael, Raguel, Michael, Saraqa'el, and Gabriel. They are God's servants who oversee the garden of Eden and watch over the cherubim who are the gate-keepers of Paradise (1 En 20).

The central angel figure in 3 Baruch is Michael, the commander-in-chief of all the angels. Five archangels are mentioned by name in the Slavonic version of 3 Baruch: Michael, Gabriel, Uriel, Raphael, and Satanael. The name Satanael (*satan-el* 'adversary-god') is modeled after the names of some of the other angels, which have *-el* 'god' for a suffix. When he fell, his name was then changed to Satan (Gaylord 1983:658).

---

[2]Authorities, powers, and dominions are also mentioned in the New Testament as spirits, good and evil (Eph 1:21; Col 1:16).

Fallen Angels

Angels known as the watchers were good angels at the beginning (Jub 4:15), watching over the earth, teaching wisdom to people, and judging the earth. But the watchers fell in love with human women, and a generation of giants was born (Jub 5:6–16). A Genesis allusion to heavenly beings having intercourse with human women (Gen 6:1–5) was transformed into a theology of fallen angels as an explanation for the origin of evil.

In these accounts, the marriages between angels and human beings led to women being instructed by their angel husbands in forbidden sciences such as magic, making weapons, and preparing cosmetics used in charms (1 En 7:1–2). Eventually the union produced evil spirits (1 En 15:8; Isaac 1983:21). Allusions to fallen angels also occur in other pseudepigraphic and apocryphal writings, as well as in the Qumran writings of the Essenes (Isaac 1983:9).

Prince of the Evil Spirits

The Scriptures speak of the prince of evil spirits as having two aspects. On the one hand, he is the servant of God (Wink 1986:11–21) and on the other, he is the agent provocateur (Wink 1986:22–30). Since Satan is God's creation, God is the source of both (Wink 1986:31–32).

Interest in a chief evil spirit became more pronounced in intertestamental times, but details varied widely. In Martyrdom and Ascension of Isaiah (a pseudepigraphic book by several authors covering several centuries), the chief of the evil spirits has three different but apparently synonymous names, Sammael (MartIs 2:1–2, 5:15–16), Beliar (MartIs 1:8–9, 2:4, 3:11, 5:1), and Satan (MartIs 2:2, 2:7). Other names for the prince of the evil spirits in this period include Satanail/Satanael (Anderson 1983:114, 131, 148, 154) and Beelzeboul (Duling 1983:937, 952–55, 964–65).

In Jubilees (second century BC), on the other hand, Mastema is the prince of evil spirits (Jub 10:8). It was Mastema who suggested to Yahweh that Abraham be tempted to sacrifice his son (Jub 17:15–18; cf. Gen 22:1–14). Mastema, rather than Yahweh, also tried to kill Moses on the way back to Egypt (Jub 48:2–4; cf. Ex 4:24–26).

The Testament of Job (between first century BC and first century AD) contains a highly developed doctrine of Satan who is depicted as a spirit (TJob 27:2). At times he is called the devil (TJob 3:3), sometimes the enemy (TJob 47:10), but his ultimate authority is derived from God (TJob 8:1–3; cf. Job 1:12; 2:6). He deceives human beings (TJob 3:3), as when he disguised himself as the King of Persia and came to Job (here called Jobab), accusing him of destroying all the good things in the earth by distributing so much food to beggars, the blind, and the lame (TJob 17:1–4).

Evil Angels and Magic

One book from the Christian era which deals extensively with Solomon's magical powers[3] contains a variety of syncretistic beliefs involving astrology, demonology, angelology, magic, and medicine. According to this testament, Solomon got a ring from God giving him the power to subdue demons. He then caught and queried each of them about their work and rank. In fact he enslaved many of them to work for him in his kingdom.

When he succeeded in summoning Beelzebul himself, Solomon asked him, "Why are you alone the prince of demons?"

The reply was, "Because I am the only one left of the ranking heavenly angels who fell. I was the highest ranking angel in heaven." The devil then claimed that he had another companion angel, but that one was already bound in Tartarus (TSol 6:1–3).

The Human Soul

In intertestamental times the survival of the human soul at death was already taken for granted, as was the separation of the righteous dead from the unrighteous. It was even suggested that human souls pre-existed in heaven and that they leave the heavenly storehouse of souls to enter human bodies at birth (3 En 43:3). These unborn souls are classified as righteous, so when children die young, their souls go to the heavenly regions.

The New Testament

So it is that we arrive at the time of Jesus and the apostles with a spirit world more elaborate than the spirit world of the Old Testament, especially the early Old Testament. Even the tenet that God is Spirit (Jn 4:24) had yet to be fully verbalized, as we have seen, but in the New Testament it was foundational. Of major importance to the development of Christianity, also, was the full realization (only partially perceived by a few Old Testament writers) that God's rule did cover all people. During the course of the New Testament, the proclamation, "Hear O Israel: the LORD our God *is* one LORD" (Deut 6:4 KJV; repeated in Mk 12:29) was universalized to include all the nations of the world (1 Cor 8:4; Eph 4:6; 1 Tim 2:5).

This radical change in perceptions of the scope of God's kingdom did not even take place during Jesus' lifetime as he ministered primarily to Jews (Mt 15:24). After Jesus died, Pentecost was a Jewish experience when the Spirit

---

[3]The view that Solomon was a magician goes back to ancient interpretations of 1 Kings 4:29–34.

of God came upon "devout men of every nation under heaven" (Acts 2:5–11 KJV), namely Jews scattered among all the nations of the known world.

The enlarged recognition of God's sovereignty in the New Testament began when a Roman centurion was converted. Peter was surprised when God reached out in this way to the Gentiles, but learning his lesson, Peter said,

> Of a truth I perceive that God is no respecter of persons; But in every nation he that feareth him, and worketh righteousness, is accepted with him (Acts 10:34–35 KJV).

This principle that God was the God of all peoples was deepened and generalized in Paul's ministry when he turned to the Gentiles as his mission field because Jews would not accept his message (Acts 13:46). Then he had to bring all of his powers of persuasion, and sometimes his wrath, to bear on convincing Jewish believers that God was truly God of the whole world.

> There is neither Greek nor Jew, circumcision nor uncircumcision, Barbarian, Scythian, bond *nor* free: but Christ *is* all, and in all (Col 3:11 KJV; Gal 3:28).

The matter was officially settled at a conference in Jerusalem, although with some reluctance on the part of many Jewish Christians. Some of them accepted the Gentiles as equal children of God only after "much disputing," and insisted on four restrictions from the Jewish law which were to be binding on Gentile Christians also (Acts 15:1–31).

As the church leadership soon passed from the apostles in Jerusalem to the church in Antioch and other places where Paul had ministered, however, the center of gravity shifted from the reluctant Jewish Christians, and this also changed the outlook of the Christian community. In time resistance died, and the knowledge was accepted that the people who belong to God come from "every nation, and kindred, and tongue, and people" (Rev 14:6).

The Trinity

The anthropomorphically presented, highly immanent God of the first chapters of Genesis had given way to a highly exalted and utterly transcendent God in the late Old Testament and intertestamental times. God was also separated from ordinary mortals by ranks of angelic servants who jealously guarded their Lord against the intrusion of the picayune and the mundane (chap. 5).

In the New Testament, however, this transcendence was suddenly and boldly challenged by radical new concepts. God was manifested in three distinct persons: Father, Son, and Holy Spirit (Mt 28:19; 2 Cor 13:13; 1 Pet

1:2). Each of these manifestations, in turn, introduced a new dimension of intimacy with human beings.

God as the Father[4] introduced a kinship dimension which greatly reduced the earlier transcendent distance. Jesus taught God's children to address God as "Our Father in heaven . . ." (Mt 6:9; Lk 11:2; Rom 8:15-17). If earthly fathers "know how to give good gifts to [their] children, how much more will your Father in heaven give good things to those who ask him?" (Mt 7:11 NRSV; Lk 11:11–13). In keeping with this relationship, God's righteousness, justice, and judgment were tempered by mercy (Rom 9:16; Eph 2:4–7), love (Jn 3:16; 2 Thes 2:16), and patience (2 Pet 3:15).

In God the Son, divine transcendence was blended with human immanence through incarnation—the Son was born of a human mother, a concept for which Greek influence helped prepare people. In the incarnate Christ, God assumed human limitations in order to demonstrate that requirements for a godly life could be fulfilled, and that human limitations did not preclude faithful execution of God's will, or even of becoming progressively more like God (Rom 8:29; 2 Cor 3:18; Phil 3:21; 2 Pet 1:4; 1 Jn 3:2).

God the Holy Spirit, immediately present in and with the believer, was also intimately related to the Son in the latter's conception (Lk 1:35), in his temptation (Mk 1:12), and in his empowerment for earthly ministry (Mk 1:10; Jn 1:32). In his final agony in Gethsemane, an angel—not the Spirit—strengthened him (Lk 22:43), but in his resurrection, the Spirit was active again (Rom 1:4).

The Spirit, God's presence in the world, has many continuing functions. The Spirit convicts people of sin (Jn 16:8), and leads those who believe into God's truth (Jn 16:13). Where the believers need encouragement, the Spirit provides it (Jn 15:26 KJV; Rom 8:16–17) and reminds believers of what Jesus has said (Jn 14:26).

In fact, all the gifts of the church as the body of Christ come by means of the Spirit of God (Acts 1:5; 2:1–13; 11:16). Speaking in tongues is called "the work of the Spirit" (Acts 10:44–48; 11:15–17). Especially in the Gospel of John, we are introduced to the Holy Spirit's function as the comforter—or helper, or advocate, depending on the English translation (Jn 14:16–20).

The visions of John in Revelation were "the work of the Spirit of God" (Rev 1:10).

---

[4]I think it incontrovertible that in the New Testament worldview God is a male parent. Old Testament anthropomorphism not only carried over, but the kinship metaphor was also based on the existing male-dominant social structure. The understanding that God is parent in more than a male sense would eventually make its appearance in societies with very different social structures.

Angels and Demons

Angels are mentioned repeatedly in the New Testament, and the intertestamental concept of a guardian angel is common (Mt 18:10; Acts 12:15; Rev 1:20).

The New Testament has a clear separation between God and evil. No longer are evil spirits sent by God.

> If a person is tempted . . . he must not say, "This temptation comes from God." For God . . . tempts no one (Jas 1:13–14 GNB).

Evil spirits, often called unclean spirits, are strictly Satan's underlings. They do the devil's bidding as they seek to undo or destroy God's work. Evil spirits possess people, often causing them serious illness (Mt 8:28–32; Mk 1:23; Lk 13:11; Acts 10:38).

By the time of the New Testament, the heaven of the birds and the heaven of the stars have been taken over by the evil spirit hierarchy, called the principalities and powers that control the air (Rom 8:38–39; Eph 2:2; 6:12; Col 1:16; Coenen, Beyreuther, and Bietenhard, eds. 1979 1:166). Their hierarchies of increasing authority culminated in the devil himself, ruler of this world (Jn 12:31).

Satan is no longer part of the "family of God" but is the supreme evil power that opposes God and everything godly. Although the name Satan is commonly used in the New Testament, he is also regularly called by the generic name "devil." He is called by the intertestamental name Belial once (2 Cor 6:15), and Beelzebul several times (Mt 10:25; Mk 3:22; Lk 11:15).

The New Testament assumes that Satan rebelled against God and was expelled from heaven, and will be punished, together with many other angels (Mt 25:41; 2 Pet 2:4; Jude 6; Rev 12:9; 20:10). Satan continues to accuse people (Rev 12:10) and tempt them (Mt 4:1; 1 Thes 3:5), but Christ, rather than Michael the archangel, defends them (1 Jn 2:1) and overcomes Satan (Jn 12:31; 14:30; 2 Thes 2:8; Heb 2:14; 1 Jn 3:8). Believers are encouraged to resist and to fight against the devil (Eph 6:12; Jas 4:17; Heb 12:4).

Wink (1984:3) sees these powers as a "confluence of both spiritual and material factors." Thus the biblical principalities and powers involve both heavenly and earthly, divine and human, spiritual and political, invisible and structural dimensions (Col 1:15). The powers need to be seen as the "withinness" of institutions, structures, and systems, the simultaneity of an outer, visible structure and an inner, spiritual reality (Wink 1986: 172–73). They are not just the spirituality of institutions, but their outer manifestations as well (Wink 1992:3). These powers are spoken of as domination systems called "the ruling spirits of the universe" (Col. 2:8). Other New Testament labels are "world," "world order," and "flesh." Wink (1986:163) sees the angels as also relating to the environment. He links environmental justice to social justice. Both depend on the overarching vision of a God who encompasses the whole, in whom all find their right relation, and in whom all things hold together (Col 1:15–18).

Resurrection and Final Judgment

At the beginning of the Old Testament, human beings were in-spirited clay. God made the body out of the dust of the earth and breathed life into it. By New Testament times, however, the breath of God in people had become the soul, the non-material dimension of the human being. Some New Testament writers pair the body with the spirit (Mt 10:28), although the Greek tripartite view of body, soul, and spirit is also present in the New Testament (1 Thes 5:23; Heb 4:12; Coenen, Beyreuther, and Bietenhard, eds. 1979 2:1117).

Like the devil and his cohorts, who will end up in the lake of fire, human beings will be judged in the end and will receive reward or punishment according to what they deserve. The earth and heaven will be renewed.

The resurrection of Jesus the messiah, the son of God, is the pivotal event in the New Testament. Before that, Jesus had resurrected dead people like Jairus' daughter (Mk 5:22–24,35–42), the son of a widow at Nain (Lk 7:11–15), and his friend Lazarus (Jn 11:44). Saints were also raised following Jesus' resurrection (Mt 27:52–53). Peter later raised Dorcas to life (Acts 9:36–41), and Paul raised Eutychus (Acts 20:9–12). Furthermore Christ promised resurrection to all who would believe in him:

> I am the resurrection, and the life: he that believeth in me, though he were dead, yet shall he live (Jn 11:25 KJV).

Belief in and hope for the final resurrection was fundamental to the thinking of the early church (Acts 24:15; 2 Cor 4:14; 1 Thes 4:16). At that final resurrection, body and the soul will be reunited, but the body will be a new heavenly body (1 Cor 15:42–44).

Such aspects of worldview may go beyond cosmology, but do not exceed it by much because the cosmology of the Jews and early Christians included the abodes of God, spirits, and human beings—dead and alive. These different parts of the universe were interrelated, and beings moved or were moved from one to another. They had no meaning except in terms of the beings who inhabited them.

Part III

God and the Sacred

Introduction

Previous chapters have surveyed selected physical and metaphysical aspects of biblical cosmology—the material and spirit worlds, including the afterlife. Now we look again from another perspective, concentrating first on views of the nature of God and God's communication with people, then on spirit possession, and finally on non-spirit power.

In *Your God Is Too Small*, J. B. Phillips (1952) pointed out that many Westerners believe in the "God of the gap." Whenever something good occurs, something which they cannot explain easily, they attribute it to the miraculous work of God. And conversely, negative events are attributed to the nefarious work of the devil.

However, as particular phenomena become explainable scientifically, God or the devil has to retreat from—becomes irrelevant to—such areas. So, in this century God has retreated from such parts of life as health and illness (mental and physical), weather control, crop fertility, and much more. The natural world is getting larger, so among religious people God is forever getting smaller. And for many non-religious people in the Western world, the material is now everything; the gap has disappeared, and God with it (Figure 3).

FIGURE 3

GOD IN RELATIONSHIP TO THE MATERIAL AND THE SPIRITUAL

material ←——————————————→	spiritual
material ←—— God ——→	spiritual
material ←——— God ——→	spiritual
material ←——————— God —→	spiritual
material ←——————————————→	

Figure 3. Unbroken continuum between the material and spiritual in the worldview of the Yaroba (first line; see below, p.134ff) contrasted with the ever smaller "God of the gap" in the West, in which the "gap" for God to fill continually decreases and finally the material realm and materialistic expectations are all-encompassing. At the culmination God is dismissed entirely.

83

For Christians, the concept of a "gap-God" is hopelessly inadequate and needs to be changed, as we will explore in chapter 19. On a different level, rethinking God can be a most liberating experience.

One time when I visited my parents I soon realized that both my mother and my step-father were severely troubled. They told me that the minister had said in the previous day's sermon that many liberals were proclaiming God to be dead. Mother and Dad interpreted this as apostasy, which indicated to them that the end of the world was near.

I thought about how I might relieve their spirits somewhat without getting into too deep a theological discussion. So I asked, "Mother, do you think of God as having hair?"

My mother at once responded in Low German, *Na, oba jo!* 'Why, of course!'

"How long is God's hair?"

"It is at least shoulder length," Mother responded confidently.

"Does God have a beard or a moustache?"

She thought for a while and then responded, "God has a beard, but I don't think God has a moustache."

By this time my step-father was getting restless. He sensed that this conversation was going into theological waters too deep for his simple faith, so he left the house. Mother, however, continued to be intrigued.

I continued to ask. "Does God wear clothes?"

"Yes, certainly!" she responded, with assurance.

"What kind of clothes does God wear—pants and a shirt?"

She thought for a while and then answered, "No, I think God wears a long flowing white robe."

"Does God wear something on his feet, like shoes?"

She pondered this for a while and then finally responded somewhat hesitantly, "Yes, I think God wears some kind of sandals."

I was quiet for a while and then solemnly said in Low German, "*Mame, dee ess doot!*" 'Mother, that one is dead!'

My mother pondered these words for quite a while. Then suddenly her face lit up, and she said, "Oh, you mean my mental picture of God isn't right. I guess that kind of a God doesn't even exist."

When I nodded in agreement, mother seemed greatly relieved and said, "Yes, yes, I agree that kind of a God is dead."

The concept of God has always been and will always remain fundamental in Christian faith and mission. At least three elementary facts make it so.

The first is that belief in God is nearly universal. All known peoples acknowledge the existence of some supernatural being or spirit power which plays a determinative role in human existence.[1] Such indigenous belief in God or gods has provided a foundation on which the Christian church has been built in societies all over the world. Where unbelief in or the denial of the existence of the supernatural is found, it is a recent import from Western secularism.

Second and equally important is the fact that human beings have within them what the Quakers call "that of God." God created human beings in the divine image (Gen 1:26–27), making them redeemable and worth redeeming. To be human means to have the capacity to know and to respond to God, and sharing God's redemption is what the Christian church is all about.

In the third place, even people created with "that of God" within them do not necessarily obey God. Human beings also have the capacity for, and are attracted to, "that which is against God," or evil. Human beings have no gene-controlled instinct—like the ones which cause chicks to peck or ducks to swim—that drives people to obey God and do God's will. Men and women in all societies must be helped to recognize both the ways in which they "fall short" of the divine design and the claims that God has on their lives. The aim of the gospel of God is "to lead people of all nations to believe and obey" (Rom 1:5 GNB). This is the essence of Christian mission.

However, in spite of the universality of belief in God, the actual conceptualizations of God are far from uniform or even similar in the many cultures of the world. The wide range of variations reflects the diversity of human cultures worldwide.

As a new missionary, I was at first greatly relieved to find the concept of a creator God among the Waunana. I was also thrilled that they were "monotheistic"—that they knew only one God, named Ewandama. I thought our missionary task was thereby greatly simplified because I merely had to tell people what the Bible said about God. I did not yet realize that before I could really teach them anything meaningful, I also needed to understand how the Waunana conceptualized God, their entire spirit world, and the sacred. Time and again they heard something entirely different from what I thought I was saying because they were filtering my words through their perceptions, thus creating enormous meaning distortions. I thought I was delivering "the truth" to them, only later to find that I had been compounding error.

In fact, I eventually learned that to avoid miscommunication, Christians must understand thoroughly not only their own theological perceptions of God, but also how their perceptions distort biblical depictions of the

---

[1]To be sure, philosophical Buddhism has no God, but deities of many kinds populate the lives of most Buddhist people.

supernatural. Then on top of that, they must be thoroughly grounded in how God and gods are understood by the people to whom they want to communicate the gospel.

7

God and Gods
in World Cultures

Christians believe that God is a personal being, that although God is not material, human metaphors are reasonable depictions of divine characteristics. Thus, God does things: God guides, God loves, God wants a relationship with human beings. In fact, God's various human-like qualities are manifested not only in one but in three persons, Father, Son (Jesus Christ), and Holy Spirit (chap. 6). Other peoples' conceptions of supernatural powers range from a completely impersonal force (often associated with magic and spells), through the animation of nature, all the way to entire pantheons of gods and goddesses structured very much like human society. In our search for a cross-cultural perspective on biblical worldviews of God, we start with some characteristic non-Christian ones. Some of them throw light on the various and changing understanding which people had in biblical times. I will defer discussion of impersonal supernatural power until chapter 13 and deal for the time being with typical conceptions of personal God, gods, and spirits.

Forms of Supernatural Beings

Impersonal and personal supernatural power are often combined, of course. Among native North Americans, for example, the Algonquin called this supernatural power *manitou*, and the Sioux *wakanda*. In most such tribes it was manifested in a person's guardian spirit which appeared to the seeker in some visible form such as a star, bird, animal, or person. In Western North America these spirit powers tended to select a human being, often by seizing and compelling him into the relationship. Among the Plains Indians, the human being usually sought the guardian spirit in solitude by his own volition. And some groups such as the Pawnee personified this supernatural power, conceiving of it as a supernatural human-like person, a sky-dwelling supreme being whose commands were executed by lesser supernatural beings or spirits.

In Central and South America, people usually believe in a personal creator, or in some cases a range of deity figures. These gods are further related to a multiplicity of other spirit powers—some evil and some good—such as the spirits who help shamans heal the sick. Frequently, even where a deity is conceived of "monotheistically," the people's concern about the other spirit powers totally overshadows the creator God.

Among Nilotic tribes of Africa, like the Nuer, people speak about *kwoth* 'spirit,' which covers a large part of the meaning domain of Hebrew *ruach* 'wind, breath, spirit.' However, *kwoth* can also be personified and spoken of as the 'spirit-of-the-sky' or 'God' (Evans-Pritchard 1967).

The Sotho-Tswana people of southern Africa speak of God as *modimo*, the vital force that permeates everything. The plural of *modimo* is *badimo* 'ancestral spirits,' the living dead. Under Christian influence some distance seems to have been introduced between Modimo and the badimo, so that the badimo are not part of Modimo, but "mediators" of Modimo. The badimo are hierarchically organized just like the Tswana tribes, with some badimo closer to Modimo than others. When people want to contact Modimo, it is wisest to follow channels similar to the ones they use to approach the king. The solicitor first speaks to his older brother, who in turn speaks to their father, who in turn speaks to their grandfather (dead or alive), until the communication reaches someone who has Modimo's ear (Setiloane 1976:64–86).

West African people like the Ewe of Ghana also see ancestral and other spirits as messengers of the wise and benevolent sky God. While it is hard to nail down this fact universally, in Africa, God is often considered the earliest ancestor. Thus the Christian usage of referring to God as our father is natural but can also be misleading. Some people, like the Nuer, prefer to say "God is the father of our ancestors" thus distinguishing the deity somewhat from the ancestors.

Functions of Supernatural Beings

Most tribal and peasant peoples experience deity at least in two (and some in many more) levels. The first is at the "high God," or God-as-a-person level (Schmidt 1965), the second is at the level of lesser supernatural beings, lesser gods, spirits, fetishes, or ancestors. Each lesser category which occurs in any particular religious system may itself comprise several separate levels of deity, which are in turn sometimes treated as personalities, or at other times as impersonal forces. Except for dead ancestors, personality is often not as distinct on lesser levels as with the high God.

Typically, the high God created the universe and usually made human beings, although frequently a more tribally related deity created the tribe. After creation, however, something akin to the fall of Adam and Eve (Gen 3) caused the high God to withdraw, leaving people under the domination of lesser gods, spirits, or shades of their ancestors.

The accounts of this rupture between God and human beings are as varied as the peoples who tell them. For the Waunana of Colombia, the 'devil' caused people to mistrust Ewandama 'high God,' and persuaded them instead to buy axes from him, so that they could raise food crops independent of God. Ewandama therefore withdrew from the Waunana and left them to fend for themselves against the devil's kin and a host of amoral spirit entities that inhabited their environment (Loewen 1969:156–57).

West Africans often speak about creation as occurring at the time when the high God's abode (heaven) was still located very close to earth. Women (shades of Eden) who did the gardening used long-handled hoes which continually poked into the sky or "God's buttocks," as one local language puts it. God told the women to use short-handled hoes, but they wouldn't listen. Finally, tired of being poked, God withdrew from the human scene, leaving people in the care of their deceased ancestors. Subsequently, everyone began using the current short-handled hoes (about twenty to twenty-four inches long), but God has nevertheless kept at a distance from human beings on earth ever since.

In another African situation, smoke from the women's cooking fires got into God's eyes and caused the deity to withdraw in a huff (Cardinall 1970:15).

Deity as Territorially Linked

Many societies experience their deities as tribally, geographically, or functionally specialized. When my wife and I began our mission work in Colombia, one of the first things we noticed was that the Waunana saw every tree, mountain, stream, spring, or even large rock as being the home of some specific spirit entity. Then, when I began to travel more widely to make a dialect survey of Choco languages in Colombia and Panama, I discovered that it was next to impossible to take people from one river or dialect area to visit another dialect group because they were afraid that the spirit powers of the alien area would steal their souls and cause their death. In group after group we heard stories about hunters in pursuit of game who had inadvertently gone beyond the domain of friendly spirits into the realm of alien spirits with dire consequences. Only a few had returned to tell the tale, and even some of them died soon thereafter because they were unable to retrieve their souls from the alien spirits who had captured them.

In many societies the spirit deities associated with various geographical or topographical phenomena are spoken of as their "owners." People never own the land but only use it by permission of the spirits—the true owners—who have adopted them (Loewen 1965a). Thus, nomadic Indians in the Paraguayan and Argentinean Chaco always consulted the spirit owners of an area before they made camp. If the response was favorable, they made camp in peace; if not, they would move to another area and repeat the process. In the case of sedentary people, spirit forces which owned the land were likewise said to own the people living on it.

A new missionary to Nigeria found out about territorially-linked deities when he built a hospital. He started each day of work with Bible study and prayer with his work crew, and long before the hospital was ready to function, all his workmen had accepted Christ. Even the construction time had been an evangelistic success.

Once the building was completed, the workmen returned to their respective home villages, but when the missionary began making evangelistic tours through some of the villages, he found that his converts were contentedly tending family deity shrines. When he confronted them with what was to him this gross incongruity with their confession of faith as Christians, they were surprised. At the mission they had prayed to Owo 'God,' who had power there. But in their home villages they had to pray to Ifa, the deity that owned that area. If they prayed to the mission God at home, Ifa would be unhappy and make too much trouble for everybody (Bunkowske 1983).

Because many tribal groups are unwilling to roam beyond the area controlled by friendly spirit owners who have adopted them, war against another tribe for the purpose of taking away their land is inconceivable. It would be suicidal to occupy land whose spirit owners had already adopted another tribe, or which was watched over and lived in by the souls of the deceased ancestors of a people other than their own.

But in other cases, if people with a strong territorial concept of God do conquer another tribe's land, they must change their religion and worship the local deities. For example, when the Zulus and related tribes of South Africa conquered tribes as far north as today's Malawi and Tanzania, they immediately changed allegiances and worshipped the local gods. Thus in modern Malawi among the Ngoni (as the conquerors are called today), it is almost impossible to find even a trace of their earlier South African deities.

In many African societies, furthermore, since the people are on the land only by permission of its real spirit owners, they consider it prudent not to abuse the land. They employ preplanting rituals, often informing the spirit owners of what they intend to plant. Then they promise to return the land to its owners after the harvest.

The earth is often spoken of as female. Some peoples even see it as sentient. In some societies, people do not dig or hoe a whole field but dig up just the exact spot where the seed is to be planted, believing that they should not tear up "Mother Earth's body" unnecessarily. They resist mechanized deep plowing for fear of injuring or hurting Mother Earth and thus endangering fertility.

A Westerner observing slash-and-burn farmers who plant in a different area each year, allowing the previous year's field to return to nature, is prone to conclude that the people do so to enhance fertility. While this may be the result, the rationale of these farmers in some cultures is to let the wound inflicted on the land heal itself. Continuous infliction of pain on the same spot may bring about an alienation of the earth, its fertility, and its spirit owners. Should this happen, the consequences would be even more disastrous than alienating the high God.

Because deities are restricted to specific tribes or defined areas, morality is also restricted. Proscriptions on negative behavior apply only to one's own group. Thus to steal from, to harm, or to kill a person from one's own group is punishable by supernatural beings; to do the same things to a member of another group may make a person a hero. Such limitation on morality is a major obstacle for newer nations of the third world to overcome in their efforts to build a national identity.

For people with strong territorial beliefs, death in an alien country is a tragedy of enormous proportions. For many African groups, the dead control the salvation of the living, while the living control the salvation of the dead. This means that the ancestral spirits guide, chasten, help, protect, and bless the living. By remembering and paying respects to the dead, the living in turn prevent the latter from becoming angry and eventually becoming evil spirits, for anger is the first step toward becoming an evil spirit. In Africa, most of the spirits that cause diseases (or cure them as helpers of tribal healers) are souls of aliens who have died away from home.

The spirits of white people who die in East Africa, far from their native lands, are especially likely to become evil spirits. When Caucasians die, they often have no one to remember them. Their souls therefore become angry and finally become malevolent spirits. Tribal healers, therefore, work with many souls of dead white people to heal especially the illnesses brought to Africa by Westerners. For example, one healer in Malawi counted seven British, Portuguese, and South African spirits among her seventeen spirit helpers.

But the relation between souls of the dead and evil spirits is not confined to white people. At a Bible translators' institute in Kitwe, Zambia, we collated and plotted on a map all the names for spirits from over thirty languages. We discovered that tribe X's name for 'soul-of-the-dead' was frequently tribe Y's or Z's name for an 'evil or disease-carrying spirit.' All evil spirits, it seemed, were of human origin, as well as geographically restricted.

Functional Specialization of Deity

In addition to being identified with ecological or topological features, deities may often be functionally specialized in their activities or roles. Deities of classical Greek or Roman mythology illustrate the phenomenon (Table 4).

TABLE 4

CONDENSED LIST OF GREEK AND ROMAN DEITIES WITH THEIR AREAS OF SPECIALIZATION

FUNCTION	ROMAN	GREEK
king of the gods	Jupiter	Zeus
god of the sun and youth	Apollo	Apollo
god of war	Mars	Ares
god of the sea	Neptune	Poseidon
messenger of the gods	Mercury	Hermes
god of wine	Bacchus	Dionysus
goddess of agriculture	Ceres	Demeter
goddess of hunting	Diana	Artemis
goddess of love	Venus	Aphrodite
goddess of the home	Vesta	Hestia

In South American tribes, such supernatural specialization is largely among evil spirits. On the other hand, among many Bantu tribes in Africa, where the spirits are usually former human souls, the specialization is often most marked in a hierarchy of protective spirits. At a personal level, for example, the West African deities Ifa or Afa control people's behavior, telling them where to go today, what they may do there, whom they should marry, and many more details of life.

At the level of the household, some deities are charged with protecting the health and safety of the family. In one "Christian" home, nine such deities from nine past generations were each represented by a small white stone. More were added when the present family members died and then revealed themselves to be family protectors.

At the village level, a village may contain more than one clan, but all the clans who live together in a place share a common peace-keeping village deity, although each clan also has its own clan deity. In other tribes, farmers, fishermen, blacksmiths, or warriors each have their own protecting and guiding deity.

People who believe in specialized deities usually add gods to their pantheon quite easily, including the biblical God whom they see as specialized in preparing people for life after death. Missionaries sometimes sense this limitation in function of the God they preach and often blame their converts for not being truly converted.

However, tribal people of South America and Africa are not the only ones who multiply specialized gods. The Catholic Church has saints with special functions ranging from Saint Joseph, the patron of carpenters, to Mary Magdalene, protector of prostitutes. In Latin American Christo-paganism, many local tribal deities have been saved from oblivion by being rebaptized with the name of a Catholic saint (Madsen 1957; Herskovitz 1937).

One God and Many Gods

Africans, including many African Christians, do not feel that their multiplicity of gods, fetishes, and spirit powers excludes monotheism. To them, one high God has divided the work of running the world among a multitude of lesser manifestations charged with attending to day-to-day affairs, but the high God remains fully in charge of the whole. Such people are quick to point out that Christians do not see Father, Son, and Holy Spirit as three deities, but as three separate manifestations of one God, so they too see their specialized deities and spirit powers as multiple manifestations of a single God. Here follows a description by one African theologian.

> A traditional Ghanaian, be he Akan, Ewe, Ga, or whatever, . . . believes he is surrounded by numerous hosts of spirit-beings, some good, some evil, who are able to influence the course of his life for good or for ill. So he believes in the Supreme Being, Gods, and ancestors, and tries to get their good will in all sorts of ways . . . (Pobee 1979:28).

> The first spirit-being is God, the Supreme Being, called *Onyame* or *Onyankopon*. He is *Oboadee* i.e., the Creator, the Sustainer of the Universe, the final authority and the Overlord of Society who has the power of life and death. Atheism is foreign to the Akan, because, as his proverb puts it, *obi nnkyere abofra Onyame*—since God is self-evident, no one teaches a child to know God. *Homo Akanus* also conceives of this God as being a big potentate who may therefore not be approached lightly or bothered with the trivial affairs of men. Consequently, God the Supreme Being has delegated authority to the *abosom* (Gods) and to the *mpanyinfo* (the ancestors) who, therefore, act *in loco Dei* and *pro Dei* (Pobee 1979:46).

In this situation lesser gods called *Nyame mba* 'children of the Supreme Being' also have power which is at once beneficent and potentially dangerous. Their values, attitudes, and thoughts are likened to those of human beings.

Apart from the High God, the ancestors, and the lesser gods, nature itself is believed to have power, even spirits. Thus the Akan may offer an egg or a mashed yam to a tree or a rock. The power of nature may both be revered and harnessed for people's benefit (Pobee 1979:47–48).

My wife and I discovered a very similar point of view in India, where we spent almost two months. We dedicated three weeks of our time to touring Hindu temples, reading Hindu literature, and talking to Hindu priests and worshipers. Some of the most thought-provoking ideas emerged in response to our question, "Why so many deities?" We learned something very similar to what the Africans say:

> Hinduism is very much like Christianity. You Christians say that you believe only in one God and worship only one God. However, in practice, you admit that this one God has been manifested in three different persons. However, when you meet multiple manifestations of God in other religions, you don't recognize them as manifestations of one God, but condemn them as idols. Now Hinduism, like Christianity, believes in only one God. Like Christians, Hindus believe that God is manifested in more than one form. In fact, in Hinduism we believe that God has been revealed in enough forms to meet all individuals, wherever they find themselves, and whatever their need may be.

While touring the cave temple on Elephanta Island near Bombay, the Hindu guide explained the various deity carvings and ended up her remarks with an idea reminiscent of Quaker thought:

> There is a part of God in every human being and the function of religion is to help this divine element develop to the fullest possible extent.

With cross-cultural perspectives from this brief background sketch, we turn now to look at perceptions of God in the Bible.

8

The God Concept in the Bible

The concept of God was not constant through all the centuries in which the Israelites lived and in which the Bible was written. Our churches, our Bible training, and our all-pervasive Western culture have obscured many of the changing perceptions of deity which are actually reflected in the Bible and have blurred the patterns which such biblical changes followed. Many of the same conceptions of deity found in various world cultures (chap. 7) are also present in the Scriptures, so we will look at the biblical evidence and consider what the changes in those conceptions mean.

Divine Specialization

In contrast with the great, transcendent universal God with which the Bible record ends, the God who called Abraham was seen as a narrowly specialized God, first a personal and household God, then a tribal and territorial God after Abraham's time. That specialized deity, however, provided the beginning points from which the concept of a universal God grew.

Personal and Household Deity

Abraham, the ancestor of the Hebrews, came from a polytheistic background in which people believed in personal and household gods in addition to a high God. While Abraham accepted Yahweh as his sole God, his relatives in Mesopotamia continued to live by their old religious tradition. Thus, when Jacob returned to his uncle Laban's place to look for a wife, he found that his uncle had personal gods, called *teraphim*, which protected his person, his household, and his prosperity. When Jacob later fled with his wives—Laban's daughters—Laban pursued him as much for the recovery of

95

his gods as for any other reason: "But why did you steal my household gods [Hebrew: *elohim*]?" (Gen 31:30 GNB).

Jacob did not know that his wife Rachel had stolen the gods; he permitted Laban to search everything in his camp. Rachel, however, saved the teraphim by putting them in her camel saddle and sitting on it, pleading menstruation as the reason for not getting up when her father searched her tent (Gen 31:35).

But when Jacob got back close to Bethel, the place where he had earlier made his covenant with Yahweh, he collected all of the other gods in his family, including his uncle's teraphim, and disposed of them under an oak tree (Gen 35:2–4). Bethel was at the border between the territories of the gods El and Yahweh, so Jacob left the alien gods there.

However, this was by no means the end of the teraphim concept in Israel. Some time later, in response to Yahweh's call, Gideon destroyed the altars of Baal and Asherah (the female consort of Baal) which his father had built up in their village, much to the anger of his fellow villagers. In their place he made an *ephod*[1] of gold and established this deity in a shrine in his home to become his family's protector (Judg 6:25–32, 8:24–27).

Likewise, a man named Micah and his mother had a silversmith make an ephod and teraphim which Micah installed in a shrine in his house with one of his sons as priest. However, when a Levite later came through his village,[2] Micah hired him as his priest and so felt that he was really doing things God's way. "Now I know that the LORD will prosper me, because the Levite has become my priest" (Judg 17 NRSV).

However, this particular personal household god later was destined to become a clan or tribal deity. Some men from the tribe of Dan learned about the shrine and came to ask the priest for a divine message. When the message proved useful, the men came back and stole the deity, persuading the priest to go along with them, saying it was better to be a priest to a whole tribe than to a single family. They all then went off and made this shrine the official shrine of the tribe of Dan (Judg 18).

Toward the Tribal God of the Hebrews

The foregoing examples may not represent the mainstream of Israelite worldview, but it is clear that in the earliest times Yahweh was seen as the

---

[1]The ephod was originally a vest in the high-priestly wardrobe, but later the term was used for a personal, family, or village deity. Ephod and teraphim are mentioned together in Hos 3:4 (NRSV).

[2]Levites were members of the tribe from which Yahweh's priests were supposed to be selected.

personal God of the individual patriarchs, Abraham, Isaac, and Jacob.[3] When Yahweh[4] selected Abram as his protégé and asked him to leave his family and his country (Ur of Chaldees) and to go into a new country, the LORD promised to give him this new land and make a great nation out of his descendants. When Abram arrived there, Yahweh confirmed that he had come to the right place so Abram built an altar and called the place Bethel 'house of *el* [God]' (not 'house of *yahweh*') (Gen 12:1–9).

At times in the early accounts of Abram, the name Yahweh is not used for God. In Canaan Abram met Melchizedek, a priest of *el elyon* 'most high God.' Melchizedek called Abram a follower of El Elyon (Gen 14:18–19). Abram swore an oath to Yahweh El Elyon 'Yahweh the most high God' (Gen 14:22). Not long after that experience, Yahweh again appeared to Abram and made a covenant with him, identifying himself by name saying, "I am Yahweh[5] who brought you out of Ur," to which Abram responded, "*adonai yahweh*," 'Lord Yahweh' (Gen 15:7–8). From then on, Yahweh was "the God of Abraham." Thus, when Eliezer, Abraham's servant, was sent to find a wife for Isaac, Abraham's son, he prayed to and spoke about '*yahweh*, the *elohim* of my master Abraham' (Gen 24:12, 27, 42, 48).

Later, Isaac prayed to Yahweh concerning his wife's barrenness, and she was blessed with twin sons, Esau and Jacob (Gen 25:21–24). When Yahweh appeared to Jacob in his later life, he identified himself as the '*elohim* of your father Abraham' (Gen 26:24). When Jacob was in the process of stealing the blessing of the firstborn from his brother Esau, he answered his father's question on how he succeeded to find game so quickly by saying, "because *yahweh* your *elohim* brought it to me" (Gen 27:20).

When Jacob had to flee Esau's wrath, while at the same time wanting to look for a wife among his mother's relatives in Haran, Yahweh appeared to him at Bethel, 'house of *el*,' on the border between Yahweh's and El's territory and said, "I am *yahweh*, the *elohim* of Abraham your father, and the *elohim* of Isaac" (Gen 28:13). For the next twenty years, Jacob lived and worked in El's territory, as shown in the use of *el* for 'God'[6] in the story (Gen 30:2,18,20; 31:5, 9). Eventually Yahweh advised Jacob to leave Laban and Haran, reminding him of the encounter at Bethel (Gen 31:11–13).

When Laban discovered that Jacob had fled, he pursued but admitted to

---

[3]The interplay between the use of *yahweh*, the personal name for God in Hebrew, and *el/elohim*, the generic term for God and gods, will be further developed in chapter 15.

[4]The text reads Yahweh at several points here in the story, but likely Yahweh has been substituted for El or Elohim by later writers or editors.

[5]Here the Septuagint has only 'God.'

[6]In most English translations God (without small capitals) translates *el* or *elohim*, and LORD translates *yahweh* (chap. 15).

Jacob that the Elohim of his father had warned him to treat Jacob correctly (Gen 31:29). After some discussion, the two men then set up a boundary marker between their respective countries and their respective gods. The gods of Abraham, Nahor (Abraham's brother, Laban's grandfather), and Abraham's father Terah would judge between them (Gen 31:53 KJV). Later, when Jacob wrestled with Elohim at the ford of the River Jabbok, he said, "I have seen Elohim face to face," and he named the place Peniel 'the face of El' (Gen 32:30).

Centuries later, when Yahweh confronted Moses at the burning bush in Midian, the LORD was identified as "the God of your ancestors, the God of Abraham, the God of Isaac, and the God of Jacob" (Ex 3:13 NRSV). God then instructed Moses to return to Egypt and tell the Hebrews that "Yahweh, the God of your ancestors, the God of Abraham, of Isaac, and of Jacob" had sent him (Ex 3:16 NRSV), but to tell Pharaoh, the king of Egypt, that he represented Yahweh, the God of the Hebrews (Ex 3:18). Thus the personal God of Abraham, Isaac, and Jacob was becoming the tribal God of the Hebrews, still specialized, but much larger than the earlier, strictly personal or family God.

Territorial Deity

The God of the Hebrews remained a tribal deity as Yahweh traveled with the people through the Sinai wilderness and into Canaan. But there God came into conflict with another kind of divine specialization, territorial deities, the gods of the land. A long period of uncertainty followed, a period of ambivalence as to what Yahweh's place was to be in this new territory, until finally Yahweh, too, was established as territorial God, centered on Mount Zion, the location of the temple in Jerusalem. As territorial God, Yahweh was still specialized, but less narrowly so than as a tribal God or a personal God.

However, the territoriality of Yahweh did not emerge brand new with the transition from desert, nomadic, tribal God to agricultural, settled, territorial God, any more than did the tribal link end then. Its roots went way back. We have already seen that after his dream at Bethel, Jacob took leave of Yahweh, the God of his father and grandfather, at the border of the territory ascribed to Yahweh in order to go to Haran where El, the God of Abraham's father, was in charge. He said:

> If *elohim* will be with me, and will keep me in the way that I go . . . so that I come again to my father's house in peace, then *yahweh* shall be my *elohim* (Gen 28:18–22 NRSV adapted).

Then when Jacob was to return to Canaan from Haran, Yahweh appeared to him in a dream, and spoke to him in territorial terms.

I am the God of Bethel, where you anointed a pillar and made a vow to me.
Now arise and go forth from this land and return to the land of your birth
(Gen 31:11–13 NRSV).

Laban and Jacob also defined a territorial boundary between the gods of their
ancestors.

Then much later, when Jacob was en route to join his son Joseph in Egypt,
he reached Yahweh's southern limit at Beersheba, and worshiped the Elohim
of his father Isaac in a farewell ceremony. But Elohim promised to go along
to Egypt with them and to bring them back.

When the Israelites did arrive back in Canaan from Egypt and the
wilderness more than four hundred years later, they found another dimension
of territoriality in operation, namely that the local territorial deities had their
shrines, their holy places, on the mountains. This aspect of divine territoriality
was not new to the Hebrews either. Yahweh had appeared to Abraham when
the latter was sacrificing his son Isaac on Mt. Moriah (Gen 22:1–14). Yahweh
appeared to Moses in the burning bush at Mt. Horeb, also called The
Mountain of God. Here God said, "The place on which you are standing is
holy ground" (Ex 3:1–5 NRSV). God made his covenant with the nation of
Israel on Mt. Sinai (Ex 19:5–8; 24:7–8).

Later on, after the Israelites had long been in the promised land, Solomon
would build the temple on Mt. Zion, which is repeatedly called the hill where
God resides (Ps 9:11; Is 8:18). To the Hebrews' enemies, Yahweh became
known as the God of the hills (1 Kgs 20:23–28).

Another aspect of territoriality was agriculture. The people of Israel had
never been a farming people. When they arrived in Canaan, they found the
Canaanite gods Baal and Asherah—the specialized territorial[7] god of the
agricultural people living there and his consort the goddess of fertility. These
deities of agriculture already occupied the strategic high places and were
specialized in the needed skills, so many formerly nomadic Israelites blended
into the local worship and adopted them. Periodically, however, Yahweh or
the prophets demanded that the deities be removed.

That night the LORD told Gideon, . . . "Tear down your father's altar to
Baal, and cut down the symbol of the goddess Asherah, which was beside it.
Build a well-constructed altar to the LORD your God on top of this mound"
(Judg 6:25–28 GNB).

When Naaman, the leprous Syrian general, was healed by bathing in the
river Jordan, he realized the power of the Yahweh of Israel and asked for two

---

[7]Asherah was not as territorially limited, but was known all over the Middle East by various
names such as Ashiru, Astarte, Asherat, Ashtareth, Ashtoreth, Athtar, Atargatis, and Ishtar.

mule-loads of Israelite earth to take home so that he could pray and worship Yahweh on a symbolic bit of Yahweh's own soil because his birth and his position condemned him to live in the domain which the god Rimmon controlled (2 Kgs 5:1–19).

Another time the Syrians under Benhadad had suffered a severe defeat at the hands of the Israelites, but within a year they rebuilt their armies and planned a new campaign. This time they took the deity residence factor into account. They reasoned,

> The Gods of Israel are mountain Gods, and that is why Israel has defeated us. But we will certainly defeat them if we fight them in the plains (1 Kgs 20:23 GNB).

When the territoriality and the tribalism of God were linked, and war occurred, it was not merely a war between two peoples, but also between their respective Gods. Just as the vanquished general turns over his "sword" to the victorious leader of the conquering army, so the vanquished God turned over the territory to the victorious God.

> But the LORD, the God of Israel, gave the Israelites victory over Sihon and his army. So the Israelites took possession of all the territory of the Amorites who lived in that country. . . . We are going to keep everything that the LORD, our God, has taken for us (Judg 11:21–24 GNB).

Battles between the respective Gods (together with their people) occur frequently in the Scriptures. The king of Assyria warned Hezekiah, the king of Judah,

> Do not let your God on whom you rely deceive you by promising that Jerusalem will not be given into the hand of the king of Syria. . . . Have the Gods of the nations delivered them, the nations which my father destroyed, Gozan, Haran, Rezeph? (2 Kgs 19:9–13 NRSV).

To this challenge, Isaiah told the king to respond on Yahweh's behalf,

> Who do you think you have been insulting and ridiculing? You have been disrespectful to me, the holy God of Israel. . . . I will defend this city and protect it, for the sake of my own honor and because of the promise I made to my servant David (2 Kgs 19:22–23,32–34 GNB).

That night Yahweh killed 185,000 Assyrian soldiers, forcing the Assyrians to retreat.

When David fled from Saul, he deplored that

> They have driven me out from the LORD's land to a country where I can only

worship foreign gods. Don't let me be killed on foreign soil, away from the LORD (1 Sam 26:19–20 GNB).

David's concern demonstrated both the problem of worshiping God away from the LORD's territory and the fear of dying outside of his homeland, away from his God's control.

The book of Daniel, written from the perspective of the captivity, contains another intriguing example of deity being perceived and spoken of as acting territorially. Daniel, a Jewish captive in exile serving as a Chaldean-Persian government administrator, is a faithful servant of God. In the course of one of his extended worship periods, he receives a vision about future events in world affairs. Since he does not understand its meaning, he asks God for an interpretation of the awesome vision. However, no answer seems to come from God for twenty-three days, but on the twenty-fourth day the archangel Gabriel finally arrives and informs Daniel that God had dispatched him on the very first day of Daniel's request, but he was waylaid and held up by the archangel (prince) in charge of the empire of Persia. The two angels had struggled for twenty-one days until finally Michael, the archangel in charge of the nation of Israel, had arrived to help Gabriel overcome the powerful archangel of Persia. Gabriel then informed Daniel that the mighty archangel (prince) of Greece was about to appear on the world stage (Dan 10:1–11:1). Thus, each nation and the territory it governs is supervised by its own powerful divine authority—here called prince or archangel—to whom God has delegated supervisory responsibility (Hammer 1976:14, 51; Wink 1984:26–35, 1986: 87–107).

From Specialization and Territoriality to Universal God

It took many centuries for the specialized, territorial Yahweh to become the universal God in the worldviews of God's peoples. And actually, God is often not fully so yet.

From Tribal to Universal

The early chapters of the Bible were not written as a step-by-step account at the time they happened, but the stories on which they were based were transmitted orally from generation to generation for some time before they were written down. As in many societies, a single orally transmitted account may develop variant versions in the course of time. Thus in the first creation story Elohim is the creator (Gen 1:1–2:4), but in a second, Yahweh is the creator (Gen 2:4–25). In the light of what we have said about African religions, we can readily equate Elohim with the high God and Yahweh (having a personal name) with the personal God of Abraham and later the tribal God of the whole Israelite people.

The high God Elohim appears in the first chapter of the Bible as the universal creator of all people, without distinction of race, ethnicity, territory, or sex, in the ideal image that God wants people to have of deity. But much of the rest of the Old Testament consists of Yahweh's struggle to become that high God of all humanity in the thinking of the people of Israel. The Hebrews were slow to learn that Yahweh is really Elohim, and that as such he is the God of all humanity.

God's universality was severely limited in much of Hebrew belief. Yahweh was their tribal God exclusively, and both poet and prophet picture him as fiercely partisan to his chosen people as his covenant with Abraham demands:

> I will bless those who bless you, But I will curse those who curse you (Gen 12:3 GNB).

In loyalty to Israel, Yahweh was pictured as destroying entire nations, despite the divine assignment to each different tribe of the specific area it was to occupy. The tribally loyal Yahweh promised to give Jacob's descendants all the land

> . . . from the borders of Egypt to the Euphrates River, including the lands of the Kenites, the Kenizzites, the Kadmonites, the Hittites, the Perrizites, the Rephaim, the Amorites, the Canaanites, the Girgashites, and the Jebusites (Gen 15:18–20 GNB).

Yahweh himself enjoined the Israelites to exterminate these people.

> When you capture cities in the land that the LORD your God is giving you, kill everyone. Completely destroy all the people: the Hittites, the Amorites, the Canaanites, the Perrizites, the Hivites, and the Jebusites, as the LORD ordered you to do (Deut 20:16–17 GNB).

Indeed, Yahweh promised to perform a lot of this destruction for them.

> My angel will go ahead of you and take you into the land of the Amorites, the Hittites, the Perrizites, the Canaanites, the Hivites, and the Jebusites, and I will destroy them (Ex 23:23 GNB).

The Israelites' country had to be destroyed, the people captured to become a minority living permanently in a country not their own, before they could conceive of Yahweh as also the God of the whole world.

As with tribal Gods elsewhere, so also for Israel, morality was largely confined to behavior within the tribe. "God's people" were free from moral restraints to outsiders; they could beat, burn, and kill, all to the glory of their God.

Later, however, some of the prophets began to see Yahweh as showing concern for other nations, although still largely as the God who will punish them for their evil deeds (Is 13–23; Jer 46–51; Ezek 25–32; Amos 1:2).

But then, sometimes Yahweh installed rulers in these other nations as instruments for either punishing or doing kindness to Israel.

> I am the one who has placed all these nations under the power of my servant, King Nebuchadnezzar. . . . But if any nation, or kingdom will not submit to his rule, then I will punish that nation by war, starvation and disease until I have let Nebuchadnezzar destroy it completely (Jer 27:6,8 GNB).

> The LORD has chosen Cyrus to be king. He has appointed him to conquer nations. . . . To Cyrus the LORD says, "I myself will prepare your way. . . . I appoint you to help my servant Israel, the people I have chosen" (Is 45:1–2, 4 GNB).

During and after the captivity in far-off lands which were outside of Yahweh's territory, a few of the prophets began to see Yahweh still differently. A few had glimpses that God included members of these nations in the divine plan of worldwide salvation.

> A foreigner who has joined the LORD's people would not say, "The LORD will not let me worship with his people" . . . And the LORD says to those foreigners who become part of his people, . . . "I will bring you to Zion . . . and accept the sacrifices you offer on my altar. My Temple will be called a house of prayer for the people of all nations" (Is 56:3,6,7 GNB).

In this Isaiah passage the condition for the acceptance of people from other tribes to worship Yahweh seems to include submission to the whole Mosaic law as a proselyte, but occasionally we also note that they will be accepted even without becoming external Jews.

> The LORD says, "The end is near for those who purify themselves from pagan worship. . . . I am coming to gather the people of all nations. . . . I will make some of them priests and Levites" (Is 66:17,18,21 GNB).

The book of Jonah is one of the most dramatic biblical illustrations of the struggle of Yahweh to be seen as the Elohim of all people. Yahweh's word came to Jonah, telling him to go to Gentile Nineveh and to warn the people there that God was about to destroy their city because of their wickedness. But Jonah believed that Nineveh needed to be destroyed and ran away from Yahweh and from the horror of preaching to Gentiles—what if they should repent? He set out on a ship bound for Tarshish (Spain), which was equivalent to the end of the world.

After Jonah's escape was unsuccessful, and Jonah was spat up by the great fish associated with his name, Yahweh told Jonah a second time to go to Nineveh, that Elohim-sized city (Jon 3:3) which took three days to walk across.

So Jonah did tell all the inhabitants of Nineveh that God was going to destroy their city, and as he feared, those Gentiles did repent. Jonah, still hopeful, went to the edge of the city to watch its destruction, only to be dreadfully disappointed when nothing happened to all the "evil" Gentile people.

Jonah was uncomfortable pouting out in the hot desert sun so God caused a plant to grow up, and Jonah was delighted to find refreshing shelter under its shade. But when God arranged for the plant to be killed, Jonah became so angry he wanted to die.

Then God pointed out the lesson,

> This plant grew up in one night and disappeared the next; you didn't do anything for it and you didn't make it grow—yet you feel sorry for it! How much more, then, should I have pity on Nineveh, that great city. After all, it has more than 120,000 innocent children in it, as well as many animals! (Jon 4:10–11 GNB).

The Jerusalem Bible concludes that this book is an Old Testament preparation for the gospel in the New. It was a hint that Yahweh was really the God of all people.

As we noted earlier, this struggle did not finish in the Old Testament. In fact, even the new covenant seemingly was not able to fully restore the original equality of all races of mankind before God. In some cases Paul still insisted,

> God will give . . . to the Jews first and also to the Gentiles (Rom 2:10 GNB).

But he also approximated the ideal when he said,

> There is no difference between Jews and Gentiles, between slaves and free men, between men and women; you are all one . . . (Gal 3:28 GNB).

Monotheism

How difficult Israel's struggle was to believe in one God and how extensive Israel's belief was in many gods is partially masked in the Old Testament by the fact that the writers and editors themselves were strong monotheists. Even so, there is no indication of true polytheism among the Israelites who never had a pantheon of semi-equal specialized gods like the Greeks and Romans. But henotheism was deeply ingrained in the Hebrew worldview and erupted at many points. This was the view that one God, in this case Yahweh, was the first among gods, the greatest of the gods. That was the level on which the struggle for monotheism was fought: "Thou shalt have no other gods before me" (Ex 20:3 KJV); "Worship no god but me" (GNB).

The Hebrews came from Mesopotamia, a culture with multiple gods. They probably worshiped the multiple gods of Egypt. They certainly intermingled the gods of the surrounding peoples with their worship of Yahweh in Canaan. The prophets cried out against idolatry. The growth toward monotheism seemed fragile for centuries.

In the first verse of the Bible, and commonly thereafter (chap. 15), the Hebrew term for God occurs in the plural form *elohim*. Taken literally, the passage says, 'gods created the heavens and the earth' (Gen 1:1). It goes on with, 'then gods said' (Gen 1:3), 'and gods saw' (Gen 1:4), and so on through the story. However, although the term for God or gods in the Old Testament is plural *elohim*, it clearly does not mean plural gods in such Bible passages as these. This plural form has been explained as a plural of majesty, such as when a king uses the plural "we" when he addresses his people. However, the problem of the plural noun is made more difficult when the text reads,

> Then God[s] said, "And now we will make human beings; they will be like us and resemble us" (Gen 1:26 GNB).

Here God uses a plural pronoun in apparently talking to some sort of a heavenly council, to which other references also occur.

> God presides in the heavenly council;
> in the assembly of the gods he gives his decision (Ps 82:1 GNB).

The Bible has two descriptions of heavenly councils.

> One day the heavenly beings [Hebrew: 'sons of *elohim*'] came to present themselves before the LORD, and Satan also came among them (Job 1:6 NRSV).

> I saw the LORD sitting on his throne, with all the host of heaven standing beside him to the right and to the left of him. And the LORD said, "Who will entice Ahab, so that he may go and fall at Ramoth-Gilead?" Then one said one thing and another said another, until a spirit came forward and stood before the LORD, saying, "I will entice him" (1 Kgs 22:19–21 NRSV).

These two descriptions do not say that the other heavenly beings were other gods, but they lend weight to seeing the plural forms as remnants of an earlier henotheistic view of creation.

Under the Sinai covenant, Israel was to have and to serve only one God (Ex 20:3–6), but other gods existed, and their worshipers were to be destroyed (Ex 22:20). The Israelites believed that Baal, the God of the Canaanites; Chemosh, the God of Moab; Milcom, the God of Ammon, and others, had power, just as Yahweh the God of Israel had power. And as we have seen, many people continued to worship more than one god. For example, Solomon later unabashedly accepted the power of other gods by building shrines for them (1 Kgs 11:4–8). The difference was that Yahweh was stronger than these other gods.

Once Israel became established in Canaan, it lost its exclusive dependence on pastoral existence and increasingly depended on agriculture for its livelihood. Shifts of residence or major shifts in economic activity such as a move from pastoral to agricultural often also have serious implications for other aspects of culture, such as social organization and religion.

So the Hebrews had doubts that Yahweh—the God of their pastoral past, the God of manna, quail, and water, the God who had made a covenant with them in the desert—really knew enough about agriculture to provide them with the needed fertility while the Baals, which were the gods of the territory into which Israel had moved, were also fertility gods who specialized in agriculture.

Yahweh therefore complained that Israel did not recognize who actually gave them the rich produce which they attributed to Baal's blessings:

> She would never acknowledge that I am the one who gave her the grain, the wine, the olive oil, and all the silver and gold that she used in the worship of Baal (Hos 2:8 GNB).

In fact, Yahweh wondered aloud whether it would help if he took Israel back to the desert where he first made the covenant.

> I am going to take her into the desert again; there I will win her back with words of love. . . . She will respond to me there as she did when she was young, when she came out of Egypt. Then once again she will call me her husband—she will no longer call me her Baal (Hos 2:14–16 GNB).

Thus Israel's need to worship the deity owners of the land with their agricultural expertise is like what we described for Africa where the conquerors felt obliged to accept the gods of the conquered because it was the latter's deities who controlled the land (chap. 7).

Agriculturalist concern about crop fertility often leads also to developing male/female deity cults whose function is to stimulate fertility. In Canaan fertility was dependent upon the annual rains, but these did not always come or were not necessarily on time, and crops were jeopardized. To add to the problem, in the fertile coastal plain which was occupied by the Canaanites and the Philistines the crops often succeeded while Israel's crops in the highlands failed. Israel therefore not only adopted Baal but also Ashera.

Another force in the pull to polytheism was Israel's social structure which was without a supreme ruler until the kingship. Societies without central leadership usually have multiple gods in some form. On the other hand, when societies develop strong centralized rule under a king or an emperor, they tend to be attracted toward monotheism (Naroll 1983:144). In Israel's experience, no sooner had David become king than he began to move toward establishing one place of worship, in Jerusalem. His first step was to bring to Jerusalem the ark of the covenant, the box in which Yahweh had traveled with the people in the desert. When his first attempt failed, he was exceedingly frustrated (2 Sam 6:1–11).

When Solomon completed the temple in Jerusalem, this "house of Yahweh" became the unique rallying point of Israelite monotheism. But apparently not until Josiah's day did monotheism succeed in rooting out most of the local polytheistic worship.

Even during the period of kingship and developing monotheism, Israel also seemed to feel a strong pull toward providing Yahweh with a female counterpart, the "queen of heaven."

> As for the word which you have spoken to us in the name of the LORD, we will not listen to you. But we will do everything that we have vowed, burn incense to the queen of heaven and pour out libations to her, as we did, both we and our fathers, our kings and our princes, in the cities of Judah and in the streets of Jerusalem; for then we had plenty of food, and prospered, and saw no evil. But since we left off burning incense to the queen of heaven and pouring out libations to her, we have lacked everything and have been consumed by the sword and by famine (Jer 44:16–19 RSV).

But monotheism also has its dangers. On the positive side, monotheism enables a society to develop a single all-embracing explanation of reality, with moral law as its one supreme arbiter. But then if the human ruler becomes closely linked to the one God, the ruler provides a single focus for loyalty, both religious and political.

Under this linkage between monotheism and social structure, the one God becomes the tribal or national deity again. If the society has aspirations to dominate others, the tribal God provides the rationale. Thus the *jihad*, the holy war, is often a direct outcome of strong monotheism. The desire of the deity to become the one universal God links up with the society's desire to dominate other people.

With the advent of monotheistic Shintoism at the turn of the nineteenth century, Japan embarked upon a course that directly led to World War II in the Pacific. When the will of God and the desire of the people became one, the moral climate for holy war had been created (Koyama 1984). The North American war cry, "for God and country," is analogous.

Thus, the Hebrews' concept that Yahweh was their one tribal God, but not a universal God, severely colored their history. When one's tribal God is seen as the only true God, all other people worshiping other gods are therefore seen as infidels. Yahweh, as the name of Israel's tribal God, was and remained an almost insurmountable wall that separated the Jews from the nations of the world. The Jews were the people of God, and the nations of the world were the enemies of God (Rosin 1956:7). When a people's conceptualization of God separates them radically from the people surrounding them, the resulting ethnocentrism and self-satisfied feeling of superiority can be most detrimental to healthy relations with others. Certainly their morality is limited to the in-group.

Such was part of the range of Israelite worldviews concerning God as seen through categories clarified by other religious systems. Personal God, functionally specialized God, territorial God, first among many gods, only God, eventually universal God—the people of Israel believed in all of these and in various mixtures of them at different times and places. Getting humans to realize the true nature of God has already taken more than two thousand years, and God is still not fully known.

9

Images of God:
Male, Female, or Both

In the West, one controversial worldview issue concerning the nature of God in the Bible and in Christian faith focuses around male and female metaphors for God. When my wife and I became missionaries to the Waunana, we were pleased not only because the people had only one God, but also because he was male, like our own God. Even after I had become a translation consultant working in "polytheistic" settings, I felt that translators should use a masculine name for God. Not until I came into contact with the Peve (Chad, central Africa)—for whom the only deity was a female God, with no alternative—was I forced to rethink my position and restudy the Scriptures on this issue.

The word for God in Peve literally means 'our mother' (Venberg 1971:68–70). If we are to take this name for God seriously, expressions like "our father in heaven" should be translated as "our mother in heaven" in the Peve language. But is this possible?

The missionaries answered "No!" and insisted on using "our father in heaven" in their preaching and in the translation of the Scriptures. To the Peve this was something like having the missionaries insist that they call their own mothers "father," or their own sisters "brother," or their own daughters "son." What kind of foreign nonsense was that? The Peve refused to accept either the missionaries' message or the Scriptures. A male God was a foreign deity, and they wanted to have no part of him.

In many Bantu languages a similar kind of linguistic violence has been perpetrated on the Spirit of God. In Bantu languages the word for 'spirit' does not belong to the human grammatical class. That is, grammatically you do not use personal pronouns or other grammatical elements for it. In

Sotho-Tswana, for example, *modimo* 'god, spirit' belongs to a class of mass nouns along with 'smoke,' 'fire,' 'wind,' 'mist,' 'lightning,' and many others and requires pronouns used in reference to such phenomena, not in reference to people (Setiloane 1976:77). Believing that the Holy Spirit is a person, missionaries taught believers to use Modimo or its equivalent in the human grammatical class rather than in that of mass nouns. This was something like a missionary from an animist tribe telling Americans that they should not use the pronoun "it" for rocks or trees because such natural phenomena have spirits in them. We must therefore speak of rocks or trees with the pronoun "him" or "her" if we are to believe in their religion. Once the local church became independent, widespread reaction arose against the grotesque distortion which foreigners had imposed on their language.

On the other hand, missionaries have sometimes seemingly succeeded in changing God's sex. Mawu was a female deity in Ewe and other related languages in Ghana, Togo, and Benin, but under German missionary influence she was converted into a male. However, after almost a century of missionary work, one still hears that some people are uncomfortable with that long-ago sex change.

As a Bible Society representative, I could not escape the responsibility of knowing for myself what name for God was used in the Scriptures I approved for publication and by what means such a name was selected. Prompted by this cross-cultural dilemma, I was forced to establish my own premises on the basis of which I could decide what the Bible was actually depicting on this subject.

First, I had to examine my own strong feeling that God was male. Why did it seem dead wrong to me to translate biblical expressions like "God our father" as "God our mother"?

I reread the Bible and saw how thoroughly saturated it was with male images. Early translations of the Old Testament, like the Greek Septuagint, showed an even stronger abhorrence for female deities than I had. The Hebrew text spoke of both male and female deities alike as *elohim* 'God, gods,' but the Septuagint translated *elohim* in reference to female deities with expressions like 'abomination,' 'thing to be ashamed of,' instead of 'goddess' (chap. 16).

As I surveyed world religions, including the non-Hebrew religions mentioned in the Bible, I discovered that most recognized a dual male-female aspect of deity, usually by incorporating both gods and goddesses. Greek mythology, moreover, not only included separate male and female deities but also one who was both male and female. One day while Hermaphrodite was bathing, his body became permanently fused with that of Salmacis, the nymph of a fountain in Caria.

Even monotheistic tribal religions like the Waunana, which have only a masculine God, usually have myths regarding God's wife, although they do not accord her divine status. It is therefore not surprising that people have elevated Mary, Jesus' human mother, to divine status calling her the "mother of God." And in rural folk Catholicism in Latin America, Mary plays a far more significant role in the every-day religious life of the people than does the stern male deity of official Roman Catholic theology.

During our recent visit to India, my wife and I were fascinated by the Hindu priests' explanation for the multiplicity of male-female deity pairs and their sexuality. Probably the most common Shiva image is the dancing Shiva. Shiva's dance symbolizes his creative activity, for as he dances, new elements of creation spring up continuously. The cause of Shiva's dancing is his encounter with his female counterpart, Parbati. Without her, Shiva is passive and unproductive. But when Parbati approaches him, Shiva is "turned on" and his creative capacity is activated.

But what does all of this have to say about God as depicted in the Bible?

Male Image of God in the Bible

Any reference to God as a person, as male or female, is a metaphor,[1] a likening of God to some aspect or another of human experience. Metaphors are the only ways we have of talking about that which we cannot see, or hear, or sense with our other physical senses. They are the only ways we have of talking about one who is spirit, so unlike us. Metaphors illumine God to us by likening some aspect of God to the reality we know about, to men and women, fathers and mothers, shepherds, judges, kings and queens. We understand deity most clearly when we perceive God in our own image, just as we, male and female, were created equally in the image of God (Gen 1:27).

Why then the lopsided imbalance of metaphors in the Bible? Why does the Bible have, relatively, so few female metaphors for God, although the ones we have are often haunting?

> For a long time I have held my peace,
> I have kept still and restrained myself;
> now I will cry out like a woman in labor,
> I will gasp and pant (Is 42:14 NRSV).
>
> Can a woman forget her nursing child,
> or show no compassion for the child of her womb?
> Even these may forget,
> yet I will not forget you (Is 49:15 NRSV).

---

[1]Metaphor is here used in a general sense for figures of speech, of which metaphor is technically one type.

As a mother comforts her child,
so I will comfort you;
you shall be comforted in Jerusalem (Is 66:13
NRSV).

Cultural Reasons

The patriarchs Abraham, Isaac, and Jacob were pastoralists, and among pastoralists maleness generally is supreme. Women are second-class creatures. Inheritance is through male offspring. Female children are not viewed as an economic benefit to the society and will be forever lost to the family once they are given in marriage to another family. Since herders usually are at least partially nomadic, wives contribute little to the family economic well-being except as they bear sons. Wives in such societies are usually either cousins or other relatives, like the wives of Abraham, Isaac, and Jacob, or they are purchased concubines/slaves like Hagar, Abraham's second wife, and the co-wives of Isaac and Jacob (chap. 2).

The male-dominant worldview of the patriarchs continues through much of the Bible and colors the general perspective, the selection of material, and the metaphors used, although with some notable exceptions. One of those exceptions is the first creation account where Elohim created both man and woman "in his image" as "male and female" (Gen 1:27 NRSV), equal images of God.

But in sharp contrast to the first creation account, the second reflects the male values of a pastoral society. In that account, Yahweh first created only the man. Only later, after failing to make a companion for the man by creating the animals, God made the woman as a companion by deriving her from the male, making the man's rib into a woman (Gen 2:4–3:24). She was an afterthought, a reflection of the man, not of God. In her manner of creation she was one step removed from God and was thus morally weaker, more prone to error. She immediately showed that she was an inferior being when she succumbed to temptation. Later on, the legal system of the nation of Israel in Exodus and Leviticus enshrined the unequal status of the two sexes.

In the first creation account, Elohim (Hebrew generic term for 'God/gods') is the creator, in the second, Yahweh Elohim ('the God [named] Yahweh,' the tribal God of the Hebrews). Throughout the Bible the people of faith struggled, usually not very successfully, to learn that their tribal male God Yahweh was in fact the universal God Elohim (chap. 8). As one element in that struggle and an example of it, the Elohim account of creation is universalist, the Yahweh account male dominant.

Beginning in the pastoral society of the patriarchs and supported by many aspects of the worldviews of surrounding peoples, the Yahweh perspective predominated. God was therefore male, the stories about God were male stories, the metaphors male metaphors.

Like the Hebrews, the people of the Arabian Peninsula, where Muhammad developed Islam, were also pastoralists. In fact, their pastoral activity was not even tempered with agriculture as was Israel's. Thus Islam not only developed an exclusively male God but also a religious philosophy in which women were the epitome of that which distracts men from God. Thus, females must be covered in public and for the most part kept from public view, enclosed in women's quarters.

Linguistic Reasons

The cultural reasons for the strong images of God as male in the Bible are foundational, but they are supported by linguistic processes as well, by fundamental aspects of the nature of language. Both of the primary linguistic supports for the images of God—metaphor or grammar—have already been mentioned, but they need a little more elaboration here.

The first is the phenomenon of metaphor. Metaphor is an important linguistic device, the means by which we communicate ideas for which our language has not yet developed literal words. Metaphors can also touch an emotional chord in the human psyche and so may have an enormous emotive impact in communication.

Metaphors have great evocative power. They stir our emotions, and they soothe our fears. On a literal level, "The Lord is my shepherd" (Ps 23:1) is patently false—I am no sheep and God is no shepherd. But the metaphorical image has provided comfort and reassurance to multitudes of people ever since the psalmist first coined it. This is true even for many of us who have had only minimal experience with shepherds. For people who have no experience whatsoever with a shepherd, the impact of the metaphor is, of course, greatly reduced, and we can predict that in due time they will feel it to be archaic or maybe even irrelevant.

When such metaphors are used frequently or when they reflect a highly valued culture trait, they often produce whole networks of associated metaphors. Psalm 23 contains images of nurture, guidance, protection, and tranquility, among others. In other contexts in the Bible the shepherd's sheep get lost and are found; they are described as belonging to different folds and they are pictured as facing dangerous animals. Such "expandable" metaphors not only broaden our conception of the referent but often function also as models which shape our thinking, feeling, and perceiving. In fact, the metaphors people use frequently provide an insight into the conceptual framework in terms of which they are organizing their experience. Such metaphors can often have far-reaching effects as models for social behavior.

Consider the lover model of God. It not only gave the Israelites a way of interpreting history, it also suggested meaningful lines of action to them which resulted in radical shifts in their political and social life. This image established the idea of covenant loyalty. On the political front this meant that international bargains, once made, should not be broken. More directly we can see that it led to the development of the monogamous marriage concept—a symbolic model which provided a framework within which all kinds of social and religious obligations and commitments had to be performed (Ferré 1983:76–87; cf. Fawcett 1971:111–27).

Metaphors also serve as grids which limit our perceptions. Once an expandable metaphor has been given prominence as an organizing model, it can become fixed, functioning as a screening device to eliminate other equally valid models or metaphors. The God-as-father metaphor, for example, with its vast network of associated metaphoric images, takes on a reality of its own. People do not perceive it as a comparison to reality but as reality. God ceases to be like a father in the respect of loving and providing, but becomes a male. Then it suppresses any other metaphor that seems to contradict the maleness. It makes some possible metaphors seem alien.

The choice of any given metaphor as focal is neither arbitrary nor fortuitous, but the product of its cultural milieu. God-as-father reflected a prevalent cultural reality in Hebrew society. Already under the Abrahamic covenant, which established male circumcision as its outward symbol, only men were marked as belonging to God. The interaction between the metaphor and patriarchal culture gave it its controlling status. But once established, this metaphor also severely limited Israel's conception of female-like aspects of God and how God related to women.

Metaphors functioning as grids therefore tend to become blinders, blocking out the perception of other, sometimes more uncomfortable, dimensions of the truth. For example, no matter how useful chess may be in teaching the basics of war strategy, it also filters out all the destruction of life and property, the enormous waste of badly needed resources, the horrible human suffering, the devastating compromise of morality. That is—to use Churchill's famous phrase—it filters out all the blood, sweat, and tears (Loewen 1983a:9–12).

Second, in addition to metaphor, some aspects of grammar may give strong support to metaphors based on person. In languages like English, once a male or female metaphor has been used, subsequent pronouns have to agree grammatically. That is, if the metaphor for God is father, it requires the pronoun "he."

Latin and Greek go farther than that. Adjectives must "agree" as well. If the noun is masculine, so must the adjective be. In the languages mentioned earlier where a female metaphor for God is basic, any words which must agree in gender must be female.

Some languages do not have the problem in this form. In Thai, for example, there is no difference in gender of pronouns when referring to man or woman. However, Thai has a complicated agreement of another kind. The second person pronoun ('you') must agree with the status of the person referred to. Different pronouns are used for addressing people socially above the speaker from those who are below the speaker, for holy people as against ordinary people, and many more.

All such factors are part of the arbitrary conventions of language. Some languages do such things one way, some another. But not to do them as is customary in the language produces sometimes violent reactions, as when some English-speaking people use the pronoun "she" for God.

The point is that we become trapped into logical circularity by our grammar. Because our prevailing metaphors for God are male, we use male pronouns whether the metaphor is explicit in what we say or not, and then, because we refer to God as "he," God must be male. Notice how we do not have as much trouble saying "it" for the Holy Spirit as we do for God whom we call "father." Spirit does not seem as male as father and creator.

God as spirit, of course, has no gender, no reproductive organs. God the creator is just as much like the provider of the egg as like the provider of the sperm. God is as much the ultimate nurturer as the ultimate protector.

Jesus, on the other hand, was a man. For God to become a human being, the incarnation had to be male or female, and for its cultural time and place to be male was more appropriate.

Such was the result of my cross-cultural examination of the possibility of female names and images for God in the Bible, and my present understanding of God is much richer as a result. I found that names and metaphors for God are equally appropriate whether male, female, or both, and as a result my vision of God has deepened. I saw that the metaphors we use to express our dim understanding of deity tend later to be taken literally and become solidified into dogma. But no metaphor can picture all of the reality it represents. As a result of these discoveries, my God is not as small as before. A cross-cultural perspective has helped clarify at least a small part of the dark mirror in which I look for God.

10

God Speaks,
Prophets Prophesy

When the Bible Societies transferred me to Africa in 1970, for the first time in my life I ran into prophecy wherever I went. Independent churches were springing up everywhere, each with a prophet as its head. In individual families, people fell into trances, and ancestors spoke through them, giving prophetic messages or divine answers to human problems.

For example, an African father employed by a colonial government was able to open a small store on the side in his home village. Since he was working away from home, he put one of his unmarried daughters in charge of the business, paying her the usual wage for her service. For years the store functioned well. The man enlarged it time and again. Eventually, he bought his own trucks and used them to bring in trade goods and haul out local produce.

Then came independence, followed by a twenty-fold jump in inflation. However, the father never changed his daughter's wages. While he became wealthy, the daughter received only a pittance for managing the store. This made her increasingly unhappy, but the culture demanded that she submit quietly to her father's will.

In this society, people sought to maintain social and material equality, so the increasing wealth of the government employee caused extensive gossip. Was the old man trafficking in the souls of his neighbors? Was he a sorcerer? If not, how was he becoming so wealthy?

Both father and daughter were members of a local Protestant church which for decades had developed along local cultural lines because no foreign missionary was in charge. As the daughter's unhappiness with her unjust wages increased, she developed symptoms of physical illness, and when "store" medicine did not help her, she took her problem to the women's society of the church. It held a special prayer service for her.

As the "spirit moved" in their midst, one of the women fell into a trance and began to speak in the name of the young woman's grandmother. "My granddaughter, you are ill because the people are jealous of your wealthy father. This jealousy has settled in your back. It is now causing you too much pain.

"In addition, I, your grandmother, am very unhappy that you have never taken a husband, so I have sent this illness to you. If you want to get well, granddaughter, you must permanently leave the store. In that way you can escape all the jealousy that is now poisoning your body. Then when some good man wants to marry you, you must take him as a husband."

The daughter obeyed the message and immediately withdrew from the store. Her father accepted her retirement as valid because it was in response to a vision from the supernatural world. He arranged with another daughter to manage the store, at current wages. Once the first daughter was out of the store and available for marriage, a local widower asked her to marry him, and she accepted.

The ancestor's prophetic intervention saved the father's face and restored the daughter's health. It also released considerable community tension about the wealth the father had accumulated.

Direct Forms of Divine Communication

In the earliest parts of the Bible, God came in person and talked with human beings face-to-face, as with Adam and Eve (Gen 3:9–20). Later God appeared to people as though slightly disguised, in a form called the "angel of the LORD." The form was human, but the presence was Yahweh (chap. 5). Then as time went on, Yahweh's immediate visible presence faded as a form of communication, but other direct forms developed, especially dreams and visions.

Dreams

The first dream messages in the Bible were those which came to Abimelech, who had unwittingly taken Abraham's wife, Sarah. God told him in a dream that Sarah was a married woman. When Abimelech recognized his mistake and pleaded for mercy to God, the latter replied in another dream, giving Abimelech instructions on how to salvage the situation (Gen 20:3–7).

In a dream at Bethel, Jacob saw the LORD, who spoke to him. He also saw a ladder to heaven with angels ascending and descending (Gen 28:12–17). Later, the angel of the LORD told him in a dream how to increase his wealth, and instructed him to return to his home country (Gen 31:11–13). When Jacob fled from his father-in-law with his wives and his flocks, God spoke to Laban in a dream, warning him to go easy on Jacob (Gen 31:24).

The story of Joseph's life was built around dreams. In dreams the sheaves of the other members of his family bowed before his sheaf, and the sun, the moon, and eleven stars bowed to him (Gen 37:5–11). Angry with the affront, his brothers sold him to be a slave in Egypt, but when Pharaoh himself had two troubling dreams, his servant suggested that Joseph could interpret them. On the basis of this interpretation, Joseph became the chief administrator of the country, and in due course his whole family did actually bow down to him (Gen 40–46).

When Gideon was military leader in Israel, he sneaked into the Midianite camp at night and overheard a soldier telling his friend of a dream about a barley loaf hitting their camp and flattening their tent. His friend interpreted it as the sword of Gideon. Gideon therefore took courage and defeated the Midianites (Judg 7:13–23).

In a dream, God promised Solomon wisdom (1 Kgs 3:5–15). Nebuchadnezzar, the pagan king of Israel's captivity, had two dreams which Daniel interpreted for him (Dan 2:1–4:27).

In the New Testament, a series of dream messages occurred around the birth of Jesus, according to Matthew's account. First, Joseph was assured in a dream that Mary's pregnancy was of God. Then the wise men from the East were warned in a dream not to return to Herod but to go back to their own country by a different route. Joseph was warned to take the family to Egypt because Herod was going to massacre all children two years and under. When Herod later died, the angel appeared to Joseph again in a dream and told him to return to Palestine. When the family did finally return and became aware that Archelaus was reigning in his father's place, Joseph felt uncertain, and the Lord instructed him in another dream to go to Galilee (Mt 1:20–2:22).

In the only other dream in the New Testament, Pilate's wife dreamed of Jesus and warned her husband not to have anything to do with him (Mt 27:19).

However, dreams were not sure-fire communications from God. In the days of Eli,

> There were very few messages from the LORD, and visions from him were quite rare (1 Sam 3:1 GNB).

And not all human dreams are necessarily messages from God.

> [False prophets] think that the dreams they tell will make my people forget me, just as their fathers forgot me and turned to Baal. The prophet who has had a dream should say it is only a dream, but the prophet who has heard my message should proclaim that message faithfully (Jer 23:27–28 GNB).

The manner in which God spoke to people sometimes suggested the degree of God's intimacy with them. God spoke to other people in dreams, but to Moses God spoke face to face (Num 12:6–8).

Visions

In the Old Testament, visions are often mentioned in conjunction with dreams, and cannot always be clearly distinguished. For example, Daniel "had a dream and saw a vision" (Dan 7:1 GNB). Technically, however, visions occur when a person is awake, sometimes during a trance, sometimes not.

In the first vision in Scripture, the LORD appeared to the patriarch, Abram (Gen 15:1). When Jacob and his family reached the border of Canaan from Egypt, the LORD appeared to him in a vision at night (Gen 46:2). When the child Samuel had a vision one night, he was afraid to tell Eli what God had told him because it involved bad news for the aged priest (1 Sam 3:15).

When Nebuchadnezzar had a dream, and none of his astrologers and magicians could interpret it for him, Daniel prayed to God and asked for the meaning which was revealed to Daniel in a vision at night (Dan 2:19). The book of Daniel also has several other visions.

In the New Testament, the transfiguration of Jesus is called a vision by Matthew (Mt 17:9). In Luke, the priest Zechariah had a vision of the angel Gabriel in the temple (Lk 1:22), and some of the disciples "saw a vision of angels" after Jesus' resurrection (Lk 24:23).

Saul, on the way to persecute the Christians in Damascus, had a vision of the risen Lord (Acts 9:3, 9:12, 26:19). Then Cornelius the Gentile had a vision (Acts 10:3), as Peter the apostle was also being instructed through a vision to give Cornelius God's message (Acts 10:9–17). When Peter was released from prison by an angel, his first thought was that the whole experience had been a vision rather than a real happening (Acts 12:9).

Paul had a vision when he was asked to come to Macedonia (Acts 16:9) and another vision in connection with his work in Corinth (Acts 18:9). He implies other visions that God had given him (2 Cor 12:1). The book of Revelation largely recounts apocalyptic visions (Rev 1:1, 1:10, 9:17).

Prophecy

The longer God dealt with his people, as reflected in the biblical record, the less God's message came through direct contact with them, and the more it came through prophets. Prophecy was God's word to the people as spoken by God's chosen spokespeople. Very often God spoke directly to the prophet by the various means we have already discussed, but that message was usually not so much for the prophet as for others (Tucker 1985:335–56).

A number of the prophets, for example, based their messages on divinely inspired visions. Obadiah spoke of having had a vision from God (Obad 1), and "Israel did not heed the visions Hosea had received from God" (Hos 12:10–14). The prophet Isaiah said that his whole prophecy was "the vision of Isaiah" (Is 1:1), as did the prophet Ezekiel (Ezek 1:1, 8:3–4, 11:24, 12:22–23, 40:2, 43:3). Perhaps this was metaphorical usage.

Such decreasing numbers of cases aside, the message which the prophets were to deliver usually came as "the word of the LORD" to them and was delivered as such to the people or the king. But then in the New Testament, God says that word was finally brought in the form of God's son: "The Word became a human being and . . . lived among us" (Jn 1:14 GNB).

Prophecy in the Early Hebrew/Jewish Setting

The Hebrew word for prophet is based on the verb 'to call, to proclaim.' Throughout the Old Testament, God was the author of all true prophecy, for God called the prophet and gave the message.

We have to recognize that the word 'prophet' is used rather loosely at times in the Old Testament. Abraham was called a prophet (Gen 20:7), as were Moses (Deut 34:10) and Aaron (Ex 7:1) and Miriam, their sister (Ex 15:20). Writers and editors, it seems, projected the term back into earlier periods when other terms were typically used.

The earliest label for a prophet in Israel was 'man of God,' that is, a person in tune with God. The "man of God" label was used for a variety of people, including Moses (Deut 33:1), David (Neh 12:24), Elijah (2 Kgs 1:9), and twenty-nine times of Elisha (beginning with 2 Kgs 4:7).

The next designation of a prophet in Israel was 'seer' (1 Sam 9:9). Here the emphasis was on receiving visions from God and then communicating these visions to the people. This emphasis produced a school of ecstatic prophets whose prophecy was equivalent to the New Testament speaking in tongues (1 Cor 14). In much ecstatic prophecy, the prophet was "seized" by the spirit of a deity and pronounced the words inspired by the deity, usually unaware of what he or she was saying. Examples include messengers Saul sent to capture David (1 Sam 19:18–24). When King Saul was informed what was happening to his messengers, he himself was taken by the Spirit (1 Sam 19:22–24).

The period of kingship in Israel marked the beginning of what might be called true prophecy, when the messengers who regularly received the word of God began their messages with the formula "Thus says the LORD."

> Thus says the LORD:
> For three transgressions of Israel,
>   and for four, I will not revoke the punishment;

> because they sell the righteous for silver,
>   and the needy for a pair of sandals—
> they who trample the head of the poor into the dust of the earth,
>   and push the afflicted out of the way (Amos 2:6–7 NRSV).

Dreams and visions were no longer necessary, although they still occurred. Instead, the prophet spoke the word of the LORD, often in the cadences of rich poetry.

New Testament Prophecy

By New Testament times, under the influence of Greek culture a subtle shift occurred in the meaning of 'prophet,' more in the direction of the interpreter of the divine message. In Greek culture, the prophet was either the one who predicted the future or who interpreted an oracle which had often been given through a medium who did not know what he or she was saying (Coenen, Beyreuther, and Bietenhard, eds. 1979:1020).

The most famous oracle in Greece was at Delphi where Pythia was the medium. Someone put a question to the supernatural which was answered by the oracle through the medium. The medium was not responsible for either the form or the content of the message but only transmitted what it received through ecstatic inspiration. The message might be totally unintelligible to the questioner and needed a prophet to interpret it. Thus, under this system, the prophet was usually chosen by the oracle, not by God. The medium was always in a trance or in ecstasy when it spoke, which greatly influenced ecstatic prophecy, but the Jews maintained their prophets' individuality and insisted that they had to be called by God.

In the New Testament, the word 'prophet' is used of John the Baptist (Mt 11:9), Jesus (Mt 13:57), Zechariah (Lk 1:67), and Anna (Lk 2:36). It is also used of Christian preachers (Eph 3:5). Finally, it is used by John in Revelation where he says that he himself was "a prophet of God" (Rev 22:9).

The Trajectory

In summary, the Bible shows a trajectory of divine purpose in its development (Hanson 1986:522, 525–46; Moltmann 1977) in the way knowledge of God came to his people in Scripture. In the earliest instances, God spoke anthropomorphically to people face to face, then to individuals through dreams. By the time of Daniel it seems as if even some heathen kings also received messages from God through dreams, but Daniel interpreted those dreams by means of visions. In time, vision became more common. During intertestamental times especially, apocalyptic visions were plentiful, as they were later in the book of Revelation.

Eventually, however, Israel began to hear its messages from God through prophecy. At first the spirit of God seemingly seized random individuals and spoke through them more or less as automatons (1 Sam 10:9–11; 19:18–24). But eventually, God began choosing individuals for this permanent role, from Samuel through the major and minor prophets of the Old Testament.

Prophecy was at its height in Israel when the Northern Kingdom went into exile in 721 BC, but after some people from the Southern Kingdom returned from exile over the period 539–440 BC, prophecy decreased altogether. The land God had given Israel was in shambles, much of it occupied by strangers. The kingship, in which God's personal representative ruled the nation, was terminated. The temple, God's house in their midst, was in ruins. God's "chosen people" were hostages, slaves and displaced people in foreign lands. And the people no longer received prophetic messages from God.

But a new form of message was developing. Beginning in the captivity, and developing slowly over several hundred years, people began turning to the oral and written records of God's dealing with them in the past. They gradually established the canon, the official selection of writings which were God's authentic word (Eliade 1982:274–75). They began with the Torah, consisting of the first five books of the present Bible, to which they eventually added the prophets, and then the "writings" (the remainder of the Old Testament). This process continued throughout intertestamental times until it finally culminated with the official approval of what we call the Masoretic text (the Hebrew text of the Old Testament as we know it) in AD 90.

Various other, later writings were also accepted by some groups as authentic messages from God. The books of the apocrypha were included in the canon used in Alexandria, Egypt, and some other writings, including Jubilees, were accepted by the Ethiopian and Coptic churches.

The early Christian church used the Greek translation of the Old Testament as its written word of God. However, to that it added the living and resurrected Word of God.

> In the past God spoke to our ancestors many times and in many ways through the prophets, but in these last days has spoken to us through his Son (Heb 1:1–2 GNB).

> The Word became a human being and, full of grace and truth, lived among us (Jn 1:14 GNB).

In time, the early church put together the sayings of Jesus, a book now lost. Eventually, so many suspect stories of Jesus' life began to circulate in the church that it began to entertain the idea of an authentic record of Jesus' life and times. The first book about Jesus now included in the New Testament was probably the Gospel of Mark. This was followed by the Gospel of Matthew. Luke suggests in his introduction that many people were telling the story of

Jesus, but that not all of them were getting their facts straight, and he tried to verify all the facts he was reporting (Lk 1:1–4). The Gospel of John did not appear until almost the end of the first century.

However, the epistles of Paul were probably the earliest books of the New Testament which circulated in the church. Other epistles followed. For a long time people felt no need for a fixed canon,[1] and as they began to want one they disagreed widely on what should be in it. The whole New Testament as we know it probably was not fixed until some time during the fourth century.

Even after that the Eastern branch of the Christian church, centered around Antioch, developed a book on the life and times of Jesus, combining the accounts of the four gospels into one. The Western church anathematized it, but it became increasingly popular in the Eastern church, and was clandestinely translated into many of the European languages of the day, becoming the basis for the evangelization of the area.

The process of developing channels through which God speaks has not ended. Among those channels is Bible translation whereby the word of God is made accessible in ever more languages. But many of the old channels continue, too. Dreams, visions, and prophecy of different kinds still flourish among God's people in different parts of the world and in different cultures.

Some channels may have grown obsolete in the thousands of years since the priests in the desert of Sinai used divining stones; others have emerged. But the effectiveness of any channel of communication from God depends in part on worldview, on what people understand to be legitimate, authentic, powerful, sacred. People of different worldviews do not necessarily agree as to what may be an authentic channel but, again, if we are to learn of God from each other we need to learn to translate God's messages between each other's channels.

---

[1]The canon of Scripture is an agreement about what books are authentically the word of God.

11

Spirit Possession and Exorcism: An African View

A chronically ill African woman had sought healing in various ways, but without success, so she went to an African independent church where the prophet-leader diagnosed her case as possession by three evil spirits sent to punish her for her continual quarreling with her husband. Two of the spirits had been sent by her deceased maternal great-grandmother, one by a deceased ancestor from her husband's family. After a number of confession and healing sessions, and a series of consultations with her husband and other relatives, the healer gave the woman an emetic so that she herself eventually vomited out all three spirits and personally identified them in her vomit. By this means she received visible evidence that the evil spirits afflicting her had been successfully exorcised.

Spirit possession and exorcism are facts of life over much of the world, and were so in biblical times, foreign as they seem to most Westerners. To understand them better, a description of the worldview of a typical African society, the one to which the possessed woman belonged, will serve as a starting point. Then in the next chapter, this worldview will be compared with some of those reflected in the Bible as well as with some Western ones.

West Africans usually conceived of their universe as fairly local, created by a now remote tribal high God. An example of such a "local" universe is the one inhabited by the Yaroba,[1] among other peoples, who share it also with nonmaterial life, for their universe is alive with spirit. All things, plants,

---

[1]Yaroba is a made-up name to represent a composite of different groups in West Africa in order to present a generalized description of a typical West African view of the spirit world. Specifics described here are drawn from de Rosny (1985), unless otherwise indicated.

animals, and human beings have their spirit dimensions, if not their actual spirit counterparts. In fact, some plant and animal spirits are considered very closely related to human spirits because the various Yaroba clans are each linked to their respective plant or animal totems.[2]

In this animate universe, elements that are essentially spirit can appear in material form, and elements that are essentially material forms like antelopes can change into their spirit dimension and disappear before the viewer's very eyes. For Yaroba, the material and the spiritual dimensions of the universe are aspects of a single continuum, both equally real (part 3, introduction).

Spirits are either good or bad, helpful or dangerous; but all spirits, except the high God in the Yaroba pantheon, regardless of their character, have their origin in deceased human souls. Good or friendly spirits derive from souls of dead ancestors who were properly buried in their home territory and who have received the proper series of funerals and other remembrances since they passed on.

Bad spirits, the equivalent of evil spirits or demons of the Bible, derive from improperly treated souls-of-the-dead. They are the angry souls of ancestors who were improperly buried, usually away from their home territory, or ones who have not been properly remembered in the required sequence of funerals. Especially evil and capricious are the souls of foreigners who died in the region and who were buried by non-relatives in territory alien to them, without anyone to remember them properly. They readily lend themselves as tools for evil to any angry person, especially to sorcerers and witches.

Possession and Illness

Every illness, mental or physical, has material and spiritual dimensions. All social, physical, psychological, or spiritual problems are caused by alien spirits and/or their "tools," namely foreign elements which invade the body. These intrusive elements may sometimes be what Westerners call germs but, whatever they are, they need to be destroyed or expelled before they kill the person they afflict (de Rosny 1985:82). Herbs and other local medicines, or even Western drugs, can be helpful in the material dimension of an illness, but no material medicines are able to heal the spiritual dimension. That must be healed by spiritual means.

The spirit dimension, furthermore, is by far the more important of the two as it is the true cause of the illness. Germs and their ilk are merely instruments

---

[2]A totem is some class of objects (usually animal or plant species) with which people believe themselves to have a close relationship of some kind. People usually do not kill or eat members of their own totem.

by means of which spirit causes express themselves. That is why only those people who are under spirit attack actually fall victim to germ infections. Without a spirit cause, germs remain inactive or non-virulent, even if present.

Human beings, likewise, have two dimensions—visible physical body and invisible spiritual soul. The soul is often spoken of as a person's spiritual counterpart, its dimensions and appearance identical to those of the physical one. Only people with "double vision" have the capacity to see the spiritual dimension of the universe and of human beings, a capacity which is dangerous to ordinary mortals because the spirit dimension does not appreciate being watched.

Of the two dimensions, the spiritual part is the ultimate essential for life. Whenever a soul leaves the body, as when it is lost or is captured by a sorcerer, the body slowly deteriorates and dies. When a soul is stolen and the body begins to deteriorate, the Yaroba's standard symptoms include sore throat, fever, great fatigue, trembling, pain that constantly moves, prickly feeling in the eyes, nightmares involving incest, paranoia, and depression (de Rosny 1985:130).

However, most minor and some other illnesses, mental or physical, are actually caused by friendly ancestral souls-of-the-dead who want to warn the living that some action with dangerous consequences has taken place in the immediate social context. Such diseases are readily cured once the offending cause has been discovered and removed.

More serious are the illnesses which result from attacks by malevolent souls-of-the-dead. Such attacks—possessions or other afflictions—may come because the victim or close kin violated some major tribal taboo. Or they may result from witchcraft or sorcery growing out of the social tensions within the immediate or extended family. A common Yaroba proverb says, "Your sorcerer is your sibling or your bodyguard" (de Rosny 1985:130).

On the other hand, unprovoked spirit attacks can also occur, as when sorcerers or witches try out their powers and strike random victims. Or people may get rich by stealing and enslaving the souls of their fellow villagers to harness their power for personal gain. Or they may buy souls, which have previously been stolen, to accomplish the same result.

Especially dangerous soul thieves are white people who move into a native community and become rich quickly. The Yaroba believe that people can get rich only by enslaving the souls of others. The self-enrichers have either themselves stolen the souls of tribespeople or have bought them from some sorcerer/soul broker who has captured them and who now sells them to the highest bidder. In fact, many Africans today also believe that independence from colonialism did not really change their lot because African souls had already been captured by their colonial masters and sold to operate the Western industrial complex.

Since the stealing of souls is an ever-present danger, people should never give their names or let any part of their body (such as hair combings and nail clippings) fall into someone else's hands, especially not into the hands of a stranger. The whole is always present in the part, so any unscrupulous stranger or tribal sorcerer can use a name or parts of a body to enslave the person's soul through magic means (de Rosny 1985:176).

Once people become aware that their souls have been stolen or enslaved, they waste away and die. Or even if they should live for a period, they never achieve anything because they have been robbed of vital essence. Since AIDS is accompanied by all the symptoms of soul loss, many Africans are sure that it is caused by soul stealing. In fact, the Yaroba believe firmly that the physical slave traffic of the past is now operating as sorcery on the level of the soul (de Rosny 1985:6).

If a fellow villager prospers, and others in the community encounter consistent bad luck or misfortune at the same time, they immediately suspect that their souls and the power within them have been stolen or bought by the prosperous person. Usually one experience of bad luck will be accepted as chance, but continued misfortune has a definite cause (de Rosny 1985:83). In fact, in the Yaroba language, sickness, misfortune, and unemployment are all covered by the same word.

In Yaroba, sin or evil is generally defined socially rather than morally. Aside from a few moral absolutes such as incest avoidance and strict observance of some tribal taboos, most actions are neither intrinsically right nor wrong. People do many things which they are not supposed to do, such as engaging in illicit sex or theft, but usually the behavior turns out to have minimal negative consequences in the society. But if people do something normally considered harmless and it produces serious negative consequences, the behavior is seen as evil. For example, a nephew may legitimately have intercourse with one of his uncle's wives, but if it happens frequently or if some of the children in the uncle's family become ill, then it has become a serious infraction of social mores.

Ordinary people are completely limited to the here and now. They cannot foresee the results of their actions farther down the road. Hence the Yaroba depend on the living dead, the souls of their deceased ancestors, to show them when and what will produce bad results. Deceased ancestors have the responsibility of warning their living relatives if and when even an innocent action will have long-term negative consequences. They must warn the living so that the harm-producing action can be undone or at least so that its effect can be greatly reduced.

Warning messages from ancestors usually come in the form of benign illness or misfortune, but they can also come in visions or dreams. When such an illness arrives and/or when such a supernatural message is not readily understood, a diviner is consulted, who consults with the deceased ancestors and determines the precise reason for the warning.

When illness is not caused by the friendly soul of a deceased ancestor who is trying to prevent a major catastrophe from developing, it may be caused by a witch or a sorcerer within the family or the village. For example, if two people disagree, tempers flare momentarily, others intervene, and no major calamity develops, then no evil consequences follow. But if one of the contending parties wishes some evil on the other, and suddenly the evil desire becomes reality in that the opponent or some member of the opponent's family becomes ill, the person who wished the evil becomes an accidental witch or sorcerer, if she or he is not already one.

Exorcism and Healing

As we saw at the beginning of this chapter, when illness has spiritual causes, cures must be spiritual cures. And because evil is social, cures must take place in the relevant social context whenever possible and must heal the social ill. In the situation described earlier, the spirits were vomited out and the family tensions were healed; the African independent church community provided the healing social context (Loewen 1976). More commonly, however, the immediate family provides the social context of healing.

The affected person may manifest only a benign form of an illness, as in the preceding example, or stronger symptoms such as capacity to speak in what appear to be unknown foreign languages, use of foul and blasphemous language, intensely violent behavior toward self and others, the manifestation of multiple personalities each with its own voice and persona, severe depression, or paranoia. However the exorcism procedure remains remarkably similar in all cases.

The cooperation of family members is considered essential for all normal healing. One healer put it this way: "There is no healing or exorcism without family reconciliation and cooperation. The healer's cannon hangs fire as long as the family of the possessed withholds the powder" (de Rosny 1985:44).

In such typical healing, other patients, friends, and visitors provide the larger social context, but the inner circle is formed by relatives who have been summoned, often from afar, because they are recognized as part of the social tension network within which this illness or possession has developed. This same context must now cooperate to expel the demons. In the later stages of the exorcism, the healer will "accuse" one or more members of the family of being the sorcerer(s) who have provoked the evil spirit invasion. The healer is often specific in the accusations based on knowledge of the social situation in general and on interrogation of the patient, but ultimately also on the basis of his double vision capacity to see the spiritual dimensions surrounding the case, invisible as they are to ordinary people.[3]

The people accused of sorcery respond, and the pattern of accusation and response usually continues until the social situation which originally sparked the illness/possession has been healed. That healing comes when all potential or actual witches/sorcerers have spoken the required release formulae for the victim in public. On the strength of the resulting social solidarity, the healer proceeds to the exorcising phase. He or she exorcises and then banishes the attacking evil spirits either by a word of command or by ritual washing or anointing, but most usually by the patient's ritual vomiting.

In Yaroba, all social tension and friction invariably involves the spirit world, leading to evil-spirit-caused illness or catastrophe. But once the healing/exorcism has been successfully concluded, the witches/sorcerers are also cleansed by it and restored to full social acceptance. The next time an illness arises in the family, the social evil causing it is usually personified in a different family member. Since all people participate in the creation of social problems, all of them must also take turns to be designated as evil witches/sorcerers who cause trouble in the social setting (de Rosny 1985:48).

Non-Social Sorcery

As mentioned earlier, however, unprovoked invasion by evil spirits is also possible, especially when sorcerers/witches try out their powers at random or when someone steals the souls of fellow villagers for personal enrichment or for resale to others. Unprovoked invasion by alien spirits may also come from neighboring clans or villages when they engage in sorcery against their neighbors. Under such unprovoked conditions, the healing/exorcism may have to be one-sided.

Even if agents of such sorcery can be identified through the healer's double vision, they may not be willing to cooperate in the healing/exorcism. If so, once healers have identified the source of the attack and have exorcised the invading spirit or spirits, they create supernatural armor for the patient, indeed, for the entire family, to deflect any additional evil spirit forces that may be sent against them. The spiritual armor provided by a healer causes any new malevolent spirits that may be sent at them to bounce off the armor and to be deflected back toward the senders (de Rosny 1985:133).

Soul stealing has exactly the same negative effects and requires healing procedures similar to those of spirit possession. The legitimate spirit inhabitant

---

[3]The Christian helper of one healer could perform most of the rituals on behalf of the recognized healer, but was deemed incapable of double vision because of his Christian upbringing (de Rosny 1985:47).

of the individual has been taken captive and enslaved by more powerful alien spirit forces. The resulting soul loss may involve the same illness symptoms as when a person falls under the control of alien spirits.

Healers in Yaroba are critically important people because they are the group's anti-sorcerers. Since healers are endowed with double vision and can see those dimensions of the world that are beyond the view and knowledge of ordinary mortals, they are able to intervene in most cases of illness, soul loss, or evil spirit invasion. The greatest hindrances to Yaroba healers are not the invading evil spirits or even the sorcerers who sent them, but the doubts which family and friends may have in their powers to heal and exorcise (de Rosny 1985:37).

Thus, the religion of the African Yaroba is basically a therapeutic one. It seeks not only to heal sick individuals, but also to heal whatever community originally gave birth to the disease-causing evil. It is thus in sharp contrast to much of evangelical Christianity which tends to deal largely with forgiveness for biblically defined moral sin and with preparing people for life in a blessed hereafter (de Rosny 1985:197–99). We will examine these contrasts in the next chapter, comparing them also to the worldviews in the Bible.

12

Spirit Possession and Exorcism: Comparison of Views

Some years ago a young Vietnamese woman immigrant to Canada became possessed by the soul of her deceased Vietnamese fiancé. She had been promised in marriage to this young man, but before the marriage could take place he had been inducted into the Vietnamese army and was killed shortly thereafter. Already devastated by the sudden death of her fiancé, the woman then lost her parents in the same war. So relatives helped her emigrate to Canada with other members of the family.

Instead of recovering in the new homeland, the young woman developed increasingly more severe depression and eventually experienced the soul of her fiancé as molesting her sexually. She was institutionalized and treated repeatedly by Canadian psychiatrists for the next five years, as her symptoms periodically increased or abated; finally, one of them mentioned the case to a Vietnamese psychiatrist who had been licensed to practice in Canada.

Meeting with her for several hours, the Vietnamese psychiatrist realized that in order to help the young woman he would have to depend on her Vietnamese view of the spirit world and enlist the Buddhist religion in the healing. So he took her to the Vietnamese Buddhist temple where the priest performed a ceremony to induct the soul of her deceased fiancé into a celibate order of monks. The inductee's soul was instructed to stay away from his former fiancée forever. The young woman herself was never addressed during the whole ceremony, but when the final blessing on the new inductee had been spoken, she walked out of the temple completely free of her possession and emotional depression.

The Vietnamese psychiatrist first shared this incident with me in confidence. It took several hours of persuasion to make him willing to recount the experience in public at a conference on refugees in Canada sponsored by

Alberta Mental Health. He was afraid that his Canadian colleagues would ridicule him, and maybe even cause his license to be taken away. However, when he became convinced of the importance of the experience in light of the problems for which he and I were trying to serve as resource people, he did tell the group.

Comparison of Worldviews and Cultural Contexts

Westerners do not hold many of the worldview assumptions about spirit possession, illness, and exorcism that were held by the Vietnamese woman and the priest who helped her, or which were described regarding African people in the last chapter. Biblical worldviews, however, lie intermediate between the African ones and ours, but closer to the African than to ours. Some of the similarities and differences between these assumptions are summarized in the tables of this chapter.

In these tables, column 1 picks up specific details from the discussion of the African Yaroba tribe in chapter 11. The assumptions of the groups represented in the other columns are listed for comparison to the first. The West has two columns in the tables, distinguishing between typical secular materialism and typical views of Christians, especially evangelical ones. However, most of these Christians, while professing loyalty to the Scriptures, do actually operate more or less fully on the general premises of the scientific and materialistic worldview of North America.

The tables are necessarily oversimplified. The Yaroba do not represent all of Africa in all respects, much less all societies elsewhere in which spirits are important. The Bible, furthermore, includes a variety of views, as we have already seen (chaps. 5–6). And both columns of the Western scene involve wide variation. There is nothing here about the assumptions of Western Jews or Muslims, New Age people, or cultists of various kinds, for example. The gross comparisons are nevertheless revealing and show how models of reality influence the interpretation of events like physical or mental illness, and how they determine the type or methods of treatment that will be considered applicable in cases of evil spirit attack.

In making these comparisons, I am not judging the rightness or wrongness of these models of reality but am trying to show that radically different models are possible and that no model can be comprehensive in the current state of our knowledge. All of them necessarily operate on selected premises, choosing and interpreting only certain features of the total reality which surrounds them. However, dissonance between the professed model and reality or the actual experience of reality potentially breeds doubt, and the resulting weak faith, or even lack of faith, seriously hinders any process of healing or exorcism. This is particularly noticeable in the reactions of Western

Christians. My own attempt to resolve the tensions between the models is presented in chapter 19.

TABLE 5

CONTRASTING FUNDAMENTAL ASSUMPTIONS
ON BODY, SOUL, AND SPIRIT

(Amplification of many of the points, including biblical references, is to be found in the text)

a AFRICAN	b BIBLICAL	c WESTERN MATERIALIST	d WESTERN CHRISTIAN
[1]The whole universe, including all matter, is alive.	The world (air) is peopled with a variety of spirit powers.	The universe is matter. "Spirit" is a superstition.	Professed belief in spirits (at least the Spirit of God) but discomfort with the concept. Spirits seldom experienced.
[2]Material things can change into spirit and spirits can be manifested in material form.	Instances recorded.	Superstition	Bible is true but such things no longer happen.
[3]Matter and spirit comprise a single continuum.	Matter and spirit comprise a single continuum.	Matter is real, spirit superstition.	Matter and spirit are separated by unbridged gap.
[4]Good and bad spirits both exist.	Good and bad spirits both exist.	No spirits exist.	At least Spirit of God exists; bad spirits more problematical.
[5]People have both bodies and souls.	People have bodies and souls/spirits.	People have bodies, life, and self-consciousness.	People have bodies and souls worth saving, but modern people are more comfortable with life and self-consciousness.

(Table 5 Continued)

[6]Soul released from body at death.	Soul released from body at death.	Life processes stop at death.	Soul survives death.
[7]Souls of dead become good or bad spirits.	God created choice between good and bad.	Superstition	Souls go to heaven or hell.
[8]Souls of the dead speak to the living.	Instances recorded.	Superstition	The dead do not communicate with the living. Consulting with the dead is "of the devil."
[9]Souls of people can be stolen, captured, enslaved.	Instances recorded.	Superstition	Souls of people can become slaves of devil/evil.
[10]People can be possessed by good spirits.	People can be filled with the Spirit of God.	Superstition	All true believers indwelt by Spirit of God.
[11]People can be possessed by evil spirits.	Instances recorded.	Superstition	Have never seen a case of possession.
[12]People can control spirits, good or evil.	Instances recorded.	Superstition	Theoretically believers have power over evil spirits.
[13]Spirits communicate with people.	Instances recorded.	Superstition	Spirit of God speaks to people, but devil speaking almost unheard of.
[14]People communicate with spirits.	Instances recorded.	Superstition	Generally unknown except in exorcism.

Sometimes amplification is needed to understand some of the terse entries in the tables of this chapter. A few examples (often representative of many others) also need to be supplied where the table simply lists "instances recorded." Such information accompanies each table. To make clear the connections between the various parts of the amplification and the tables themselves, rows of entries have been given superscript numbers in the tables, and the columns are considered to be lettered a, b, c, and d. Thus, amplification [2]b refers to the corresponding cell of the table.

Amplification of Table 5

[1]d. Charismatic Christians and some others do claim to experience the Spirit of God, and a smaller number claim to experience evil spirits.

[2]b. Moses and Elijah appeared with Jesus when he was transfigured (Mt 17:3–7); dead saints appeared to the followers of Jesus in Jerusalem (Mt 27:52–53); Jesus appeared several times after his death (Jn 20:14–29; 21:4–14; Acts 1:3–9; Mt 28:9; Lk 24:28–51); an angel appeared and freed Peter from prison (Acts 12:6–11); Philip disappeared when the Spirit of God took him away (Acts 8:39); Aaron's rod became a living snake (Ex 7:10).

[3]b. The resurrected Jesus walked through closed doors (Jn 20:19,26); Philip disappeared (Acts 8:39).

[3]c. The discovery of quarks raises the question of spirit again (chap. 19).

[4]b. Good spirits include the Spirit of God and angels; evil spirits include Satan and demons (chaps. 5–6).

[6]b. Jesus "gave up his spirit" and died (Mt 27:50 KJV); the Spirit of God struck Ananias and Sapphira dead when they lied (Acts 5:3–5, 8–10).

[7]b. Choice for angels (2 Pet 2:4; Jude 6); for human beings (Prov 1:29–30; Is 65:12; Josh 24:15; 1 Kgs 18:21).

[8]b. Jesus talked to his disciples after his death and resurrection (Jn 20:26–29); dead saints appeared to disciples at Jerusalem (Mt 27:52-53); witch conjured up Saul's soul (1 Sam 28:11–12); consultation with mediums and necromancers condemned (Deut 18:10–11).

[9]b. Souls of people sold by merchants to the city of Babylon (Rev 18:11–13); people are slaves of the devil (2 Tim 2:26).

[10]b. People can be filled with the Spirit of God (Acts 2:4; 1 Cor 6:19); people can be led by the Spirit of God (Rom 8:14).

[11]b. A dumb man was possessed by a demon (Mt 9:32–33); a Canaanite woman's daughter was possessed by a demon (Mt 15:22); after an evil spirit was exorcised it brought back seven others to reinhabit the person (Mt 12:43–45); Satan entered Judas (Jn 13:27).

[12]a. A Malawi healer had seventeen spirit helpers.

[12]b. Jesus' disciples are given power over evil spirits (Mk 6:7; Lk 9:1; Acts 5:16); Jewish exorcists tried to exert power over spirits and failed (Acts 19:13–16); Paul had authority over a spirit which predicted the future (Acts 16:16–18).

[13]b. Spirit of God took Jesus to the desert (Mt 4:1); the Spirit communicated with Philip (Acts 8:29), Paul (Acts 16:6), all who believed in Jesus Christ (Rom 8:16); the devil or his cohorts communicated with Jesus (Mt 4:1–9), to sons of Sceva (Acts 19:15), to Judas (Jn 13:2).

[14]b. Jesus spoke to devil (Mt 4:4–10), to evil spirits (Mt 8:32; Mk 9:25); Paul commanded evil spirits (Acts 16:18); exorcists spoke to evil spirits (Acts 19:13).

TABLE 6

CONTRASTING ASSUMPTIONS ABOUT SIN, SICKNESS, AND HEALING

a AFRICAN	b BIBLICAL	c WESTERN MATERIALIST	d WESTERN CHRISTIAN
[1]Creation of human beings with capacity for choice leaves evil as possibility.	No clear statement on origin of evil, but freedom of choice demands that it exist.	Good and evil exist; little speculation about origin.	Evil comes from the devil.
[2]Sin usually socially defined.	Sin sometimes morally defined, sometimes socially.	Right and wrong relative rather than intrinsic.	Sin divinely and morally defined.
[3]Evil spirits cause physical illness.	Instances recorded.	Germs, viruses, mechanical malfunctions, etc., cause illness; growing awareness of psychosomatic illness.	Hesitantly believe that evil spirits cause illness in the Bible, but germ view more convincing.
[4]Evil spirits cause psychic illness.	Instances recorded.	Malfunction or imbalance causes psychic illness.	Hesitantly believe that evil spirits cause emotional disturbance.

(Table 6 Continued)

[5]Wrong doing, sin, result in illness, affliction.	Instances recorded.	Guilt may cause emotional problems which predispose people to illness, but does not cause it.	Reluctant to believe that own sins cause illness, but see some illness as God's judgment.
[6]Evil spirit helpers can heal or kill.	Instances recorded.	Superstition	Some fundamentalists believe in Satanic miracles.
[7]Friendly (ancestral) spirits cause illness.	Instances recorded.	Superstition	Theoretically believe Bible view but not African.
[8]All illness is caused by spirit or by spiritual means.	Some illness caused by spirits.	Superstition	Evangelicals theoretically believe Bible view; charismatics have stronger belief.
[9]Illnesses resulting from deeds which lead to evil social consequences may strike the sinner or his/her relatives.	Instances recorded; children suffer from ancestral sins; but sin also treated as a personal matter.	Psychiatrists believe that children often act out parents' unresolved problems.	Is a personal matter; however, people allow that children suffer from ancestral sins.
[10]Religion is therapeutic.	Religion therapeutic and provides salvation.	Religion largely left-over superstition.	Religion provides salvation.

Amplification of Table 6

[2]a. For example, in Africa the violation of a virgin is not a moral offense but may be a social one.

[2]b. Morally defined sins: actions are either right or wrong (Ex 20:1–17); socially defined sins: actions are violations of social obligations (Eph 4:31–32; Acts 5:28; Jas 4:1–5).

[3]b. Bent woman (Lk 13:11); blind and dumb people (Mt 12:22; Mt 9:32).

[4]b. Epilepsy (Mt 17:14–21); insanity (Mk 5:1–13).

[5]b. Who sinned to cause blindness? (Jn 9:21); misuse of communion leads to being weak and sickly (1 Cor 11:29–30); sin is punished with illness (Lev 26:15–16); Herod killed because of pride (Acts 12:23); people suffer because of sin (Ps 107:17).

[5]d. The particular illnesses depend on what seems especially frightening at the time; now AIDS is seen as divine judgment on homosexuality.

[6]b. Satanic miracles (2 Thes 2:9; Rev 13:13, 16:14).

[7]b. Saul's emotional illness caused by a spirit sent by God (1 Sam 16:14); Paul's "thorn in the flesh" allowed by God to keep him from becoming proud (2 Cor 12:7–9); God sent diseases (Deut 7:15).

[9]b. Who sinned, he or his parents? (Jn 9:2; see also Job 21:19; Is 14:21; Lam 5:7); children complete ancestors' sins (Mt 23:32–33); sin treated as a personal matter (Jer 31:29–30; Ezek 18:19–20).

[10]b. Religion therapeutic (Lk 4:18; Jer 30:17); provides salvation (Rom 10:13; Jn 3:16).

TABLE 7

CONTRASTING ASSUMPTIONS ON RELATIONSHIPS
BETWEEN SPIRITS AND LIVING PEOPLE

a AFRICAN	b BIBLICAL	c WESTERN MATERIALIST	d WESTERN CHRISTIAN
[1]Ancestral spirits concerned about living relatives.	Parallels recorded.	Superstition	Theoretically possible but practically unbelievable.
[2]People can see spirits when they have "dual vision."	Instances recorded.	Superstition	Theoretically believe the Bible but have not seen any.
[3]People can enslave soul power of others for self-enrichment.	Instances recorded.	Superstition	Incredulity
[4]Certain people are mediums who communicate with spirits.	Instances recorded.	Superstition	Forbidden by Scripture.

(Table 7 Continued)

[5]Spirits serve as messengers, helpers of ancestors, healers, or sorcerers.	Instances recorded.	Superstition	Angels are messengers, but most people have not experienced them.
[6]The living dead protect the morals and health of the living, while the living provide eternal "goodness" for the dead.	Those who died in faith form a cloud of witnesses who watch the faith of the succeeding generations.	No relationship between the dead and the living.	The dead are irrelevant to an individual's personal salvation and health.

Amplification of Table 7

[1]b. Christ is our older brother (Heb 2:11,16–18; Rom 8:29). Ancestors in the faith are "a cloud of witnesses" (Heb 12:1). Such a biblical passage may seem metaphorical to many North Americans but when I taught a course in African religion at an American University, twenty to thirty African students came to me with questions about ancestors and Bible passages like this one and 1 Samuel 28:7. These passages were very important to them because of their experience with and views concerning spirits.

[2]b. Balaam saw an angel after the LORD opened his eyes (Num 22: 31–34); Paul saw the risen Christ (1 Cor 15:8); Jesus saw Satan fall from heaven (Lk 10:18); Elisha's servant saw the heavenly host (2 Kgs 6:17); believers can discern whether a spirit is of God or not (1 Jn 4:1–3).

[2]d. "Dual vision" is probably equivalent to the New Testament gift of discernment of spirits, the ability to distinguish evil spirits from the Spirit of God or even from a human spirit. Some say they have the capacity to physically see the evil spirits which are afflicting the individual (White 1987).

[3]b. Human souls as slaves (Rev 18:13); people enslaved to spirits (Gal 4:3).

[4]b. Medium at Endor (1 Sam 28:7); prohibitions against communicating with the spirit world (Lev 19:31; 20:6; Mic 5:12; Gal 5:19–20).

[4]d. See 4b.

[5]b. God sent Spirit (Gal 4:6); Gabriel (Lk 1:26); messenger of Satan caused Paul's "thorn in the flesh" which was either a spirit harassing him or a physical ailment caused by the devil (2 Cor 12:7).

[6]b. See latter part of amplification on 1b.

TABLE 8

CONTRASTING ASSUMPTIONS
ON WITCHCRAFT, SORCERY, DIVINATION, AND MAGIC

a AFRICAN	b BIBLICAL	c WESTERN MATERIALIST	d WESTERN CHRISTIAN
[1]People can practice witchcraft, sorcery.	Instances recorded.	Superstition	Incredulity
[2]Close relatives are the most frequent sorcerers.	Instances recorded.	Superstition	Incredulity
[3]Name has power.	Instances recorded.	Superstition	Incredulity, but use formulas like "In the name of the Father," "in Jesus' name."
[4]Name is used for witching, magic.	Instances recorded.	Superstition	Incredulity
[5]For power transfer, whole is present in the part.	Instances recorded.	Superstition	Incredulity
[6]Actions can have magic effects.	Instances recorded.	Superstition	Actions only ritual.
[7]Words can have magic effect.	Instances recorded.	Superstition	Incredulity but use religious formulas.
[8]Thoughts can have magic effect.	Sin begins with thought.	Bad thoughts are harmful to the thinker.	Bad thoughts are harmful to the thinker.
[9]Amulets and charms have magic effect.	Instances recorded.	Superstition	Some people use amulets and charms.

(Table 8 Continued)

[10]Diviners can divine future or the humanly unknowable.	Instances recorded.	Superstition	Some charismatics claim prophetic gifts.

Amplification of Table 8

[1]b. Sorcerers (Deut 18:10; 2 Kgs 17:17; Gal 5:20; Rev 21:8; 22:15); practice of magic (Acts 8:11; 19:19).

[2]b. Family members involve younger generation in witchcraft (Deut 18:10; 2 Kgs 17:17; 21:6).

[3]b. Holy is his name (Lk 1:49); believe in his name (Jn 1:12); "By what power or by what name did you do this?" (Acts 4:7 NRSV); ask in my name (Jn 14:13); no other name saves (Acts 4:12); a blasphemous name (Rev 13:1).

[4]b. Sons of Sceva attempt exorcism in Jesus' name (Acts 19:13–14).

[5]b. Woman healed by touching hem of Jesus' robe (Mt 9:20–22, 14:36); people healed by touching Paul's handkerchiefs and aprons (Acts 19:12).

[6]b. Anointing with oil consecrates (Ex 29:36; 1 Sam 10:1), heals (Mk 6:13; Lk 10:34; Jas 5:14); laying hands on someone blesses (Mt 19:13–15; Acts 6:6; 1 Tim 4:14; 2 Tim 1:6), heals (Mk 6:5; Lk 4:40; Acts 28:8).

[6]c. Examples believed by "superstitious" people: danger in walking under a ladder; crossing fingers when lying; success by use of champagne in ship launching.

[6]d. For some Christians anointing and laying hands on someone results in healing.

[7]b. Curses (Acts 23:3; Gal 1:9); blessings (Rom 16:20; 2 Cor 13:13; Jude 24); prayers (Jn 15:7; Jas 5:15).

[8]b. Sin begins with thought (Mt 15:19; Prov 23:7).

[8]c. Bad thoughts lead to depression, paranoia, and eventually to physical symptoms.

[9]b. Books used in the study of magic (Acts 19:19); Simon practiced magic (Acts 8:9–11); Pharisees wore phylacteries 'protectors' for protection against evil (Mt 23:5); use of amulets (Is 3:20), charms (frontlets Ex 13:16; Deut 6:8), idols of gold and silver (Rev 9:20).

[9]d. St. Christopher medals, crucifixes, used for protection.

[10]b. Ability to divine the future (Gen 44:15; 1 Sam 6:2; Jer 27:9; Is 2:6; Acts 16:16); use of lots to know God's will (Acts 1:26).

TABLE 9

CONTRASTING ASSUMPTIONS ON EXORCISM

a AFRICAN	b BIBLICAL	c WESTERN MATERIALIST	d WESTERN CHRISTIAN
[1]The family is the all-important social unit, the basis of self-definition and salvation.	The family is the basic social unit, but the family in Christ is the ultimate social context.	The individual is more important than the family.	The individual is responsible for his/her own salvation.
[2]Expulsion of demons is a family effort.	Instances recorded.	Psychiatric healing non-coercive. See also chapter 19.	See chapter 19.
[3]Exorcism is accomplished as the victim vomits the spirits out and identifies them.	Jesus expected faith from the victim's guardian.	See chapter 19	See chapter 19.
[4]Exorcism is a normal, expected happening.	Numerous instances recorded, but observers marveled.	Psychiatry frowns on exorcism because does not accept existence of demons.	Church at large skeptical, but some Catholics, charismatics, and others are exorcising.
[5]Exorcism without community support requires armoring victim and family against further attack.	God provides spiritual armor.	Immunization and medication provide material armoring.	Immunization, medication, and prayer for protection provide armoring.

Amplification of Table 9

[1]b. Family as social unit (Deut 4:9; Prov 22:6; 2 Tim 1:5); family of God (Jas 5:13–16; 1 Cor 12:24–27).

[2]b. Expulsion of demons by divine power and authority with family support (Mk 9:20–27; 7:26).

³b. Faith from the victim's guardian (Mk 9:22–24; 5:22–23,36; 7:24–30).

⁴b. Exorcism by Jews (Acts 13:6-9; 19:13; Mt 12:27); by Jesus (Mt 8:16; 9:33; Mk 7:29); by disciples (Mt 10:1; Mk 6:13); by apostles (Acts 16:18); by people who did not follow Jesus (Mt 7:22).

⁵b. God's spirit fortifies people, builds "armor" around them against spirit attacks (Eph 6:10–17).

Summary of the Comparative Listing

The most salient similarities and differences between the four world-views summarized above, together with their resulting social contexts, may now be summarized as follows.

African Worldviews

1. The spirit dimension pervades all of life and functions as the supernatural dimension of all material phenomena.

2. Sin and evil are defined in social terms: everything that has negative effect on society is evil and can result in illness.

3. All persistent misfortune, illness, or bad luck is caused. Benign afflictions are usually caused by friendly ancestral spirits who are seeking to prevent greater calamity. Serious illness and misfortune result from sorcery, usually within the family itself.

4. The immediate family and the local community provide the social context which provides healing. All actual and potential sorcerers must speak the required release formula before the victim can eject the invading evil spirits. The healer is the catalyst to bring about personal and community healing.

5. Religion is basically therapeutic in the here and now.

6. Descendants are responsible for salvation of those in the beyond, just as those who have passed on hold the welfare of the living in their hands.

7. Life and ritual are pervaded by magic.

New Testament Worldviews

1. The universe, especially the air above, is peopled by hosts of hierarchically organized spirit forces, both good and evil. While there seems to be some material/spirit alternation, the pattern is not as all-pervasive as in the African situation.

2. Sin and evil are defined both morally and socially. A strong link exists

between evil and illness. Illness is frequently seen as resulting from specific sins or evil deeds.

3. The church theoretically functions as the accepting healing community. Both the therapeutic and salvationist dimensions are present in Scripture, but the former is often Old Testament, the latter New Testament.

4. Healing of illnesses of all kinds and exorcism of evil spirits are both heavily based on power. The sufferer has faith in the healer, or God, and the healer is endowed with divine power and authority to "cast out" the demons.

5. There is a recognizable decrease in the amount of magic involved in religious ritual between the Old and the New Testaments.

6. Over all, the similarities between the New Testament context and the African one are so extensive that Archbishop Milingo in Zambia found that he could operate more or less literally in the New Testament way (Milingo 1984), even though Western charismatics do find some difference.

North American Scientific Worldviews

1. The universe is a giant material machine with no place for spirits, good or bad, unless quarks (energy without mass) should turn out to be spirit.

2. Evil is usually contextually defined so there are no absolute rights or wrongs, and everything is relative. Furthermore, evil and good are highly personal matters. Only the individual culprit can be punished. Legal technicalities often prevent punishment from being meted out even to those who are obviously guilty.

3. Individual self-fulfillment is usually more important than the welfare of family and society at large. Social responsibility is largely a memory of the past so individuals often feel alone and abandoned. Loneliness expresses itself in increasing mental and emotional breakdown and in alienation from fellow human beings. Yearning for community has spawned various cults and group therapies. However, no true therapeutic community exists for those who need it.

4. All illness, physical and mental, is materially caused, either by invading organisms or by mechanical or chemical malfunction within the organism itself. Healing thus involves destroying or eliminating invading organisms, or correcting malfunctions or chemical imbalances. On the other hand, psychosomatic interaction has been receiving increasing attention.

5. While the Western scientific context officially has no place for religion or magic, remnants of magic still abound. The degree of magic which still remains in the West seems to be about equal to the non-supernaturalism that makes its appearance in the New Testament in contrast with the Old.

North American Christian Worldviews

1. The fundamental characteristic of North American Christianity is an acute schizophrenia. Theoretically the church "believes" in the New Testament spirit world: Spirit of God, angels, evil spirits, demons, and Satan. In practice however, most people experience no evil spirits and little, if any, of the Spirit of God. In everyday life North American Christians are firmly rooted in, and for all practical purposes are operating on, the premise of a material universe.

2. North American Christianity is also schizophrenic in its definition of evil (Walsh and Middleton 1953:117–26). Doctrinally it accepts a moral definition of evil, but practically it interprets evil relatively and contextually.

3. North American evangelical Christianity operates in terms of the "God of the gap." All good phenomena with unknown causes tend to be interpreted as miracles of God. But each time science offers a new materialistic or mechanistic explanation, God gets smaller. Likewise, each new discovery of chemical or material malfunction in the brain or nervous system reduces the realm of Satan and of demon possession.

4. Charismatic Christians, deeply aware that God is growing too small, are actively trying to resurrect the New Testament spirit model. However, unlike the New Testament, where spirits are pervasive, they see demons as operating in only a percentage of the cases of mental illness (chap. 19).

5. Theoretically, North American Christianity views the church as the accepting, healing context, but few actually find community in the church as a whole. Some find it in smaller cells or prayer groups, but even these offer limited refuge in times of trouble.

6. On the whole Christians seem to consider that "original sin" by far outweighs the image of God in each human being. Thus, the salvationist emphasis by far outranks the therapeutic one, and the church readily defers therapeutic functions to secular specialists or social agencies. Christians often seem uncomfortable with such passages as the following, because they emphasize the behavioral and the therapeutic rather than the salvationist approach to Christianity.

> The Spirit of the Lord *is* upon me, because he hath anointed me to preach the gospel to the poor; he hath sent me to heal the broken hearted, to preach deliverance to the captives, and recovering of sight to the blind, to set at liberty them that are bruised, to preach the acceptable year of the Lord (Lk 4:18–19 KJV).

> When the Son of man shall come in his glory, and all the holy angels with him, then shall he sit upon the throne of his glory; and before him shall be gathered all nations: and he shall separate them one from another, as a shepherd divideth *his* sheep from the goats: and he shall set the sheep on his

right hand, but the goats on his left. Then shall the King say unto them on his right hand, "Come, ye blessed of my Father, inherit the kingdom prepared for you from the foundation of the world: for I was ahungered, and ye gave me meat: I was thirsty, and ye gave me drink: I was a stranger and ye took me in: naked and ye clothed me: I was sick and ye visited me: I was in prison and ye came unto me" (Mt 25:31–36 KJV).

7. The "chosen people" complex and the conviction of the uniqueness of their approach to God keeps most evangelical Christians from recognizing people in other faiths who live like Christians, even if they do not bear a Christian label.

The critical question which these comparisons raise for many Western Christians, and especially for me, is how to understand the spirit world within the framework of a modern worldview, or an adaptation of one. How can I translate the various spirit worlds of the Bible into my modern worldview? I see the biblical spirit worlds more clearly because I can compare them with the Yaroba. How can I translate that greater clarity for my own time? That issue will be discussed in chapter 19.

13

Impersonal Power:
Holiness, Taboo, Magic, Divination

In world cultures, sacredness is a wider phenomenon than only direct association with God and the spirit world. Usually for personal supernatural power the appropriate metaphors used all over the world are anthropomorphically based on human personalities. In contrast, metaphors for impersonal supernatural power are mechanical (Wink 1984:3, 1986:172–73; 1992:4–6, 63).

An irregularly-shaped rock outcropping lying at a dangerous place on the trail may be powerful either because it has a spirit which causes harm, or because it is in its nature to be powerful. If a spirit is associated with that rock and someone trespasses on or near it without an appropriate acknowledgment of its power, the spirit may *do* things like intentionally *causing* the person to stumble and break a leg. On the other hand, if the rock has impersonal power rather than spirit power, anyone who trespasses automatically trips and breaks a leg. The power does not consciously do it or cause it; nor does the injury happen by chance. The result lies in the nature of that special rock with its impersonal power to avenge itself.

Belief in impersonal power is commonly a significant factor in worldview. For example, in the West, as well as in many other parts of the world, many people practice astrology, which is based on an assumption of impersonal power. The positions of the stars or planets, the "sign" under which someone was born, and various other mechanical factors combine to set the person's fate. No spirit in the stars consciously does this, but in their very nature the stars and various other factors associated with them bring about the results (Douglas 1985:41–57).

Luck and fate, to the extent that we believe in them as affecting our lives, represent impersonal power. If we escape injury in a serious accident, we may attribute our continued well-being to luck (impersonal power), or the intervention of spirit in some form or other (like God's will). Or we may ascribe no supernatural power to the situation at all. In the latter case, we believe that the impact of our moving car against the telephone pole, together with many other physical factors, were such that our bodies were held in place by seat belts and did not strike surfaces on which they would otherwise have been injured. The last of these ways of looking at the accident is a naturalistic one, the first two supernatural. As the gap God of the West becomes smaller or disappears (part 3, introduction), spirit power is being replaced by belief that natural forces explain everything and/or by belief in impersonal power, the latter often partly in the form of astrology.

Almost all major religions in the world are based primarily on spirit power, on God and/or other supernatural, sentient, active spirit beings. Impersonal supernatural power is usually mixed in as well, as we shall see, but the overall basic power is personal.

In theoretical Buddhism, however, the basic power is impersonal. What I do or what I did in past lives sets my fate. I was born a man and not an insect because of my accumulated *karma*, the merit I gained in past incarnations. In my next incarnation, I may be born on a lower level (like a woman or an animal), or on a higher level (like a wealthy powerful man), again the fruit of my accumulated karma, including merit I gain both in this life and in previous ones. In Buddhism as it is actually practiced by ordinary people, however, a great many spirits are also mixed in with the impersonal power.

The difference between spirit power and impersonal power is contrasted in the concepts of what made a king in medieval Europe and in modern Thailand. Europe believed in the "divine right of kings," which meant that it was God who established the king. The king was validated by spirit power. Thailand believes that the king validates himself. He is king because his enormous karma from the past makes him king. The fact that he is king proves the karma. Spirit power has nothing to do with it.

Holiness

The most general form in which impersonal power is manifested in religious worldviews is in the concept of holiness or sacredness. In the Bible, holiness is ascribed both to spirits and to inanimate places and things. God is holy, and so is God's temple. Holiness is impersonal power, however, even when it is a characteristic of spirit beings, and even when the presence of the spirit being induces the holiness. Holiness does not have a spirit in it, but is a characteristic of some spirits as well as some physical objects.

Holiness involves being separated from the ordinary, being special, being unusual in some way. It is "other," beyond the natural. Some objects or people are holy because they are consecrated to God and therefore out of the natural. In some religions, holiness is associated with purity and cleanliness, but this is not universal; neither is holiness necessarily associated with morality or righteousness.

Holiness often induces awe or fear and stimulates worship. In the Bible people are pictured as trembling in the presence of God, not necessarily because they think God wants to harm them but because God is holy.

Ordination to the Thai monkhood produces remarkable holiness:

> I once heard a new monk use honorific language to an old woman. She replied, "Oh, don't your holiness! You're a *phra'* ['holy one, monk, Buddha'] now, a human being no longer." Her words were beyond a manner of speech. In her eyes he had become something quite different from what he had been before, apart from his fellow men (Wright 1978:121).

The power of this otherness in the Thai monks is further demonstrated in their lives after ordination.

> Buddhist monks in Thailand preserve their celibacy to an admirable and incredible degree. I am prepared to vouch for this. As anyone knows who has attempted celibacy, mere moral advice, "Thou shalt be chaste," is no help at all. Only a psychic notion of immense depth can preserve one in so hard a state. . . .
>
> The celibacy of Thai Buddhist monks could be called heroic if it did not seem to come so easily. . . . The monks know themselves to be more than men, not in moralistic or rational terms, but in magical terms (Wright 1978:121).

The secularism of the West has greatly reduced our capacity to sense holiness. Holiness is disappearing with the gap God, although it permeates the Bible. But there is more to holiness in the Bible than we ordinarily think of.

For example, in Hebrew culture holiness was sometimes associated with war, like the Muslim *jihad* 'holy war.' Thus, when Israel went to war at Yahweh's command, all the enemy people and all their belongings were considered "devoted," dedicated to Yahweh. They could therefore not be plundered. Taking something "devoted to God" carried the death penalty in Israel. Thus, when Israel attacked the city of Jericho during their conquest of Canaan, and Achan took and hid some of the devoted valuables, God withheld all further help from Israel until this violation had been punished (Josh 7:1–26).

Conversely, once God had commanded King Saul to fight the Amalekites, these people and their belongings were devoted to God, this time requiring their total destruction. When King Saul saved the life of the Amalekite King

Agag and allowed the Israelites to keep the best of the Amalekite cattle for sacrifices, God withdrew all further help from him (1 Sam 15:1–33).

Religious prostitutes, male and female[1], were holy in the early religions in the Middle East, especially the Canaanite religions, with powerful effect on Israelite behavior and religion, as denounced by the prophets.

> [The LORD says,] "As a result, your daughters serve as prostitutes, and your daughters-in-law commit adultery. Yet I will not punish them for this, because you yourselves go off with temple prostitutes, and together with them you offer pagan sacrifices" (Hos 4:13–14 GNB).

Taboo: Self-Avenging Holiness

One manifestation of holiness is taboo, or self-avenging holiness. Violations of taboo bring automatic retribution. The holiness of which taboo is an expression is often traditionally called *mana*, the term used in Melanesia, where mana was first recognized by Western scholars. The taboo object, or "mana container," is usually hedged about by behavioral rules which, when broken, will automatically avenge themselves on the culprit (Codrington 1965; Handy 1965; Ellis 1965).

The most prominent holy object to which self-avenging taboo was attached in the Old Testament was the ark the of covenant, the box which contained the stone tablets on which the Ten Commandments were inscribed. Its holiness and resulting taboo can be seen in a series of incidents such as when the sons of Eli took the ark with the troops when going to war against the Philistines (1 Sam 4:1–7:1). When Israel was defeated, the ark of the covenant was captured by their enemies, who were ecstatic because they recognized it as Israel's most sacred object.

The Philistines put the ark in the temple of their God, Dagon, assuming that since he had defeated Yahweh, the tribal God of Israel, the Hebrew taboo would be inoperative. But next morning they found Dagon off his usual high pedestal, lying face down on the ground, prostrate in front of the box. The Philistines thought this must have been an accident and put their Dagon back in his proper place. But the next day Dagon was again lying face down on the ground in front of the box, this time with his extremities broken off.

So the Philistines realized that the Israelite ark was too holy, too taboo for them to keep. They were also suffering from plagues because the ark dedicated to the LORD was in their country. So they returned it to Israel.

The Israelites, of course, were overjoyed, and began to celebrate. Some

---

[1]Examples of references to devoted male prostitutes are Deuteronomy 23:18; 1 Kings 14:24; 15:12; 22:46; 2 Kings 23:7; Job 36:14, and of female prostitutes are Genesis 38:21–22; Deuteronomy 23:18; Hosea 4:14.

of them were so intrigued by what the ark of the covenant might contain that they looked inside it, and some 50,070 people died as a result (1 Sam 4:12–6:19 KJV).[2] As a consequence of ignoring the holiness of the box, they were killed by its taboo. The ark was then quietly stored at a private person's home for a number of years.

Later, King David wanted to consolidate his reign by bringing the ark of the covenant to Jerusalem, his new capital city. So the ark was put on a cart, and the people sang and rejoiced as they accompanied it to its new home.

Uzzah was walking alongside the cart when it became unsteady and looked as though the ark might get tipped off. He quickly reached out to steady it, not wanting it to come to any harm, but in spite of his noble intention, the holiness of the box killed him (2 Sam 6:1–11; 1 Chr 13:1–11). The taboo force in this instance is obvious although the incident was rationalized as Uzzah having angered God by touching the ark.

Taboo is more prominent in some societies than in others, and the evil results of breaking taboo are stronger in some than in others. Queen Sunanda of Thailand was drowned when her river boat capsized in 1881. So great was her royal holiness that no commoner could touch her, so her boatmen looked on helplessly as she drowned. To have rescued her would have defiled her and have brought calamity on those who did so. High-caste Brahmins in India used to be defiled if even the shadow of a low-caste person touched them. Among the Khmu' people of Laos, a standard result of breaking certain taboos is for the teeth of the guilty person to fall out and for him or her to die young.

Taboo Places

When Moses was herding sheep in the desert, he saw a bush which burned but was not burned up. When he went to investigate, he heard the LORD warn him from within the bush, "Take off your sandals, because you are standing on holy ground" (Ex 3:5 GNB; see also Josh 5:15). Had Moses not removed his shoes, the holiness of that place would have harmed him.

Later, God came down on Mt. Sinai to give the law to the Israelites. At that moment, the mountain became charged with divine holiness, and all the people had to be warned not to go higher than the foot of the mountain. In fact, a fence was built to keep both people and animals away because whoever or whatever strayed onto this holy ground would be killed. Only Moses and Aaron (and once the seventy elders) were exempt from this taboo (Ex 24:9–11).

---

[2]The ancient Jewish historian Josephus says only seventy people were actually killed (Josephus n.d.:178).

The holy of holies was the most sacred part of the wilderness tabernacle (God's personal tent) and later of the temple at Jerusalem. No ordinary people, not even priests, could enter this taboo place except for the high priest at a specific time of the year. Should unauthorized people go into the holy place in the tabernacle at any time or an authorized person at an unauthorized time, they would die (Lev 16:2).

Taboo Actions

Such trespassing in holy places was a taboo action. Another taboo action was looking at God's face, or even seeing God.

> Then Moses requested, "Please let me see the dazzling light of your presence."
>
> The LORD answered, "I will make all my splendor pass before you . . . [but] I will not let you see my face, because no one can see me and stay alive, but here is a place beside me where you can stand on a rock. When the dazzling light of my presence passes by, I will put you in an opening in the rock and cover you with my hand until I have passed by. Then I will take my hand away, and you will see my back but not my face" (Ex 33:18–23 GNB).

God made many appearances to various Israelites in the form of the angel of the LORD (chap. 5), but some of them frightened people because of their fear of seeing God.

> When the flame [of the sacrifice] went up toward heaven from the altar, the angel of the LORD ascended in the flame of the altar while Manoah and his wife fell on their faces to the ground. . . . Then Manoah realized that it was the angel of the LORD. And Manoah said to his wife, "We shall surely die, for we have seen God" (Judg 13:20–22 NRSV).

This taboo became more marked as Israel grew in understanding of God's transcendence. Eventually seeing God was simply stated as an impossibility (1 Tim 6:16).

God's covenant with Abraham included the obligatory rite of circumcision. Every male in Hebrew households, whether born in the family, brought in as a slave, or married into the family, had to be circumcised, or he would automatically be excluded. This time the taboo would be activated by the lack of action on the part of those responsible (Gen 17:1–14).

Moses had probably been circumcised at some time, even though he had been raised by Pharaoh's daughter. But his son had not been circumcised after he was born in the desert of Sinai to Zipporah, a non-Hebrew mother. After God appeared to Moses in the burning bush and sent him back to Egypt to lead the Hebrew people, Moses was confronted with this failure on the way.

When they stopped for the night, the LORD met Moses and was going to kill him, even though he had just sent him off on his task. So Zipporah took a sharp stone and circumcised her son, touching Moses' feet with the bloody foreskin.[3] In this case, violation of circumcision was portrayed by the later writer as punishment by God (spirit power), although it was a taboo which, if not avoided, would avenge itself (impersonal power).[4]

Taboo Objects

As when circumcision was neglected, frequently the penalty for breaking taboos associated with objects in the tabernacle was banishment from among God's people. Anointing oil and incense were to be used to make objects holy, and inappropriate use of these same ingredients on unworthy objects or people were to result in the same punishment (Ex 30:22–38). The altar in the tabernacle was completely sanctified so that anyone or anything that touched it would be harmed by the power of its holiness.

Clothing which the priests wore in the temple was holy. As soon as the priests entered the gateway of the inner courtyard of the temple, they were to put on priestly clothing consisting of turbans and linen trousers, but no belt. Then at the conclusion of their duties, before they returned to the outer courtyard where the common people were, they were to take off the holy clothing and leave it in the holy inner rooms in order to keep the sacred clothing from harming the people (Ezek 44:16–19).

Another penalty for violating taboo was contamination, pollution, defilement, becoming unclean. In the dietary laws of the Old Testament, certain animals were classified as unclean (Lev 11). Also unclean were women after childbirth (Lev 12), leprosy and certain other diseases (Lev 13:1–46), mildew in clothing or houses (Lev 13:47–59; 14:33–53), and bodily discharges together with objects soiled by them (Lev 15). Many of these also have corresponding analogous taboos in other cultures. The Hebrews followed purification rites to cleanse the defilement, as specified in the Old Testament. After a struggle, some of these taboos were dropped by Christians in the early years of the church.

Taboo Names

The name Yahweh, the personal name of the God of the Hebrews, was so sacred that the people were afraid they might accidentally defile it by

---

[3] "Feet" here is probably a euphemism for his genitals.

[4]It is worth noting that in some of the pseudepigraphic books the attempt on Moses' life is attributed to Satan (Mastema), not to Yahweh (Jub 48:1–4).

pronouncing it. The law itself warned the people not to use the name of God "in vain" (Ex 20:7 KJV)—or "for evil purposes" (GNB)—or dire consequences would follow. As the people's awe for the holiness of God's name increased, they simply stopped pronouncing it. Eventually, when reading the Scriptures they would substitute a word written in the margin as a suitable replacement for the taboo name Yahweh in the text.

At the earliest time, before scribes had written such alternatives in the manuscripts, people merely said "the name which one does not pronounce" or "the unspoken name" when they saw Yahweh in the text. Eventually this was reduced to just "the name." Then over time, other replacement words began to be used like "glory," or "majesty." Eventually, *adon* 'Lord' became the regular replacement, so that whenever the taboo name Yahweh occurred, *adon* or *adonai* (its plural) was given in the margin. Eventually Adonai came to be used conventionally for the taboo name, very much as Elohim, the plural of El 'God,' was used for the one God (Loewen 1984).

Most English translations have adopted the practice of substituting LORD (all capitals) for Yahweh right in the text, although the taboo name had never been taken out of the Hebrew text itself. In modern times, this convention of using LORD, no longer based on a sense of taboo, is rarely understood by readers of Old Testament translations. When modern readers see such an expression as LORD God, they ignore the small capitals, take the word to be a strong honorific term followed by God's name, rather than the holy, taboo personal name of the God of the Hebrews, followed by Elohim 'God.'

In the New Testament, the old Hebrew taboo against pronouncing the holy personal name of God sometimes even came to be attached to *theos*, the Greek generic noun for 'god.' This development was encouraged by the fact that the early church used the Septuagint version as its Bible. This Greek translation of the Old Testament, made by Jews in Alexandria, Egypt, used Adonai—'Lord' as a translation of the Hebrew Yahweh. Thus, Jewish Christians and some others avoided using Theos, just as they had formerly avoided Yahweh. In addition to using 'Lord' they said things like "I have sinned against heaven" (Lk 15:18 KJV). Matthew uses "kingdom of heaven" rather than "kingdom of God" more than thirty times (for example, Mt 3:2; 4:17; 5:3; 5:10). Other examples include "a sign from heaven" (Mt 16:1 KJV; Lk 11:16 KJV), "from heaven or of men" (Mk 11:30–31 KJV; Lk 20:4–5 KJV), "from heaven" (Lk 9:54; Jn 3:27), "swear by heaven" (Mt 5:34; 23:22), "the Blessed One" (Mk 14:61).

The Septuagint also extended this Hebrew name taboo in another direction. Wherever the Hebrew text used the word *elohim* for a female god, it was translated with the word *bdelugma*—'abomination.'

Evil holy names became taboo as well. The names Ishbosheth and Mephibosheth, listed as descendants of King Saul in 2 Samuel (3:14 KJV, 9:6), incorporated within them the word *bosheth* 'shame.' However, when these same descendants of Saul are mentioned elsewhere, they are called Eshbaal and Meribaal (1 Chr 8:33–34). Baal was the name of the Canaanite god, for which 'shame' had been substituted.

When words for unholy or unclean items are avoided and replaced by other words which are pronounceable without danger or embarrassment, such a replacement is called a euphemism. The penalty for not using euphemisms instead of taboo words is often no more than social censure and embarrassment, much weaker than the retribution of impersonal power, but in some societies audibly saying some taboo words brings real danger.

In the Bible the name Satan—'accuser, adversary'— developed a taboo. As a result we find references to him like "the Evil One" (Mt 6:13 NRSV). Words for hell or Hades were likewise sometimes replaced by euphemisms like "darkness" (1 Pet 2:9; 2 Pet 2:4,17; Jude 6,13) or "outer darkness" (Mt 8:12; 22:13; 25:30). In the Old Testament, Sheol, the place of the dead, was sometimes replaced by various euphemistic expressions such as "the land of silence" (Ps 88:12, 115:17 GNB) or "the land where the gates are shut forever" (Jon 2:6).

Certain body parts are referred to only by euphemisms in Scripture. When Abraham sent his servant Eliezer to find a wife for his son, he told the messenger, "place your hand under my thigh" ("between my thighs" GNB), where 'thigh' is a euphemism for the genitals (Gen 24:2,9; 47:29). I first became aware of the meaning of this example when I began working with African translators. The first time they met it in their translation work, they gasped and said, "So the people in Bible times also had that powerful oath. That is very powerful indeed!"

The sons of Noah found their father drunk with his "nakedness" uncovered, another euphemism for genitals (Gen 9:22; see also Ex 20:26; Lev 18:6–19; Hos 2:9; Hab 2:15). Some Bible scholars feel that "feet" is a euphemism for genitals in Exodus 4:25–26 (GNB).

The most common euphemism to replace words for sexual intercourse in the Old Testament is "know," as in "Adam knew his wife" (Gen 4:1; see also Gen 4:17; Judg 11:39 KJV; 1 Sam 1:19; Mt 1:25 KJV). Others include "come/go unto" (Gen 16:2, 29:23), and "to touch a woman" (1 Cor 7:1). Rape, likewise, was referred to with euphemisms like "he forced her" or "he humbled her" (2 Sam 13:22 KJV). Even the word "prostitute" picked up a taboo and was sometimes replaced by a euphemism such as "sinner" (Lk 7:39). Homosexual intercourse was referred to euphemistically as "shameless acts" (Rom 1:27).

Words for menstruation were replaced by euphemisms because a woman's period (an English euphemism) was thought of as polluting: "It had ceased to be with Sarah after the manner of women" (Gen 18:11); "The way of women is upon me" (Gen 31:35; Loewen 1981).

A number of biblical euphemisms refer to going to the toilet (an English euphemism again): "cover the feet" (1 Sam 24:3 KJV; Judg 3:24 KJV); "on a journey" (1 Kgs 18:27 KJV).

Words for death are likewise often replaced by euphemisms in many languages. Examples in English include "passed away," "is no more." In West Africa, speaking the word for death in reference to a chief is especially taboo, and in some places the euphemism is "the big tree has fallen." Euphemisms for death in the Bible include "give up the ghost" (Mk 15:37), "breathe his last" (Mt 27:50), "return to the ground" (Gen 3:19), "gathered unto his people" (Gen 25:17), and "close your eyes" (Gen 46:4).

Reverse Taboo:
Protection through Association with Holiness

It is not called taboo, but persons in many cultures seek to shield themselves by the proximity to or the association with holy objects. Such objects are used for protection, to ward off evil or bring good fortune. Such objects are holy because they are different, or because they have been made holy through a ritual, or because they are pictures of—or otherwise symbolically represent—a holy person or thing. Often called amulets or talismans, protective objects may be worn on a chain around the neck, or placed on a special shelf in the house, or propped on the dashboard of a car. They are common in taxis all over the world.

Following biblical instructions literally, many Jews put amulets in their homes, on their arms and on their foreheads (Deut 6:8–9; 11:18,20). These were short passages of Scripture encased in protective coverings. The ones worn on the body were called phylacteries, and others were attached to the door posts. They were to provide protection against the devil and evil spirits (Ausubel 1964:391). A sixteenth-century computation of Talmudic laws based on oral tradition lists one hundred sixty laws that relate to phylacteries, amulets, and talismans (Ausubel 1964:459).

Magic and Divination

A Toba woman from the Argentine Chaco was seriously injured by a sorcerer and plotted revenge. She saw a chance when she had occasion to serve some watermelon at a gathering which the sorcerer also attended. She bewitched the seeds in a piece of watermelon, putting a death curse on them. The watermelon was sent to the offending man, but by some fluke of fate the bewitched piece was placed before the woman's son instead. When the woman saw the misplacement, she screamed, for she had no way to undo the curse. Her son died. Did this magic really work? Ask the missionary who witnessed it (Loewen, Buckwalter, and Kratz 1965:255–56)!

The type of magic found in the Bible consists of magic acts like "evil eye," casting spells, and other kinds of sorcery used to harm someone, or amulets and charms to heal and protect. In some societies, such magic can be performed by anyone, but in others a specialist like a wizard, witch, or sorcerer must act. Sometimes people become sorcerers without knowing it, or without intending to do so.

In the Bible, various practitioners of different kinds of magic are mentioned. Magicians, enchanters, and diviners, for example, are mentioned as part of the Babylonian court where Daniel served (Dan 2:27, 4:7 NRSV). In general, such people are not looked upon favorably but are seen as rivals to Yahweh.

> No one shall be found among you . . . who practices divination, or is a soothsayer, or an augur, or a sorcerer, or one who casts spells, or who consults ghosts or spirits, or who seeks oracles from the dead. For whoever does these things is abhorrent to the LORD; it is because of such abhorrent practices that the LORD is driving [the Canaanites] out before you. You must remain completely loyal to the LORD your God (Deut 18:10–13 NRSV; see also 2 Chr 33:6).

Magic is not the same as miracle. Magic is done with impersonal power, miracle with spirit power. Jesus performed miracles of healing, not magic. On the other hand, in parts of the Old Testament which record early events, the line between magic and miracle is more tenuous because the people who wrote down and edited the oral tradition may well have reinterpreted some magical acts as miracles. For example, when Yahweh instructed Moses to go back to Egypt and free the Hebrews he gave him a magical/miraculous sign. He told him to throw his staff on the ground, and when he did so it became a snake. Obviously God's doing, and therefore a miracle?

But when Aaron, Moses' brother, threw down his staff in front of Pharaoh, king of Egypt, and it became a snake, the response by the Egyptian magicians, at least, was seen as magic.

> Pharaoh summoned the wise men and the sorcerers; and they also, the magicians of Egypt, did the same by their secret arts. Each one threw down his staff, and they became snakes; but Aaron's staff swallowed up theirs (Ex 7:11–12).

Divination. In many cultures, including biblical cultures, acts of divining occur constantly, acts intended to find out supernaturally what is happening, the meaning of what is happening, what will happen, and what people should do. Divination is sometimes carried on entirely through non-personal power, sometimes through personal power, and sometimes mixed. At the two extremes, people who consult their astrological signs are divining through non-personal power; people who pray to God to show them what to do are divining through spirit power. The mixed form may be seen when an act involving impersonal power is used to determine God's purpose (spirit power).

As for the Bible, some cases which may have actually been carried out under impersonal power have later been reinterpreted as personal power by writers and editors, so that separating the two kinds of power is nearly impossible. I will therefore not try to distinguish between them here.

Gideon's use of a fleece, the skin of a sheep, is a clear case of divination. God wanted him to lead Israel in a war against the Midianites. So, one night Gideon placed a fleece on the threshing floor and specified that if there was dew on the fleece in the morning, but not on the surrounding ground, he would know that God would use him successfully to free the Israelites from the Midianites. The next night he reversed the criteria, and if the fleece was dry and the ground wet, he would know what God wanted him to do. In both cases his conditions were met, so he was sure of God's direction (Judg 6:36–40).

Casting lots was a common way of finding God's will in various biblical worldviews, an action similar to our picking names out of a hat, tossing coins, or throwing dice. It was sometimes used in ritual, as when the priest selected which of two goats was to be sacrificed to Yahweh and which was to be sent out into the desert to bear away the sins of the people (Lev 16:8).

On a lower level, the land in Canaan was divided by a combination of clan size and lot (Num 26:54–56; Josh 14:2; 18:6). The priests were organized by lot (1 Chr 24:5). Sailors cast lots to see who had brought on the severe storm that threatened them, and Jonah was chosen (Jon 1:7).

In the New Testament, the apostles cast lots to find a replacement disciple for Judas who had hanged himself (Acts 1:23–26). However, Paul did not consider the lot-casting to have indicated the real will of God because he considered himself to be the twelfth apostle and the special apostle to the Gentiles (Rom 1:1, 11:13; 1 Cor 9:1–2; 15:8–9; Gal 1:1–2).

Occasionally, lots were used negatively, even for gambling (Ps 22:18 [see GNB]; Joel 3:3; Obad 11; Nah 3:10).

Attached to the breastplate of the high priest's garments were objects called *urim* and *thummim*, used to ascertain the will of God, probably in a manner similar to casting lots (Ex 28:30). When King Saul realized that his troops no longer had God's favor because of sin, he set about finding the perpetrator by use of urim and thummim. He divided the group between himself and Jonathan (his son), on the one hand, and the troops on the other. Urim was to indicate that the troops had sinned, Thummim that he or Jonathan had done so. Thummim turned up, so the next division was made between Saul and Jonathan, and Jonathan was shown to be guilty (1 Sam

14:41). Later, after God had rejected Saul, the king no longer got any answers— "not by dreams, or by urim, or by prophets" (1 Sam 28:6 NRSV).

Dreams and their interpretation were sometimes ways of divining, as well. Joseph was sold into Egypt in part because he learned in dreams that all his brothers and even his parents would bow to his superior status, in spite of the fact that he was almost the youngest among his siblings (Gen 37:5–11). Then, in Egypt he rose to power by interpreting the king's dreams (Gen 41:25–45). Eventually his brothers came to Egypt seeking food and bowed before Joseph, not knowing who he was (Gen 42:6–17).

Joseph, Mary's husband, was warned in a dream to take the family and escape to Egypt (Mt 2:19–20). The apostle Peter was alerted in a vision that some of the Old Testament taboos were no longer in effect and was thereby prepared to go to the house of Cornelius, a non-Jew (Acts 10:9–22). Ananias was sent to minister to Saul in much the same way (Acts 9:10–16).

The ordeal is another way of deciding about the truth in some societies. It was used in the Old Testament, for example, to test whether or not a wife had been unfaithful in cases where there was no evidence. If her husband suspected her, she was required by the priest to drink water mixed with dust from the ground in front of the altar. If she had not committed adultery, no harm would come to her, but if she had, the water would cause harm to her reproductive system (Num 5:17–31).

The prophet Samuel and some others were called seers, diviners who could see into the future. This category eventually developed into the prophets who were more clearly God's mouthpieces and not so much diviners (1 Sam 9:6–12; chap. 10).

This is only a small sampling of the use of impersonal power (and related phenomena) in the Bible. In the development of Israel's worldview, magic and divination diminished as Israel's understanding became more transcendent and more universal, but it did not entirely disappear. For the most part, spirit power—the acts of God—replaced impersonal power; miracles and the word of God revealed God's will to prophets and other individuals. We may feel that the worldviews became more sophisticated with the changes, but impersonal power is still a great force among many peoples of the world. And, in the naturalistic, materialistic West, impersonal power in the form of evolution has supplanted spirit power as the dominant explanation of creation.

Therein lies a profound worldview shift which has taken place over the past few centuries. And although many evangelical Christians repudiate "evolution" as an explanation for the origins of animate beings on the earth, they gladly embrace radical forms of social and economic evolution. Classical capitalism is a prime example of a belief in impersonal power. Under a capitalist worldview, the "market"—impersonal power—controls human economic well-being. This is in sharp contrast to most biblical worldviews, where economic state is the result of God's direct action.

Part IV

The Significance of Names

Introduction

To look at all aspects of biblical culture in this one book is, of course, impossible. And the topics which I am discussing are naturally ones which are particularly salient to me because of my experience, as summarized briefly in Chapter 1. Thus my study of the significance of names comes out of my concentration on the problems of Bible translation. But a cross-cultural view of names in the Bible is not important only for translators. Seeing the place of names in biblical culture clarifies another bit of the clouded mirror in which we see God.

I first ran into the significance of certain Bible names in Waunana, the first language in which we did any translating in South America. It came up in a passage where the biblical text itself draws attention to the fact that Peter's name has meaning. When Peter made his confession that Jesus is the Christ, the Son of God, Jesus commended him for it and said, "You are Peter [Greek: *petros* 'rock'], and upon this rock [Greek: *petra* 'bedrock'] I will build my church" (Mt 16:18).

The Waunana have two words for rock: 'gravel stone, pebble,' and 'bedrock.' 'Gravel stone' is seldom more than two inches in diameter, found in the beds of rivers, and 'bedrock' exists in rock cliffs or as pieces broken from them. Many people use such rocks as surfaces on which to pound their laundry.

So one possible translation was, "Your name is 'pebble' and upon this 'bedrock' I will build my church." Another was, "Your name is Peter (which means 'a piece of bedrock') and upon this 'bedrock' I will build my church." After the church had prayed, asking how God would have said this if the Bible had been written in their language in the first place, the people decided that the text had a bit of a pun on the name Peter. So they rendered it, "Your name is Peter (which in their language[1] meant 'pebble'), and upon this 'bedrock' I will build my church."

---

[1] "Their language" in the Waunana translation meant "the language of the people in Bible times."

In this Waunana case, the translators opted for keeping the proper name Peter and clarified the passage by including a translation of its meaning. However, I later found that in many African languages such a solution does not work well, and that people prefer not to use the proper name Peter at all but to make a name for him out of the word for rock in their language. An English parallel might be, "You are Rocky, and upon this rock I will build my church."

Meaningful names are far more frequent and significant in the Old Testament than in the New, extending even to God's personal name, Yahweh (chap. 15). In parts of French-speaking West Africa, people were used to the French Segond translation which uses l'Éternel—'the eternal one' where English has LORD. Africans have many praise names for God and decided that the English usage of LORD and the French usage of l'Éternel were functioning as praise names, so they also made a praise name with which to translate Yahweh. Thus, in many such West African languages the divine name was rendered with such expressions as 'the ever-being one,' 'the causer of all being,' 'the eternal one,' or 'forever owner.'

14

The Names of People and Places

In order to more fully introduce the topic of this chapter, consider the following English sentences:

Heather is intelligent.
Heather grows in the soil of Scotland.
Heather is beautiful.

We sense that the intelligent Heather is a person, that the growing heather is a plant, and that the beautiful Heather/heather could be either. The name has an associated meaning.

In many languages of the world, all or most names have such associated meanings. In that respect, a personal name like Heather or Rose or June is less usual in English than in many other languages, as are place names like New Haven or Painted Post. More generally, we have names like William or Charles or Connecticut which have no English function other than as the name for individuals or places. In English, furthermore, we capitalize our names when writing them so we can identify in print whether a word is a name or not. So we are often not sensitive to how meanings can play into the use of names in other languages.

A major example of a name with meaning in Hebrew is *adam* (Hebrew does not distinguish between capital and lower case letters), which means 'man' or 'human being, human kind' but is also the name of a person. The context often indicates whether the Hebrew word should be understood as a specific person or as a generic term, but sometimes the text remains unclear about which is intended. This means that whenever Hebrew *adam* occurs, the translator has to decide whether the generic 'human being' is indicated, or the text refers to an adult male, or to a specific person named Adam, or ambiguously to more than one of these. How four different translations have rendered *adam* in the first chapters of Genesis may be seen in Table 10.

TABLE 10

HEBREW *ADAM* 'MAN, HUMAN BEING'
IN FOUR ENGLISH TRANSLATIONS
NOTE: "Man" alone, without an article, is intended in a generic sense; with the article, "the man," it refers to a single adult male.

GENESIS	HEBREW	KJV	NASV	NRSV	GNB
1:26	adam	man	man	humankind	human beings
1:27	the adam	man	man	humankind	human beings
2:5	no adam	not a man	no man	no one	no one
2:7	the adam	man	man	man	a man
	the adam	man	man	the man	the man
2:8	the adam	the man	man	the man	the man
2:15	the adam	the man	the man	the man	the man
2:16	the adam	the man	the man	the man	him
2:18	the adam	the man	the man	the man	the man
2:19	the adam	Adam	the man	the man	the man
	the adam	Adam	the man	the man	he
2:20	the adam	Adam	the man	the man	the man
	adam	Adam	Adam	the man	him
2:21	the adam	Adam	man	the man	man
2:22	the adam	man	man	the man	—
	the adam	the man	man	the man	him
2:23	the adam	Adam	man	the man	the man
2:25	the adam	the man	man	the man	the man
3:8	the adam	Adam	man	the man	they
3:9	the adam	Adam	man	the man	the man
3:12	the adam	the man	man	the man	the man
3:20	the adam	Adam	man	the man	Adam
3:21	adam	Adam	man	the man	Adam
3:22	the adam	the man	the man	the man	the man
3:24	the adam	the man	the man	the man	anyone
4:1	the adam	Adam	the man	the man	Adam
5:1	adam	Adam	Adam	Adam	Adam

No two of these translations introduce the name Adam at the same point in the story. The King James Version introduces it first in Genesis 2:19, followed by the New American Standard Version in 2:20, the Good News Bible in 3:20, and the New Revised Standard Version not until 5:1. In many of these passages the difference between "Adam" and "the man" does not make much difference, but note the confusion which would result if "Adam" were used in the following passage:

> And God said, Let us make Adam in our image, after our likeness: and let them have dominion over the fish of the sea.... So God created Adam in his own image, in the image of God created he him; male and female created he them (Gen 1:26–7 modified from KJV).

Some modern translations do attempt to help the readers understand names that carry meaning. In the Good News Bible, for example, the first time the translators use the name Adam, it is marked with a footnote, "This name in Hebrew means 'mankind'" (Gen 3:20).

Other Old Testament examples of names with meaning include Abram, 'high or exalted father,' for the father of the Hebrew nation. Its extended form, Abraham, probably means 'the father of a multitude.' The name of Abraham's wife, Sarah, means 'noble lady' or 'princess,' which contrasts with the slave position of Hagar, who bore Abraham's first son.

Ishmael means 'God hears,' "for the LORD has given heed to your affliction" (Gen 16:11). The name Isaac, at the prediction of whose birth Abraham laughed (Gen 17:17), means 'he laughs.' After Isaac made peace with Abimelech, and God rewarded his effort with another well, he called the place Beersheba—'well of the oath/vow' (Gen 26:33). After Jacob had a vision of the ladder on which God's angels ascended and descended and at the head of which God stood, he called the place Bethel—'house of God' (Gen 28:19). After Jacob struggled with a messenger from God, he said, "I have seen God face to face," so he called the place Peniel—'the face of God' (Gen 32:30). Rachel suffered hard labor while delivering Benjamin, so she called him Benoni, 'son of my sorrow,' before she died. But Jacob wanted to change his son's luck and called him Benjamin, 'son who is fortunate' (Gen 35:18 GNB). Gideon tore down the idols of Baal, and the people wanted to punish him for it, but his father intervened and said, "Let Baal defend himself," so the people called Gideon Jerubbaal, 'let Baal defend himself' (Judg 6:28–32 GNB). Since the second son of Adam and Eve lived only a short time, his name was Abel, 'transitory' (Gen 4:48). Cain, who killed his brother, was called 'spear' (Gen 4:1–5). Methuselah, 'man of God,' was the name of one who lived in fellowship with God (Gen 5:22 GNB).

Meanings of Names

Actual or Suggested Meaning

In some languages, people pun on names far more than we do in English where puns are deprecated as a low form of humor. Even in English, however, in a sentence like "Jerry was buried in Fuller Theological Seminary," the similarity of sound between seminary and cemetery might well carry implications concerning Jerry's state, or that of the seminary, or both. Biblical writers often intentionally used such "sound alikes" in names.

For example, Hebrew *adam* not only means 'man, human being,' as we have just seen, but also suggests the meaning of the similar-sounding Hebrew word *adamah*, 'ground.' Thus, the LORD God formed *adam* from the soil of *adamah* (Gen 2:7). An English analogy might be "formed an earthling from the soil of the earth." The Good News Bible tells us in a footnote that "the Hebrew words for 'man' and 'ground' have rather similar sounds."

Eve's name sounds like 'life' and suggests that Eve is 'the mother of the living' (Gen 3:20). An English analogy might be "The man named his wife Life because she was the mother of all who live."

Among other such names, Seth sounds like 'God given'; Noah sounds like 'relief' or 'to find comfort'; Japheth sounds like 'to find increase'; Peleg sounds like 'to divide'; Zoar sounds like 'small'; Jacob sounds like 'to cheat'; Israel sounds like 'he struggles with God'; Moses sounds like 'to pull out'; and Eliezer sounds like 'God helps me.'

However, translation usually destroys any meaning associated with a name so that the frequent use of the meanings of biblical names—or their sound-alikes—and the subtle implications of their use are lost to us as we read in English. Biblical names are usually transliterated into modern languages rather than translated, which means that the translators try to match the letters of the Hebrew or Greek with the letters of the translation language. In our example above, *adam* is transliterated "Adam" (not translated "human" or "man") when the translator believes the word is a proper name, and the transliterated name Adam simply does not mean "human being," or sound like "ground," to us. Although modern translations do try to point out associated meanings in footnotes, that is a weak substitute. Losing the associated meanings of names is usually a significant weakness in a translation, especially of the Old Testament.

Names with Special Meanings

Names of people or places are sometimes used with special meanings in a particular book or passage of the Bible, meanings of which readers need to be made aware if they are to understand the passage correctly. One of the most striking and extended uses of names in this way is in the book of Hosea. Note the differences in the ways translators have handled these names, including footnotes:

TABLE 11
NAMES WITH SPECIAL MEANINGS

Hosea	KJV	NRSV	GNB
1:6	Call her name Loruhamah: for I will no more have mercy on the house of Israel	Name her Lo-ru-hamah,[b] for I will no longer have pity on the house of Israel [b]That is *Not pitied*	Name her "Un-loved," because I will no longer show love to the people of Israel
1:9	Call his name Loammi: for ye *are* not my people	Name him Lo-ammi,[c] for you are not my people [c]That is *Not my people*	Name him "Not-My-People" because the people of Israel are not my people
2:1	Say unto your brethren, Ammi; and to your sisters, Ruhamah	Say to your brother, Ammi,[i] and to your sister, Ruhamah[k] [i]That is *My People* [k]That is *Pitied*	So call your fellow-Israelites "God's People" and "Loved-by-the-Lord"
2:23	I will have mercy upon her that had not obtained mercy; and I will say to *them which were* not my people, "Thou *art* my people"	I will have pity on Lo-ruhamah,[r] and I will say to Lo-ammi,[s] "You are my people" [r]That is *Not pitied* [s]That is *Not my people*	I will show love to those who were called "Unloved," and to those who were "Not-My-People" I will say "You are my people"

The name Jezreel ordinarily refers to a specific town in Israel but is also sometimes used as a historical reference to the fact that Jehu, one of the Israelite kings, murdered his predecessor and family there (2 Kgs 10:1–11; Hos 1:4–5). Thus, when Hosea uses the name Jezreel instead of Israel (Hos 2:21–22 GNB), he is indicating that the nation of Israel is guilty of murders like the one Jehu committed.

In Hosea the name Bethaven, 'house of evil,' is sometimes substituted for Bethel, 'house of God,' the name of the city in which the northern kingdom of Israel worshipped (Hos 4:15, 10:5). The shift implies that Israel now worships idols instead of the true God.

Names of the towns Meshech and Kedar carry the connotation of 'savage.' "Living among you [liars and deceivers] is as bad as living in Meshech or among the people of Kedar" (Ps 120:5). The mountains of Bether really means 'the rugged mountains' (Song 2:17).

Occasionally such words as exile, slavery, captivity are replaced by other expressions as, for example, in "Off with your veil! Strip off your fine clothes! Lift up your skirts to cross the streams" (Is 47:2 GNB). "Cross the streams" probably means 'go into exile (beyond the great river Euphrates).' The same thing is true of several occurrences of the word Egypt in Hosea. When God says "they must not return to Egypt," he is really saying, "I will send them into captivity, slavery, or exile," and that not necessarily in Egypt (Hos 11:5).

Another place name that alludes to evil action performed there is Gibeah where a concubine was raped repeatedly until she died. So Hosea refers to Israel as sinning like at Gibeah:

> They are hopelessly evil in what they do, just as they were at Gibeah (Hos 9:9 GNB).

> The people of Israel have not stopped sinning against me since the time of their sin at Gibeah. So at Gibeah war will catch up with them (Hos 10:9).

The region of Bashan in Israel was a fertile pasture area so that cows raised there were fat and sleek. The prophet Amos used this association between Bashan and fat indolence to express his contempt for the rich women of Samaria who were oppressing the poor. Note how much better the Good News Bible captures that connotation than does the King James Version:

> Hear this word, ye kine of Bashan, that are in the mountain of Samaria, which oppress the poor, which crush the needy, which say to their masters, "Bring, and let us drink" (Amos 4:1 KJV).

> Listen to this, you women of Samaria, who grow fat like well-fed cows of Bashan, who ill-treat the weak, oppress the poor and demand that your husbands keep you supplied with liquor (Amos 4:1 GNB).

The issue of the meaning of names is even more complicated in a few cases in the New Testament, which was written in Greek, but in which the sayings of and about Jesus were probably originally made in Aramaic, the language of Palestinian Jews of the time. For example, Jesus' name, spoken in Aramaic, was Jeshua, which means 'Yahweh saves' or 'God saves.' Today, many people insist that there is "no other name [than Jesus] . . . whereby we must be saved" (Acts 4:12 KJV). But "Jesus" was transliterated into modern languages from the Greek of the New Testament in which the name was earlier transliterated from the Aramaic 'God saves.' Therefore the passage in Aramaic says there is no other name than 'God saves' under which we can be saved, which puts a different spin on it. I do not want to build too much theology on this fact, but it does suggest muting the battle cry of many evangelical North American Christians.

Double Messages

Certain biblical passages, even whole books, have a double message, one carried by the text, the other in the proper names.

For example, in the book of Ruth, Ruth, 'friend,' was the name of a woman who left her homeland to accompany and befriend her mother-in-law Naomi, 'happy, happiness.' Accompanied by his family, Naomi's husband, Elimelech, 'God is my king,' an Israelite, 'he will rule as God,' had earlier left Bethlehem, 'house of bread,' in the kingdom of Judah, 'worship with extended hands,' to go to Moab, for which some suggest the meaning 'he is the bastard of my father.' Two sons, Mahlon, 'sickly,' and Chilion, 'weakly, consumptive,' both died. Ironically, the family had moved from 'house of bread' because of famine. Later 'happiness' asked that people call her Marah, 'bitter,' but eventually all turned out well when 'friend' married Boaz, 'by God's strength,' who came from the town of Ephrata, 'fruitfulness.'

One time, when I drew the meaning of the names in the book of Ruth to the attention of a group of six or seven African translators working in different languages, they became so excited that they stayed up most of the night retranslating the book into their languages and incorporating names that carried actual or suggested meanings of the original. Instead of just using transliterated proper names like Ruth, they made names which expressed the meaning of the Hebrew names. I have seldom seen people as excited about a passage of Scripture as these Africans were about the book of Ruth, which suddenly became new and richer for them. "We never realized that the Bible could be so rich with meaning," they said. Unlike ours, their culture had made them sensitive to this style of communication through naming.

15

Some Names for God:
A Cultural Tension

As new missionaries to the Waunana, my wife and I were thrilled to discover that they had only one word for God, namely Ewandama. I had heard missionaries from Asia describe their difficulties when trying to choose a name for God in a culture that had many divine names.

Our enthusiasm soon cooled, however, when we realized that Ewandama was not a class noun referring to God/gods, but a personal name like John or Peter. In biblical terms, the Waunana had an equivalent for God's Hebrew personal name Yahweh, but not for God's class or generic designation, El or Elohim. This became apparent when we tried to form such sentences as 'there are many Ewandamas,' or when we attempted to speak of 'the Ewandama of the Empera,' their tribal neighbors. The Waunana rejected all such statements outright saying that there was only one Ewandama and that he existed exclusively for the Waunana people. Emperas prayed to Ankone and not to Ewandama. In fact, they even rejected the idea that Ankone was the Empera way of saying Ewandama. Ankone and Ewandama were two totally separate personalities.

As among the Waunana, God's name is also a personal name rather than a class noun in many tribal societies of South America and Africa. This lack of a generic word can create serious problems for people's understanding of Scripture, especially in Genesis, and maybe even for the Old Testament in general. And how do you translate 'gods' when referring to deities other than God?

As in the Waunana case and repeatedly in the history of the spread of Christianity, the name of the local cultural deity (like Yahweh for the Jews) is rightly used for God when the gospel is introduced. Without such an association, the message would be rootless and relatively meaningless.

Nevertheless, all translation loses something from the original, and translation of the implications of names is especially difficult.

Struggling with this problem has led me to realize that readers of the Bible in English may have a similar difficulty in understanding some issues. The various names for God in the Bible have been coalesced through translation, so that we are not aware of them all and do not realize their implications.

For one thing, 'God' in English is both a personal and a class noun. When we say "God is the God of the whole world," we use it in the first instance as a personal name and in the second as a class noun. This hides from us the fact that not only are two different words frequently used for God in such a sentence in the Old Testament, but also the use of the two terms is often part of an important growth in the Hebrews' understanding of the nature of God.

To give an example of this partially different Hebrew usage, note the Hebrew terms for God in the two Genesis creation stories. Bear in mind that Hebrew does not differentiate between capital and lower-case letters (unlike English God and god), and that *elohim* is usually translated into English as "God" and *yahweh elohim* as "LORD God" (note the small capitals in LORD).

> In the beginning elohim created the heaven and the earth. . . . And elohim said . . . And elohim saw the light . . . and elohim divided the light . . . And elohim called the light . . . And elohim said . . . And elohim made . . . . And elohim called . . . And elohim said . . . And elohim called . . . and elohim saw that it was good . . . [plus twenty more occurrences of elohim] (Gen 1:1–2:3 KJV adapted).
>
> . . . in the day that yahweh elohim made the earth and the heavens . . . for yahweh elohim had not caused it to rain . . . And yahweh elohim formed man *of* the dust of the ground . . . And yahweh elohim planted a garden . . . made yahweh elohim to grow every tree . . . (Gen 2:4–10 KJV adapted).

So in the first creation story, Elohim is named as the creator, while in the second one 'Yahweh the Elohim' or 'the God Yahweh' is the creator.

In English, translators have found artificial ways around these and related problems of the Hebrew names for God, such as the use of LORD for Yahweh. But readers do not usually notice the difference between LORD (in small capitals) and Lord (without small capitals but with a different meaning), and the various names are all one jumble.

The Names of God in the Old Testament

I suddenly began to understand the depth of this issue when I read the words of an early British traveler in Africa, "I learned from the natives that the God the missionaries were preaching made sense to them because, they said, 'Our Mawu is none other than biblical [Yahweh]'" (Ellis 1890:35–36). The translations of the Bible in these languages, as it were, began with, "In the beginning Our-Tribal-Deity created the heaven and the earth" rather than as the Bible actually says, "In the beginning The-Universal-Deity created the heavens and the earth." In such societies, part of the process of learning the Good News is learning to realize that the local cultural God is none other than the God of the universe. Perhaps the juxtaposition of Genesis 1 and 2 is the way that Israel's theologians and scribes made the connection between the two, the universal and the particular God, as discussed earlier (Gordon Matties, personal communication).

One principal word for God found in the Old Testament, as we have seen, is some form of elohim, including *el, eloah*, as well as elohim, all of which can mean 'God, god, gods' depending on the context. In pre-Hebrew times, el may have been the personal name of a particular God. We occasionally see relics of this in statements like,

> . . . el, the elohim of Israel (Gen 33:20 KJV adapted).

> I *am* el, the elohim of your father (Gen 46:3 KJV adapted).

But by biblical times Elohim had become a class noun whose most frequent reference was to the one true God:

> . . . *there is* no elohim in all the earth, but in Israel (2 Kgs 5:15 KJV adapted).

Much less frequently, Elohim refers to the God of another people:

> The Philistines gathered them together for to offer a great sacrifice unto Dagon their elohim (Judg 16:23 KJV adapted).

Twice it refers to a female deity:

> Solomon went after Ashtoreth, elohim of the Zidonians (1 Kgs 11:5, 11:33 KJV adapted).

Somewhat more frequently, it refers collectively to the deities of all the nations surrounding Israel:

> [Do not] serve . . . the elohim of the people which *are* around you (Deut 13:6–7 KJV adapted).

Occasionally, it denies the deity of alien gods, emphasizing that they are not gods at all:

> The kings of Assyria have destroyed the nations, and their lands; and have cast their elohim into the fire, for they *were* no elohim (2 Kgs 19:17–18 KJV adapted).

After Abraham had been called by God and had left off worshiping many gods, he and his Hebrew descendants used the name Elohim basically to refer to the "one supreme God," somewhat as when the pagan king Nebuchadnezzar said to Daniel:

Your elohim is elohim of elohim (Dan 2:47 NRSV adapted).

The singular forms: The generic Hebrew word for God has two singular forms, el and eloah. Both occur in the Old Testament but el is by far the more frequent. The two singular forms are matched by two plural forms, elim and elohim, but elim is rare in the Scriptures. It is elohim, the plural of eloah, that occurs almost everywhere.

The singular form el appears alone in such expressions as "the el of Bethel" (Gen 31:13 KJV adapted): "O el, I beseech thee" (Num 12:13 KJV adapted). However, we see it more frequently in composite names like el shaddai, 'God Almighty' and el elyon, 'the Most High.' It also occurs frequently in compound place or personal names, such as Bethel, 'house of El,' Peniel, 'face of El,' Elijah, 'Yah is my El,' Elimelech, 'my El is king,' Elisha, 'El is my savior,' Eltekon, 'El is firm,' and many more.

Occasionally el in the singular is used for other gods:

Yahweh alone did lead him, and *there was* no strange el with him (Deut 32:12 KJV adapted).

. . . the el Berith (Judg 9:46 KJV adapted).

They hire a goldsmith, who makes [gold and silver] into an el (Is 46:6 NRSV adapted).

In the last instance, el means 'idol.'

The singular variant eloah does not have great importance or a truly distinctive function in the Old Testament but seems to occur mainly in poetic passages (Deut 32:15–17; Job 3:4; Ps 50:22). In the time of captivity, the Babylonian variant elah became prominent.

The plural forms: When elohim (the plural of eloah) occurs with plural verbs and plural modifiers (showing clearly that it is intended in a plural sense), it never refers to high gods but rather to a class of beings which people worship:

Thou shalt have no other elohim before me (Ex 20:3 KJV adapted).

Our elohim is greater than other elohim (2 Chr 2:5 NRSV adapted).

These are the elohim who struck the Egyptians (1 Sam 4:8 NRSV adapted).

Have the elohim of the nations delivered them? (2 Kgs 19:12 NRSV adapted)

You are our elohim (Is 42:17 NRSV adapted).

When elohim refers to nations known to worship more than one God, it must also be interpreted as plural, as in

I will execute judgment on all the elohim of Egypt (Ex 12:12 KJV adapted).

. . . the elohim of Syria, and the elohim of Zidon, and the elohim of Moab, and the elohim of the children of Ammon, and the elohim of the Philistines (Judg 10:6 KJV adapted).

Since the gods of other nations often had visible representations or images, the plural form includes the meaning of 'idols.'

All the elohim of the nations *are* idols (Ps 96:5 KJV adapted).

All the images of her elohim (Is 21:9 NRSV).

However, by far the most frequent occurrence of the plural form elohim is with singular verbs and/or singular modifiers, and in such instances it always refers to the one and only high God:

In the beginning elohim created . . . (Gen 1:1 KJV adapted; singular verb).

. . . the righteous elohim (Ps 7:9 KJV adapted; singular modifier).

This use of the plural form with singular meaning is sometimes called the "plural of intensity" (Eichrodt 1961:184–85), or "plural of majesty" (as when the British queen refers to herself as "we"). A few scholars insist that the plural is a relic of an earlier, polytheistic stage in the Hebrews' religious development. Except for isolated references like Jeroboam making two calves and saying, "Here are your elohim . . . who brought you up out of the land of Egypt" (1 Kgs 12:28 NRSV adapted), there is little evidence that a polytheistic view of God was still held in Israel in biblical times.[1]

Where elohim is not clearly marked by verbs or modifiers it is difficult to decide whether it means 'God' or 'gods,' as in "your eyes shall be opened and you shall be as God/gods" (Gen 3:5 GNB and KJV respectively). Furthermore, sometimes even where a plural verb occurs, commentators sometimes still differ on whether elohim means singular or plural. Many scholars hold that the golden calves made by Jeroboam (mentioned above) were not really idols but the base on which God was to descend, somewhat like the ark of the covenant in the temple in Jerusalem. Where those who hold to the idol meaning render elohim as "gods," those who hold to the meaning of stools render it "God":

---

[1]Passages like "let us make man in our image" (Gen 1:26 KJV) probably refer to some kind of "heavenly council" (chap. 8).

Behold your God/gods which brought you out of Egypt (1 Kgs 12:28 singular: GN, FC, plural: KJV, GNB).

Yahweh

The personal name of the God of the Hebrews, the name which set God apart as the only true God, is found in the Hebrew Old Testament with several variants, spelled *yhwh*, *yhh*, *yhw*, and *yh*. Ancient Hebrew writing did not show the vowels of its words, so these strings of consonants represent what the names look like in classical Hebrew writing.

Scholars believe that the original pronunciation of yhwh was "yahweh." The spelling Jehovah, which appears in the American Standard Version and a few places in the King James Version (Ex 6:3; Ps 83:18; Is 12:2), is a mixture, combining the consonants of yhwh with the vowels of adonai 'Lord.' The Hebrews avoided pronouncing yahweh when they read the Scriptures aloud and substituted adonai instead in order not to risk breaking the third commandment by using Yahweh's name in vain (chap. 13). Some Christians for a time mistakenly tried to pronounce the consonants *yhwh* with the vowels of adonai.

Precisely when the Israelites began using this name is hard to say. Logically, we might assume that they began to do so when Yahweh first revealed himself to Abraham and called him to leave his country, his family, and his polytheistic setting to follow Yahweh into the new land where he would worship Yahweh exclusively:

> Now yahweh said unto Abram, Get thee out of thy country . . . unto a land that I will shew thee: . . . So Abram departed, as yahweh had spoken unto him . . . and passed through the land unto the place of Sichem. . . . And yahweh appeared unto Abram, and said, Unto thy seed will I give this land: and there builded he an altar unto yahweh, who appeared unto him (Gen 12:1–7 KJV adapted).

But the following biblical record does not unambiguously corroborate that. For example, when God began to speak to Moses in the desert several hundred years later,

> [Elohim said] "I *am* yahweh: and I appeared unto Abraham, unto Isaac, and unto Jacob, by *the name of* el shaddai ['God Almighty'], but by my name yahweh was I not known to them" (Ex 6:2–3 KJV adapted).

This would appear to suggest that only to Moses did God first reveal the name Yahweh. Yet in Genesis,

> After these things the word of yahweh came to Abram (Gen 15:1 KJV adapted).

The situation is further complicated in Genesis 4:26, where human beings first began to worship God using the name Yahweh, although Genesis 2:4–24 says that Yahweh created the world.

Probably the best explanation for these apparent contradictions lies in a combination of two historical processes: (1) The content of the Old Testament was transmitted orally over a long period of time, with some variations, before it was finally put into written form, and (2) the Hebrew compilers of the Old Testament books often wanted to emphasize that Elohim and Yahweh were the same God (Gottwald 1985b:211-13; Moberly 1992:26–27). Thus, even if the name Yahweh was indeed first revealed to Moses, it soon became associated with earlier events like the call of Abraham and the creation of the universe.

Or, if the name Yahweh had already been revealed earlier, then the Exodus statement would suggest that the full meaning of that name and of Yahweh's purpose had not been revealed until Yahweh spoke to Moses.

Elohim explained the meaning of the name Yahweh to Moses:

> But Moses said to elohim, "If I come to the Israelites and say to them, 'The elohim of your ancestors has sent me to you,' and they ask me, 'What is his name?' what shall I say to them?"
> Elohim said to Moses, "I AM WHO I AM."
> He said further, "Thus shall you say to the Israelites, 'I AM has sent me to you.'"
> Elohim also said to Moses, "Thus shall you say to the Israelites, 'Yahweh, the elohim of your ancestors, the elohim of Abraham, the elohim of Isaac, and the elohim of Jacob, has sent me to you'" (Ex 3:13–15 NRSV adapted).

In addition to the interplay between the class name Elohim and personal name Yahweh, this passage also suggests a sound-alike association (chap. 14) between Yahweh (written yhwh) and the verb 'to be' (written hyh and pronounced "hayah" or "ehyeh"), depending on the tense. Yahweh itself may mean "the one bringing into being" (Brown, Driver, and Briggs 1978:218). Others define it as "independent underived existence" (Douglas, ed. 1974:475). It also expresses eternal existence (probably the reason for the use of "l'Éternel" in the French Segond translation), existence which is active rather than passive (Eichrodt 1961:190). It may also mean, "I act as the one who acts" (Coenen, Beyreuther, and Bietenhard 1979:598–99).

As their own worldview developed, so did the use of the terms Elohim and Yahweh as God's class name and personal name, respectively. During the time of the kings the prophet Elijah called upon the people to choose once and for all:

> If yahweh is elohim follow him; and if Baal, then follow him . . . the elohim who will answer by fire, he is elohim (1 Kgs 18:21 NRSV adapted).

And when Yahweh does send fire, all the people shout:

> Yahweh indeed is elohim (1 Kgs 18:39 NRSV adapted).

Later, during the time of the divided kingdom, prophets like Hosea echoed God's cry:

> I *am* yahweh thy elohim from the land of Egypt, and thou shalt know no elohim but me: for *there is* no savior besides me (Hos 13:4 KJV adapted).

Shorter forms of Yahweh: The name Yahweh also appears in a shortened form, transliterated Jah (pronounced yah) in the Revised Version and the American Standard Version, either in the text or footnote: "my song is Jah" (Ex 15:2); "by Jah, his name" (Ps 68:4); "I shall not see Jah in Jah's land" (Is 38:11). It is common also in such often untranslated compounds as hallelujah 'praise jah' (Ps 135:3, 146:10, 148:14), and in proper names like Elijah, 'my God is jah,' Adonijah, 'my Lord is jah,' Isaiah, 'jah has saved.'

This shorter form, written yh, seems to have had several variant pronunciations, such as "yau" and "yaho." These show up in the writings of several Christian church fathers and in earlier versions of the Septuagint which transcribed the name Yahweh as "iao" (Eichrodt 1961:187, footnote). Apparently the Greeks thought that they could avoid the taboo on pronouncing Yahweh by making up a word that was pronounced much the same.

Elohim and Yahweh, Some Implications

All this variation between forms of Elohim and Yahweh reflects a struggle between the concepts exemplified by the two names. As the earlier oral traditions were collated and put together into written form, some of these sources used Elohim as the term for the Hebrew God, others Yahweh. These separate oral traditions, and others, were eventually fused into a single written account which we today know as the Hebrew text of the Old Testament. That this merging of sources led to some leveling in the names of God is easily understood. But there was more to the struggle than that.

When Elohim, the God of the world, created all of mankind "in his image," he created them "male and female," and did so as the crowning act of creation (Gen 1:27). Elohim created all races and all peoples of the world from a single stock, and all are equal in God's sight. Males and females were also created as equals, both equally images of Elohim.

In the very next chapter, however, Yahweh first created the male alone. Only later, almost as an afterthought, did Yahweh also make the female. This second account then proceeded to show that the woman was inferior as she immediately succumbed to temptation. Later on, in Exodus and Leviticus, the unequal status of the two sexes was enshrined in an extensive legal code.

In disregard of the equality of races suggested by Genesis 1, Yahweh selected one tribe of people among all the tribes of the world to be Yahweh's own favorite people (Gen 12:1–3), and later said:

> I will establish my [everlasting] covenant between me and you . . . to be elohim to you and to your offspring after you (Gen 17:7–8 NRSV adapted).

The sharp contrast between the Elohim of Genesis 1 and the Yahweh who unfolds in the early parts of the Old Testament is striking, but later on Yahweh is sometimes depicted more like that initial Elohim, as we shall see. If the high God Elohim presented in Genesis 1 is the ideal universal image that God wants people to have, then much of the rest of the Old Testament can be seen as Yahweh's struggle to become equated with that high God of all humanity. In other words, God had all along tried to teach the Hebrews that Yahweh is really Elohim, the God of all.

However, just as the Hebrews believed that females were an inferior sex, so they struggled with God's universality. In common with worldviews all around them, Yahweh was exclusively their own tribal God. Both poet and prophet pictured Yahweh as fiercely partisan to this chosen people, just as Yahweh's covenant with Abraham demanded:

> I will bless those who bless you,
> But I will curse those who curse you (Gen 12:3 GNB).

Before people recognized God's universality, Yahweh was shown as willing to destroy entire nations on Israel's behalf and as promising to give Jacob's descendants all the land "from the border of Egypt to the Euphrates River" (Gen 15:18–20 GNB).

In fact, Yahweh was pictured as enjoining the Israelites to exterminate all such people totally:

> But when you capture cities in the land that yahweh your elohim is giving you, kill everyone. Completely destroy all the people: the Hittites, the Amorites, the Canaanites, the Perizzites, the Hivites, and the Jebusites, as yahweh ordered you to do (Deut 20:16–17 GNB adapted).

Indeed, Yahweh promised to go ahead of the Israelites and perform a lot of this destruction:

> My angel will go ahead of you and take you into the land of the Amorites, the Hittites, the Perizzites, the Canaanites, the Hivites, and the Jebusites, and I will destroy them (Ex 23:23 GNB).

As we earlier pointed out for tribal deities (chap. 7), so for Israel, their moral code was largely confined to behavior within their own tribe. Outside, among worshipers of false gods, "God's people" were free from the moral restraints which applied in their home community; they could beat, burn and kill, all to the glory of Yahweh.

By the time of the major prophets, however, Yahweh showed more concern for other nations, largely as the God who will punish the nations for their evil deeds (Is 13–23; Jer 46–51; Ezek 25–32). In this development also, Yahweh is sometimes pictured as installing rulers in other nations as his instruments for either punishing or doing kindness to Israel:

> I [yahweh] am the one who has placed all these nations under the power of my servant, King Nebuchadnezzar. . . . But if any nation, or kingdom will not submit to his rule, then I will punish that nation by war, starvation and disease until I have let Nebuchadnezzar destroy it completely (Jer 27:6–8 GNB).

> Yahweh has chosen Cyrus to be king! He has appointed him to conquer nations. . . . To Cyrus yahweh says, "I myself will prepare your way. . . . I appoint you to help my servant Israel, the people I have chosen" (Is 45:1–4 GNB adapted).

But before Israel became willing to concede that Yahweh was, indeed, the God of all peoples, their home country and its temple had to be destroyed, many of its people carried away captive, and the "chosen people" oppressed as a minority living in exile, in a country not their own—one in which they believed Yahweh had no jurisdiction. That shifted their perspective somewhat and brought occasional recognition that Yahweh did include members of other nations in God's great plan of world-wide salvation:

> A foreigner who has joined yahweh's people would not say, "yahweh will not let me worship with his people." . . . And yahweh says to those foreigners who become part of his people . . . "I will bring you to Zion . . . and accept the sacrifices you offer on my altar. My Temple will be called a house of prayer for the people of all nations" (Is 56:3–7 GNB adapted).

These conditions for accepting people from other tribes to become worshipers of Yahweh seem to include submission to the whole Mosaic law; but in the end, light begins to dawn that other nations will be accepted even without becoming external Jews, if their hearts are right with Yahweh:

> Yahweh says, "The end is near for those who purify themselves from pagan worship. . . . I am coming to gather the people of all nations. . . . I will make *some of them priests and Levites*" [my italics] (Is 66:17–21 GNB adapted; Kaiser 1987:41–46, 1978:212–19).

In this same train of development, Paul, the converted Jew, was eventually to say,

> From one ancestor [God] made all the nations to inhabit the whole earth, and he allotted the times of their existence and the boundaries of the places where they would live (Acts 17:26 NRSV).

Transformation of God's Name

We have been examining the enlargement of the Hebrew view of God, as reflected in Hebrew names for deity. Similar transformation has taken place all over the world, including among some of our own ancestors in Europe or elsewhere, as the personal names of local cultural deities have come to stand for the name of the God of all peoples. My wife and I saw this transformation take place again at the height of our frustration with translating Ewandama, the Waunana personal name for God.

As we began our translation efforts, I traveled across a range of mountains to visit one of the oldest living Waunana. He was a famous storyteller, and I wanted to learn much from him. Usually he and I spent the entire day talking together because everyone else left the house to hunt, fish, or work in the garden.

One day I asked him to retell the account of how the Waunana god, Ewandama, threw out his uncooperative wife and married his sister-in-law. Such a marriage may be quite acceptable in our culture, but the Waunana consider it incest, one of the three unpardonable sins that damage the person's blood and turn the perpetrator into a devil. Since I knew the story well, I could respond with the appropriate audience reactions a good storyteller expects. The old man rose to the occasion and delivered the story in an exciting way.

Until he finished, I behaved as a believing Waunana hearing the story ought to behave. But then I suddenly dropped that role, banged my fist on the floor, jumped up and down, assumed a horrified expression and said, "I know you are a wise old man; I know you tell the truth; but my spleen is upset because I cannot believe that the Ewandama who made the Waunana people was evil enough to commit incest and so to become an unredeemable devil." I paused dramatically, looking hard at the old man.

For a while he was stunned, and then suddenly he questioningly proposed, "Maybe there is more than one Ewandama. I think I agree with you that the Ewandama who made the world surely wouldn't commit incest; it must have been someone else also called Ewandama." It was our first inkling that Ewandama might become a class noun.

Several years later, I overheard a group of Waunana discussing the Ewandamas of the various people they knew, and then I knew that what once had been only a personal name was now functioning as a class noun, at last.

It is not surprising that an isolated people should have only a personal name for their God, and that they should lack a class noun for gods in general. In fact, it may be necessary for a people to become aware of many gods before they feel the need for a class noun to speak about such beings. Once this happens, they may develop a class noun based on a personal divine name by the same linguistic process as North Americans have generalized the brand name Kleenex into a class noun for all tissues, or Xerox as a synonym for photocopy.

Although the process was similar for the Hebrews, it was also intellectually, theologically, and psychologically more difficult. Israel had the task of equating two names sometimes seen as the names of different beings. Their struggle was not one of generalizing Yahweh or Elohim, but of equating the one Yahweh with the particular, ungeneralized Elohim. That story is the story of their growing understanding of the nature of God taking place over the centuries. And that story is reflected in the tensions and inconsistencies we sometimes see in the use of these names in the Old Testament. It is, furthermore, made vague and obscure by the difficulty of translating names. But that story became one of the foundations of the Christian understanding of the God of all peoples. To read the Bible cross-culturally we need to hear the significance of the names for God.

16

Cultural Bias
in Translating God's Names

During my early years as translation consultant with the Bible Societies in South America, I had the privilege of checking the Maquiritare language (Venezuelan) translation of the New Testament. I was much impressed with its quality, but as we worked through book after book, I became increasingly uncomfortable with the use of the loan word *Diyo* (from Spanish *Dios*) as the name for God.

Finally, I said to the translators, "I know you have told me that *Wanaari* [the local name for God] is too encumbered with negative mythology, but please check and listen very carefully once more to see if we cannot use the local name in the Bible. If you will try for one more month and finally decide that it is impossible, I will authorize printing your New Testament with *Diyo*."

So the translators accompanied a group of evangelists to a section of the tribe which had not as yet heard the gospel. They noticed that as soon as the evangelists moved beyond the area where people had been exposed to Spanish, they suddenly switched from using *Diyo* in their preaching to *Wanaari*. When the translators asked the evangelists to explain what had caused them to change, they replied, "Oh, we use *Diyo* where the people know Spanish and know that it means God, but the people way back in the jungle have never heard Spanish, and they haven't the faintest idea what *Diyo* means."

"But how could you use *Wanaari*?" asked the translators. "Hasn't the church decided that *Wanaari* did too many bad things? What about all his immorality? What about all his cheating?"

"Oh," the evangelists said, "you mean those stories? Didn't you know that all of them were stories which the devil invented so that the people wouldn't follow God?"

A mythology had been reinterpreted. In the end, the translators decided to use *Wanaari* rather than *Diyo* for God in the New Testament that was ready for the press.

Translation as a Cross-Cultural Process

Before we look at cultural bias in the translation of divine names, we need first to think about cultural presuppositions about translation in general, especially translation of sacred books. Such presuppositions vary between cultures, between subcultures, and between different religious backgrounds.

Scriptural Language as God's Language

The use historic Christianity has made of translation as against the practice of other major religions with sacred books is fundamental. On the one hand, translation has been the foundation of much of the spread of the Christian faith right from the beginning. Christians have usually believed that translations have as much power and authority as the texts in their original language. But followers of other religions which have sacred books generally believe that the books must be transmitted untranslated, left in their original language, because they consider translations not to have the same authority and power as the original.

This difference in cultural presupposition can be seen most clearly in the contrast between Christianity and Islam, two major religions, both of which have a strong missionary dynamic. Christianity has spread in good measure along with translation of the Bible and evangelization in vernacular languages. Islam, on the other hand, has spread along with memorization of the Qur'an in Arabic, regardless of whether the memorizers understand that language or not (Sanneh 1989:211–35).

The Bible which the early Christian church used as it spread from the Middle East into Europe was a translated Bible—the Old Testament in Greek, not in the original Hebrew. This translation, called the Septuagint, had been prepared by Greek-speaking Jews in Alexandria, Egypt, about 250 years before Christ. New Testament writers therefore generally quoted from the Greek translation rather than from the Hebrew original as they wrote the documents which became books of the Greek New Testament. Even Jesus' words in this Greek of the New Testament were translations of his words in Aramaic, the language which he normally spoke.

The young Christian church continued its spread in the first centuries of its existence primarily by using three major languages: Greek, Latin, and Syriac, each with its own translation of Scripture.[1] In time, these translations

---

[1] In the case of Greek, only the Old Testament existed in translation. The New Testament, of course, was originally written in Greek.

as such became hallowed in various parts of the church. In the Western church, the Latin language in its Vulgate translation eventually became sacred. The Latin Mass continued to be celebrated in the Catholic church until well into the twentieth century. Meanwhile, in the east the Orthodox church to this day regards the Greek as inspired, not the Hebrew.

Slowly, however, translations were also made into other languages. Then at the beginning of the nineteenth century, translations of the Bible suddenly began to proliferate in Asian, African, Latin American, and other languages. As a result, Hebrew, Koine Greek, Latin, and Syriac, important as they still are for biblical scholarship, no longer play much of a direct role in the life or expansion of the Christian church.

As Islam spread, on the other hand, the perpetuation of Arabic was assumed. This was the sacred language of the Qur'an which Muhammad had copied from the original in heaven. The Qur'an was considered to be holy because it consisted of the literal words spoken or written by God in Arabic. To translate them made them no longer God's immediate words. Classical Arabic and the Qur'an were, and are, inseparable.

These two different cultural assumptions concerning the place of translation in the expansion of a religious faith are founded, of course, on assumptions concerning the nature of the faith itself. In Christianity, God is revealed through human media, through human messengers, through the incarnation, in the experience of the people of God through history, and through the use of vernacular language worship. In Islam, God is transmitted through a theoretically unchanging historical form, a classical language which even native speakers of Arabic must today learn in school. It is a divinely dictated book which only the specially educated can read with understanding.

The underlying dynamic of the Christian perspective is communication of the faith. Its power rests in human beings understanding the message and responding to it. Application of this perspective has strengthened vernacular languages throughout the world. The underlying dynamic of the Islamic perspective, on the other hand, seems to be adoption of the divine message as a talisman. Its power rests in words, formulae, magic, and ritual. Application of this perspective has sometimes reduced the significance of vernacular languages in those parts of the world where Islam predominates (Sanneh 1989:88–155).

On the other hand, at times throughout Christian history its communication presupposition has been opposed and weakened by powerful forces within the church itself. At such times, the church has veered from its historical reliance on understanding the message toward an Islam-like view of the form of the text as sacred.

One such deviation lay in the development of classical church languages, and the feeling that the gospel could not be expressed except in these languages. Greek, Latin, and Syriac, already mentioned for their sacred translations, stood in the way of using the vernaculars. They were considered

God's languages in their respective areas. In effect, they were in their time somewhat the Christian counterparts of Arabic for Muslims in our time.

Those classical languages ultimately gave way but, at later times in its history, parts of the Christian church have resorted to establishing official church languages which have stifled translation and even evangelization in the vernacular. English occupied such a place in the early missionary work in Sierra Leone, not to speak of such work among many of the native peoples of North America. In Latin America, Spanish or Portuguese has often overridden the vernaculars as church languages. In one tribe in Africa, the missionary's personal incorrect way of speaking the local language, derisively called *ChiMcMinn* ('McMinn language,' after the missionary's name) was the church language for half a century. In these situations, also, the church was partially following the Muslim pattern rather than the Christian one.

Perhaps the most serious and nearly universal impediment to communication in translations is literal translation in which the word order and the phraseology of the source language are retained to such a degree that the translation is difficult, unnatural, and/or unclear. In keeping with the Muslim-like assumption that the language of the Bible is God's language, many literal translations include gibberish like

> For even that which was made glorious had no glory in this respect, by reason of the glory that excelleth. For if that which is done away *was* glorious, much more that which remaineth *is* glorious (2 Cor 3:10–11 KJV).

> O *ye* Corinthians, our mouth is open unto you, our heart is enlarged. Ye are not straitened in us, but are straitened in your own bowels. Now for a recompense in the same, (I speak as unto *my* children,) be ye also enlarged (2 Cor 6:11–13 KJV).

Compare more meaningful translations of the same passages:

> In fact, the new agreement is so wonderful that the Law is no longer glorious at all. The Law was given with a glory that faded away. But the glory of the new agreement is much greater, because it will never fade away (2 Cor 3:10–11 CEV).

> Friends in Corinth, we are telling the truth when we say that there is room in our hearts for you. We are not holding back on our love for you, but you are holding back on your love for us. I speak to you as I would speak to my own children. Please make room in your hearts for us (2 Cor 6:11–13 CEV).

Manifestations of Bias

With this background on the importance of communication in biblical translation and of the counter-pressure to reduce the historic place of translation to a perspective more like that of Islam, we turn now to summarize some specific types of cultural bias found in the translation of God's names in the Bible. Different cultural assumptions about translation and the nature of the Bible of course produce different biases.

Bias in Translation Theory

Translators follow a theory of translation, a set of principles for cross-cultural communication of a text. Sometimes the theory is carefully thought out, sometimes it is an implicit, unconscious one, but every translation theory includes a set of beliefs that one way is better than others.

The belief that translations should follow the form of the sacred original language as literally as possible is such a theory, sometimes called "formal correspondence translation" (Nida and Taber 1969:27–28,173; Nida 1964:159–79). Under this theory, explicitly or implicitly held, the words, grammar, and other forms of the translation are made to correspond fairly closely to the forms of the original. This theory emphasizes the words and grammar over the meaning.

One of the ways in which this theory of translation manifests itself is in the figures of speech in the text. For example, the expression "by their fruits ye shall know them" (Mt 7:20 KJV) means 'you shall know them by their actions.' Translated literally into other languages, "their fruits" may be puzzling because the figure requires the reader to see a person as a tree or bush which bears fruit. But readers in some languages are more likely to see it as the person carrying fruit. In several African languages the translation actually said, 'You will know people by the fruit they carry.' One language specifically used a word meaning 'to carry in a basket on the head.'

In much modern Bible translation, such a theory of literal or formal correspondence translation has been replaced by dynamic equivalence translation. Under that theory, the meaning of the translation is made equivalent to the meaning of the original. This theory emphasizes the meaning over the words and grammar.

Various cultural reasons cause some translators to prefer formal correspondence. One is the fear of syncretism—of diluting the Bible's message with local "pagan" words and ideas. Any accommodation to the vocabulary of the existing religious culture is often resisted. This was apparent in the Maquiritare hesitation to use God's name, Wanaari. It is also evident in the older worldwide practice of transliterating the names of God.

Some syncretism always takes place as the gospel spreads, sometimes distorting the gospel, and sometimes greatly enriching people's understanding of God. The changes in Israel's worldviews discussed in early chapters were often syncretistic, both those in which they turned to the fertility gods of their neighbors and those in which they began to understand the meaning of immortality and resurrection (chap. 8).

Modern speakers of English are usually unaware of the amount of syncretism that took place in our past and tend to be adamant against any syncretism in languages into which we bring the Scriptures. How trivial syncretism can be, as seen from a later time, is illustrated by the fact that the word "Easter" comes from the name of a pagan deity and that the great statue of Zeus from Greek religion became the model for the victorious Christ in early Christianity. Much more importantly, the assumption of Mary into deity was proclaimed in Ephesus, the very place in which the goddess Artemis was supreme (Acts 19:27–28, 34–35).

The problems of literal translation become really acute for concepts that are unknown in the language of the translation. In many literal translations the source language word has simply been transliterated, like "baptize" from Greek *baptidzo*, "apostle" from *apostolos*, "angel" and "archangel" from *angelos*.

Related to that tendency is the long and widespread tradition of transliterating names rather than translating them, even when the translators knew that the original word had meaning. The names of the gods of the people with whom Israel had contact were all transliterated, like Baal (1 Kgs 18:21), Dagon (Judg 16:23), Rimmon (2 Kgs 5:18), Ashtoreth (1 Kgs 11:5 KJV), Succoth Benoth, Nergal, Ashima, Nebhaz, and Tartak (2 Kgs 17:30 KJV). Even obviously meaningful names of gods like Adrammelek 'splendor of the king' and Anammelek 'the prince/son is king' (2 Kgs 17:31 KJV) have been transliterated.

On the other hand, translators have transliterated the names of the God of the Hebrews only under special circumstances.[2] In the King James Version, for example, *el* was transliterated when it was part of a place name, like Bethel (Gen 12:8) or the name of an object, like *El-elohe-Israel* (Gen 33:20). *Yahweh* was transliterated *Jehovah* or *Jah* when the emphasis of the passage was on the form of the name (Ex 6:3; Ps 68:4), or in place names like *Jehovah-jireh* (Gen 22:14); *Sabaoth* 'hosts, armies' was transliterated in expressions like Lord of Sabaoth (Rom 9:29; Jas 5:4).

Some translations have nevertheless helped the reader to realize the meaning of names in various ways. Some, for example, make explicit the fact that a deity bears the name, as by translating "the god Rimmon" where the Hebrew text only has Rimmon. The fact that the name is the name of a god is, of course, already implicit in the text, a part of the meaning. Then again, sometimes translators explain the meaning of names where they do have significant meaning, as is done in the notes of such translations as the Good

---

[2]Appendix C consists of a comparative listing of the ways in which Hebrew names of God have been translated or transliterated in a number of European translations, as well as in the Greek Septuagint.

News Bible, the New English Bible, and the Jerusalem Bible.

A few translators do sometimes translate the meanings of some names. One example of wide variation between translations in this respect is the range of translations of *el berith*, from "El-Berith" through "the god Berith" to "Baal of the covenant" (app. C, 5a). 'Sons of god' is translated as "supernatural beings" in the Septuagint, the Good News Bible, and the Français Courant (Gen 6:2). 'El the Elohim of Israel,' which was transliterated *"El-elohe-Israel"* in the King James Version, as mentioned above, was partially translated as "El, the God of Israel" in the Good News Bible and more fully translated as "Mighty God" in Luther's translation (Gen 33:20; app. C, 2b). The French Segond translation regularly uses l'Éternel 'the Eternal One' for Yahweh. The Septuagint has 'absolute master' for adonai Yahweh, 'lord Yahweh' (Gen 15:2; app. C, 31b).

Ethnocentric Culturo-Religious Bias

People widely interpret the religions of other people from their own religious points of view, or within known religious categories. Thus, people with a monotheistic religion tend to see religions with multiple gods as having idols. They are often not aware that in Hinduism and in African religions, both of which have multiple deities, many people view these deities as expressions of one God, as lesser manifestations of a single deity.

This attitude is quite visible in the Hebrew Scriptures themselves with their slowly developing monotheistic outlook in a context of pagan religions with multiple deities. The multiple gods of non-Hebrew peoples tend to be called "idols" (Ps 96:5).

Individual deities were sometimes also denigrated in the Hebrew Scriptures. Since Baal had been such a temptation to the Israelites, eventually the word "Baal" became taboo and was avoided so that the word *bosheth* 'shame' was substituted (chap. 13). We see the substitution in such names as Mephibosheth/Meribbaal (2 Sam 4:4, 9:6; 1 Chr 8:34) and in Ishbosheth/ Eshbaal (2 Sam 2:8, 3:7, 4:5; 2 Chr 8:33). Both pairs of names refer to the same individuals.

Beyond that, the gods of the other peoples in the Bible have been denigrated even more in some translations. The Greek Septuagint, for example, frequently translated elohim with derogatory terms when it referred to the god/gods of other nations. It used terms like 'statues' (Is 21:9), 'temples of divinities' (2 Sam 7:23), and 'demons' (Ps 96:5), for example.[3] It reserves its strongest disdain for the female deity Ashtoreth by translating elohim as 'abomination' when it refers to her, rather than the expected

---

[3]See the comparison with other translations in Appendix C, 13a, b, c.

'goddess' (1 Kgs 11:5; app. C, 12a). The French Segond also avoids the word 'goddess,' and uses the sexless 'divine one' instead.

The ethnocentric bias of the Hebrews against other peoples did not stop with their gods but also extended to the Gentiles themselves (Ex 34:24; Num 21:3; Deut 2:32–34). It continued in the synoptic gospels of the New Testament, as well (Mt 10:5–6; Mk 7:26–30).

On the other hand, the Gospel of John, written after the Christian community had become heavily Gentile, seems to show a bias against Jews (Bratcher 1975:401-409; Jn 5:16, 18, 7:1, 10:31, 20:19). The synoptic gospels also had an anti-Pharisaic bias (Mt 3:7, 15:1–9, 23:2–36, Lk 18:10–14).

Bias in Theological Presuppositions

The editors of the Hebrew text sometimes blurred the distinction between Elohim, the supreme God of the world, and Yahweh, the God of the Hebrews (chap. 15; app. C, 9a, 22b, 25a, 29b,c, 30a, 31a,c, 32a, 34a,b,c, 35a, 36a, 37a,b, 55a). The Septuagint translation took this tendency much farther, apparently making a conscious effort to minimize the distinction between these two names.

Thus, in the first Hebrew creation account Elohim is the active agent, but in the second, it is Yahweh Elohim (chap. 8). However, the Septuagint continues with the same word 'god,' which it had used in the first story, through the first four verses of the second, and only in Genesis 2:8 does it introduce the combined names Yahweh Elohim as 'lord the god.' Elsewhere, the Septuagint sometimes reduces Yahweh Elohim to 'god' as well (Ex 3:18; app. C, 21c).

Then again, the Septuagint uses the combined name 'lord the god' sometimes even when Yahweh or Elohim occurs alone in Hebrew: 'call on the name of Yahweh' was translated 'call on lord the god' (Gen 4:26); 'Yahweh saw' and 'Elohim saw' were both translated 'lord the god saw' (Gen 6:5; Gen 6:12).

This seemingly intentional blurring between Yahweh and Elohim is marked in the story where Jacob left Yahweh's land and said to the deity:

If elohim will be with me [so that I] . . . come back again to my father's house in peace; then yahweh shall be my elohim (Gen 28:20–21 NRSV adapted).

The Septuagint, however, begins Jacob's vow with 'if lord the god will go with me . . . ,' which masks the distinction which the original narrator made. The four common language translations cited in Appendix C have all likewise blurred this distinction (app. C, 28a).

The Septuagint renders both Yahweh and adon/adonai 'lord' as 'lord.'

The practice rests at least in part on the fact that Adonai had become a favorite oral replacement for the taboo Yahweh when Scriptures were read aloud in public. In Hebrew 'appeared Yahweh' is translated 'lord appeared' in the Septuagint (Gen 17:1). For 'said Yahweh to Jacob' the Septuagint has 'lord said to Jacob' (Gen 31:3).

In passages where 'El, the Elohim' occurs in Hebrew, the Septuagint usually drops the first el. 'I am El, the Elohim of Israel' becomes 'I am your God Israel' (Gen 33:20). For 'I am El, the Elohim of your fathers,' the Septuagint merely says 'I am the God of your fathers' (Gen 46:3). It also does the same sometimes with 'Yahweh the Elohim,' so that 'Yahweh, the Elohim of the Hebrews' is translated 'the God of the Hebrews,' and 'Yahweh, our Elohim' is rendered only as 'our God' (Ex 3:18).

More curious is the fact that when Yahweh and adonai occur side by side, both are rendered Lord. 'Oh Adonai, oh Yahweh' is translated 'Lord my Lord' (2 Sam 7:28; app. C, 31c).

Bias Against Recognizing God in Other Religions

Unfortunately, some translators do not take the God or gods of the religion of the local people seriously enough, nor study them thoroughly enough, as we have already seen in the Maquiritare translation. At least in Africa, many languages which were said to have only a personal name for God do, in fact, have an equivalent class name for god/gods (chap. 15). However, in the dictionaries which record these languages (dictionaries often prepared by missionaries), such words have been translated as 'fetish' or 'idol' rather than 'god,' and that classification ruled them out from further missionary consideration.

Thus, the Akan of Ghana recognize Onyame or Onyankopon as the supreme God, with names which are personal and cannot be pluralized. But the Akan also recognize the *abosom*, called 'idols' or 'fetishes' in the earlier dictionaries, but now translated as 'god, gods' by Akan scholars (Pobee 1979). By dismissing this class of gods in the Akan religion, missionaries reflected their bias against taking the religion seriously and missed an important word for their translation.

In many if not most West African societies, the local word for 'gods' covers the domain of Hebrew words for both 'gods' and 'idols.' However, Akan Onyame does not belong to the class of abosom even though both may be worshiped. They are felt to be completely separate categories.

As in the case of Maquiritare, many translators face the problem that the local name for God is encumbered with myths which may ascribe characteristics alien to the biblical concept of a moral and just God. How they respond often reflects their bias against taking the local gods seriously. A name borrowed from a local trade language may appear to be neutral, but its very foreign origin often encumbers it with an alien identity which prevents it from being an effective evangelistic tool.

We have seen how the Spirit of God can deal with the unsavory aspects of a tribe's mythology, but bias against recognizing the gods in the local religion is often more serious than that. Most important is the fact that God has always been present in the society, although not known from a Christian perspective. The use of God's local name powerfully places the society within the scope of God's dealings with all people, as reported in the Bible, as no foreign name can do. God is their God, not just an imported God of foreigners. The Bible, in turn, enables people to gain a truer picture of the God whom they had partially misunderstood.

Bias Against "Lower" Languages

In most parts of the world where more than one language is spoken, those languages form a hierarchy in the sense that adults learn languages they consider more advantageous, but not ones which are less useful to them (Smalley 1994:69, 343–45). Thus, in East Africa, many people whose native language is Kikuyu, a tribal language, also know Swahili, and some may know English, but other speakers of Swahili and English do not normally learn Kikuyu.

This nonreciprocal language hierarchy often produces a bias against the lower languages, the feeling that they are inferior, that they do not have adequate resources for an adequate translation of the Bible. The bias may be held only by speakers of the higher languages, including translators, or may infect native speakers of the lower languages as well.

The Maquiritare case illustrates such bias. During my years of overseas service, I have been surprised at how many groups I have met that either began to hear or are still hearing a gospel in which God's name is a loan word, sometimes borrowed from a neighboring or a related tribal language, sometimes from a trade or a colonial language.

In some cases, early missionaries claimed that they had not been able to find a local name for God and so were forced to use a loan word from a neighboring language. The search is not necessarily easy. Once I had to work for several months before I found the local name. Giving up the search too soon reflects a bias that the name is probably not to be found.

In a number of languages in sub-Saharan Africa, the influence of Islam makes people refuse any name other than the Arabic Allah for God. Even many non-Muslims may be hesitant to use their local name for God because of the strength of the reaction of their Muslim fellow members of the tribe. They have absorbed the belief that their language is inferior to Arabic.

In Central Africa, missionaries originally moved into new areas from the south. Often they were accompanied by African evangelists from established churches who felt much more at home using their home language name for God than using the name in the language in which they were to evangelize. As a result, for example, the early Lozi evangelization in Zambia was done using the Zulu name for God.

All such reasons reflect a bias against the lower language, even if it is only that the name in the higher language is easier for the translator to use. I personally have yet to find a tribe which has no indigenous name for God. Even though the local name often seems to be encumbered by many negative associations, the Bible will usually put this name in its own context, and the influence of this context can eliminate many of the negative things that were earlier associated with that name. Myth-changing is a constant process and, as in the Maquiritare case, it can often provide sanctification of the divine name. Furthermore, we need to recognize that the local name always has a "home-feeling"; it is "our God." Even groups that have used a loan word for the divine name for decades confess that it never fully loses its foreign flavor.

Theoretically, however, sometimes a loan word must be used as a name for God in spite of its weaknesses. If there absolutely is no name for God in the language, or if the strength of feeling against the indigenous name is strong, an imported name probably cannot be avoided. In the second of these cases, the bias against the lower language or religion may be too strong to overcome.

If a loan word is absolutely necessary, then the choice of language from which it is taken may be critical. The name for God from a trade language (one step up in the hierarchy) is often better than the name from a higher colonial language because if a reaction should ever develop against the colonial language, the negative feeling would certainly also extend to God's name. Likewise, a name from a neighboring tribe (on the same level of the hierarchy) is often better than the name Allah, which is often loaded with theological and cultural ideas strongly supported by Islamic influence in the culture, and so not as amenable to being cleansed of old associations.

Some languages have more than one name for God, which may provide a rich resource for translating the multiple names of God in the Bible. The African language I know best is ChiChewa, spoken in Malawi and Zambia, which has a series of names for God: Mulungu, Chiuta, Mpambe, Mlezi, Chanjira, used in different contexts in the local religion and with different functions.

Mulungu is the most widely used such name and the one most people automatically assume is also the God of the Bible. It cannot be pluralized or abstracted as a class noun; it is the personal name of God.

Chiuta is basically a praise name that refers to the great spaces in the sky which are God's domain. The sign that Chiuta puts in the sky to show that he is there is the rainbow which he stretches out from one end of the sky to the other. An English equivalent of Chiuta might be 'the chief of the universe.' It can be used to translate Hebrew 'most high.'

Mpambe is based on the verb 'to excel' and occurs in contexts of rain, thunder, and earthquakes. It seems to be a good translation of 'almighty.'

Mlezi is based on the verb 'to sustain, to care for,' and thus could be used for 'the one who sustains, the one who nourishes.' This name is most likely related to the name Leza which is very widely used for God in Central Africa. Mlezi would be a good term for Yahweh, 'the one who causes to be,' at least in part of its meaning.

Overcoming Bias Through New Perspectives

When the Jews began to recognize that Yahweh and Elohim were one and the same God of the world, not just the God of the Hebrews, they took a first step in overcoming prejudice against other peoples and their God/gods. To the degree that we today recognize that we are dealing with the one God of the world, to that degree we also will be able to recognize that God was present in other cultures and religions long before Christian missionaries got there.

When my wife and I felt that we were bringing the truth for the first time to the people to whom we had been sent as missionaries, we did not realize that these people already had long-standing contact with God and that much of the truth that we wanted to bring to them was already known to them. Thus in the first message to the Waunana we were able to find many points of contact in what the people already knew of God (Loewen 1961; Loewen 1995).

To the degree to which we recognize the truth of Paul's statement—

What we see now is like a dim image in a mirror; then we shall see face-to-face. What I know now is only partial; then it will be complete—as complete as God's knowledge of me (1 Cor 13:12 GNB),

to that degree we will humbly be open to understand the point of view of people who are different from us. Especially if this understanding is accompanied by a learner's attitude rather than the ethnocentric feeling of knowing the whole truth and nothing but the truth, we will be better able to communicate the message of Scripture sympathetically. At the same time, we will be enriched in our own understanding of Scripture.

A giant step toward overcoming bias in translation has been taken as native speakers have become translators of the Bible into their own languages. Mother-tongue speakers are often aware of where their language differs from the home language of the missionary or even from the colonial language through which the nationals got the word of God. For the few who have learned Greek and Hebrew, this awareness applies also to the original languages in which the Bible came. As they face the differences and look to God for guidance in those matters where their languages require clarification of details not indicated in the Greek or Hebrew, they have to learn to trust the Spirit of God, to pray, "God, how would you have said this if you had said it in our language in the first place?"

Native speakers need to overcome their biases too, of course, biases of the same types as those of missionaries, but sometimes differing in content. But to the degree to which native speakers and foreign missionaries do overcome biases, to that degree we will be able to manifest the mind of Christ in communicating God's word in other languages and cultures.

Part V

Some Implications
of Cross-Cultural Perspective

Introduction

I was raised in a Mennonite Brethren family to be a nonresistant Christian, a pacifist refusing to take up arms in war (Mt 5:39). But not until I saw myself in the mirror of Lengua (Paraguay) culture did I realize how seriously we Mennonites have perverted Menno Simons' original vision of a life of peace. We have reduced it from a broad lifestyle ethic of abstaining from force and coercion down to a narrow restriction on refusing to bear arms in war (Loewen and Prieb 1997). When I met the Lengua, I found a truly pacifist people.

Once its earlobes have been pierced at eight days so that it comes under the Lengua tribal covenant, a baby's personality and its wishes are sacrosanct to the other members of the society, even to the mother. A Lengua does not violate another person, no matter how young.

When Lengua come to see a Mennonite colonist and the Mennonite asks them impatiently what they want, the Lengua are bound to say that they do not want anything because they perceive that the other person's "innermost" is already agitated, that they have no right to agitate it more by voicing a request. They must remain quiet until the agitated person returns to complete equilibrium (Loewen 1965b).

Or, if a Lengua mother has a baby who is seriously ill and needs an injection from the missionary nurse, she takes it to the dispensary but does not force the child to take the injection if the child does not want it. She puts her baby in the arms of the nurse and runs away, not to return until her own innermost has recovered from the violence that she has inflicted on her sick child.

The Mennonite immigrants to Paraguay failed to recognize their own ideal of a lifestyle without force and coercion as manifested in the Lengua and instead taught them to be more self-assertive, if not aggressive. One missionary even specialized in teaching Lengua Christians to spank their children. Where parents were still "too unspiritual," he spanked the children for them every weekend.

Thus far in this book we have been looking at the Bible through the lens of cross-cultural experience, but in this part of the book I want to focus also on ourselves as Western evangelical Christians, using both the Bible as set in ancient Eastern cultures, and life in modern non-Western cultures to give us a stereopticon view of ourselves.

The treatment will be sketchy, with only a few selected topics. We will consider the implications of culture differences and culture change for our assumptions about the universality of some of our customs like marriage. We will consider the many and variable gods of North American Christians. We will also go back to the issue of demon possession (chaps. 11–12) and search for a Western way of understanding it. And finally, I will outline the bases of my faith, my testimony, to round off the views and assumptions I have exposed in this book, trying to express what all this means to me personally.

Some of my conclusions here are tentative; probably all of them controversial, seen darkly through the glass of cultural presuppositions and stereotypes and of limited humanity. But they are nevertheless my attempt to see, an attempt to open all of our eyes to the poor match which now exists between the message of the Bible and the reality of Western Christianity.

17

Culture Change:
The Case of Biblical Marriage

We call our own marriage customs "Christian marriage," and our missionaries to the third world have duplicated them widely. But how "biblical" are they, and how "Christian" are the marriages we see in the Bible? The marriage and family patterns described there are vastly different from our own in some ways and have changed radically during the two thousand years of biblical history.

Marriage Customs in the Bible.

In the first Genesis creation story, the first human beings—male and female—were created equally in God's image (Gen 1:26–31). Then in the second story, the woman was created later than the man, but with God's direction that "a man leaves his father and his mother, and clings to his wife" (Gen 2:24 NRSV). Whether or not God performed a special ceremony or ritual to mark the formation of this first couple is not recorded.

Following creation, the earliest marriages pictured in the Bible are the polygamous ones of Abraham and his immediate descendants. Abraham himself was married to his half-sister, Sarah, a child of his own father but of a different mother (Gen 20:12). She seemed not to be able to bear children, so she urged Abraham to take on her slave, Hagar, as concubine (a minor wife or servant wife) to bear children for her. That union was successful in producing a much-wanted son, Ishmael, but it also produced intense jealousy in Sarah, which led to the eventual expulsion of Ishmael and Hagar after Sarah miraculously did finally give birth to her own son, Isaac (Gen 16:1–15; 21:8–21).

When Isaac was old enough to be married, Abraham sent his senior servant, Eliezer, back to his original home in Mesopotamia to get a wife for the young man from among the women in his extended family. With Yahweh's help, Eliezer selected Rebekah, Abraham's grandniece, Isaac's cousin's daughter (Gen 24:15–27). He gave gifts (technically a brideprice or dowry) to the bride and to other members of her family, such as her brother and her mother (Gen 24:53). The father had apparently already died.

Later, when Jacob was also looking for a wife in his uncle Laban's family in Mesopotamia, he had to work for fourteen years to earn the brideprice for the two wives (two of his cousins) that his uncle provided for him (Gen 29). Rachel, the younger cousin, was the one Jacob really wanted to marry, but his uncle insisted that the older had to be married first, as was the custom.

Why the older daughter had to be married first is explained in one of the pseudepigraphic books:

> And Laban said to Jacob, "It does not happen thus in our land, to give the younger woman before the elder." And it is not right to do this because thus it is ordained and written in the heavenly tablets that no one should give his younger daughter before the elder because he should first give the elder and after her the younger. And they will write it down as sin in heaven concerning the man who acts thus. And no one who does this thing will be righteous because this deed is evil before the LORD (Jub 28:6).

Note that the Hebrew writer projects his belief in Yahweh onto Laban, to whom Yahweh was actually a foreign God.

The two wives each had their slave maid serve as a concubine for Jacob as well. In fact, when Rachel could not become pregnant she had Jacob sleep with her slave Bilhah so that Bilhah would have a child which would be considered Rachel's own (Gen 30:1–8).

Marriage under the Mosaic Law

As a culture changes, its marriage patterns often change with the rest. Thus, the Hebrews entered Egypt with the marriage customs of the pastoralist patriarchs, but when they left more than four hundred years later, God commanded a radically different marriage pattern in the desert at Sinai. In fact, marriages like Abraham's would have brought severe punishment under the new law of Moses.

> If a man marries his sister or half sister, they shall be publicly disgraced and driven out of the community. He has had intercourse with his sister and must suffer the consequences (Lev 20:17 GNB).

Elsewhere in the law, God is portrayed as putting a curse on anyone who marries a sister or a half-sister (Deut 27:22).

One important marriage custom from the period of the patriarchs did carry over to the new law. It was the levirate, a requirement that if a brother dies, a living brother—usually a younger one—must marry the dead brother's wife. The children of such a union would be counted as children of the deceased brother. The levirate marriage was recognized in Israel as being commanded by God and being expected of all true followers of God (Deut 25:5–10). It was also widespread among other peoples in the Middle East (Hastings 1901 3:269).

The levirate underlay a sordid event in the life of Judah, one of the sons of Jacob, ancestor of one of the twelve tribes of Israel, and ultimately of Jesus. Er, Judah's oldest son, married a woman named Tamar, but God soon killed him because his "conduct was evil, and it displeased the LORD" (Gen 38:7). Judah therefore instructed his second son, Onan, to marry Tamar and raise her children as Er's children. Onan, however, who knew that at least Tamar's first son would be counted as his dead brother's son, "let the semen spill on the ground, so that there would be no children for his brother" (Gen 38:9). This violation of the levirate so displeased God that he killed Onan also.

Judah had another son, Shelah, who was too young to marry, so he told Tamar to go back to her father's home to wait for her next husband. But by now Judah was afraid that Shelah would also come to harm if he married Tamar so he neglected having them married.

When Tamar realized that her father-in-law was not going to fulfill his legal duty to her, she dressed as a religious prostitute with a veil over her face, and waited beside the road where she knew Judah was going to pass. Judah's wife had died, so when he came by and saw the prostitute he had intercourse with her. As an assurance that he was going to pay her for her services, he left her his signet ring and his staff, but when he later sent someone to deliver the payment and to collect his belongings, the messenger could not find any trace of her.

In time, Judah discovered that his daughter-in-law was pregnant and ordered her burned to death as a whore. But Tamar showed Judah the signet ring and the staff and said, "I am pregnant by the man who owns these things."

Then Judah recognized the seriousness of what he had done in not carrying out the levirate and admitted, "She is in the right. I have failed my obligation to her—I should have given her to my son Shelah in marriage" (Gen 38:6–26 GNB).

The later Mosaic law, on the other hand, provided that if the younger brother did not want to perform his levirate duty he could avoid it with a humiliating ceremony. The woman was to take off one of his sandals in public, in front of the town leaders and spit in his face, and "His family will be known in Israel as 'the family of the man who had his sandal pulled off'" (Deut 25:7–10 GNB).

At a still later period, Elimelech, a Jew, left his country with his wife Naomi and his sons and went to neighboring Moab during a famine. There his two sons married Moabite women but then died, leaving their widows childless. After Elimelech also died, Ruth—one of the wives—accompanied her mother-in-law back to Israel where Naomi sent her to a relative to ask him to marry her because he was someone who could redeem the family property now in other people's hands.

This man, Boaz, then arranged for a meeting with a still closer relative and proposed that the latter redeem Elimelech's land. The closer relative at first agreed, but when he learned that he also had "to do a brother's duty" and marry the surviving widow in order to carry on Elimelech's family line, he decided not to. So Boaz fulfilled the duty. But in order to signify publicly that the closer relative had relinquished his legal right, the relative had to take off his sandal and give it to Boaz (Ruth 4:8). In this case there is no indication in the story that this was a particularly humiliating experience (Nidich 1985:452–53).

In the New Testament, the Sadducees tried to use this ancient Jewish custom to embarrass Jesus about his belief in resurrection. Obviously the custom had fallen into some disrepute by this time as the Sadducees felt that they could have some fun with an old cultural practice which they no longer considered important. They told Jesus about a woman who had seven husbands in succession, seven brothers, each of whom died before the woman had any children. Each brother tried to fulfill the purpose of the levirate for the oldest brother, but each failed. Finally, the woman died also.

Then the Sadducees, who did not believe in life after death, smugly asked Jesus, "Now on the last day when the dead shall rise to life, whose wife will she be? All seven brothers were married to her."

Jesus used the occasion to teach the Sadducees how little they knew about God's design. First of all, he told them that in the life to come people will neither marry nor be married. But as far as the resurrection from the dead was concerned, he said, "Have you not read what was said to you by God, 'I [God] am the God of Abraham, the God of Isaac, and the God of Jacob'?" Jesus then added the punch line, "[God] is God not of the dead, but of the living," implying that the patriarchs were indeed alive in the afterlife (Mt 22:23–32, quoting Ex 3:6).

Communal Recognition of Marriage

The human community is described in the Scriptures as supporting and recognizing the institution of marriage with a series of events.

First came the wedding procession. The bride and the groom were dressed up (Is 61:10; Ps 45:14–15) and paraded through the streets, followed by their entourage of the groom's friends and the bride's "virgin" friends (Mt 25:1–13).

> In her colorful gown she is led to the king, followed by her bridesmaids. . .
> With joy and gladness they come and enter the king's palace (Ps 45:14–15 GNB).

Then the community participated in a wedding feast, perhaps a quasi-religious ceremony in connection with marriage (Hastings 1901 3:272). Jacob's wedding included a feast (Gen 29:22), as did Samson's (Judg 14:10) and Esther's (Esth 2:18). Most examples are of royalty or foreigners but the many figurative references to wedding processions and feasts in the Old Testament are evidence of their prevalence among the Hebrews. Wedding feasts are also mentioned in the New Testament (Mt 22:2–14; Jn 2:1–10).

As part of the wedding feast, the dressed-up wedding couple was seated under a canopy, while the guests celebrated (Joel 2:16 NRSV; Ps 19:5 NRSV). The canopy was probably originally an actual tent, since the early Israelites were nomadic.

There is no mention of a religious ritual to mark the actual marriage event. What made the marriage binding was the solemn covenant in which the bride and the groom pledged themselves to each other (alluded to, Deut 20:7; Lk 1:27). In late Judaism, however, especially in intertestamental times, this covenant was written:

> Raguel said to Tobias, eat and drink, and make merry: for it is meet that thou shouldest marry my daughter: nevertheless I will declare unto thee the truth. I have given my daughter in marriage to seven men, who died that night they came in unto her: nevertheless for the present be merry. But Tobias said, I will eat nothing here, *till we agree and swear one to another*. Raguel said, Then take her from henceforth according to the manner, for thou art her cousin, and she is thine, and the merciful God give you good success in all things. Then he called his daughter Sara, and she came to her father, and he took her by the hand, and gave her to be wife to Tobias, saying, Behold, *take her after the law of Moses*, and lead her away to thy father. And he blessed them, and called Edna his wife, and *took paper, and did write an instrument of covenants*, and sealed it (Tob 7:9–14, italics mine).

The consummation of marriage was itself an important part of the marriage (Deut 20:7). In the law, a tribunal was set up to investigate disputed cases of marriage consummation when the woman was accused of not being a virgin (Deut 22:13–21).

Biblical Divorce

In early Israel, divorce was an exclusively male prerogative (Deut 24:1–5; Is 50:1; figuratively, Jer 3:8). Later in Judaism and intertestamental times, however, even females were permitted to initiate divorces (Coenen, Beyreuther, and Bietenhard 1979:196).

When Abraham was forced by his wife, Sarah, to divorce the maid, Hagar, there was no legal transaction. Abraham just gave gifts to the rejected woman and her child, and sent them away (Gen 21:9–14). Later, a written certificate of divorce is mentioned in the legal code and referred to occasionally.

> Suppose a man marries a woman and later decides that he does not want her, because he finds something about her that he doesn't like. So he writes out divorce papers, gives them to her, and sends her away from his home (Deut 24:1 GNB).

> Do you think I sent my people away
> > like a man who divorces his wife?
> Where, then, are the papers of divorce? (Is 50:1 GNB).

As valid reasons for divorce, the Jews officially recognized childlessness and infidelity (Ausubel 1964:132). A couple was considered childless if they had no offspring after ten years of marriage, a tragic predicament for them. Rachel cried out in anguish when she found herself childless, "Give me children or I shall die" (Gen 30:1 NRSV). Elkanah loved his wife Hannah very much, but when she turned out to be childless, his other wife, Peninnah, tormented and humiliated Hannah, causing Hannah to cry to Yahweh to have mercy upon her (1 Sam 1:5–18). The result of her prayer was the birth of Samuel, the prophet.

The New Testament seems to recognize only one basis for divorce, namely infidelity (Mt 5:32). In Judaism, however, a husband could eventually divorce his wife for almost any reason, such as that her cooking was not good. Some rabbis even permitted divorce when the man found a woman who was prettier (Ausubel 1964:131–33).

Cross-Cultural Light on Biblical Marriage Customs

The marriage customs of other peoples help to throw light on the meaning and sometimes on the importance of such biblical references to marriage as we have seen so far. I have already occasionally used terms like concubine and brideprice from the anthropological study of marriage patterns, and in this section I will elaborate from other cultures on some such customs found in various biblical marriages.

Polygamy

In Africa, the reasons for polygamy[1] are not at all what most missionaries expect—not men's excessive sexual libido—but fear of childlessness. Thus among the Zulu, if a brideprice has been paid for a woman who turns out to be barren, the family is obligated to provide a sister to replace her because children are expected in return for a brideprice (Radcliffe-Brown and Forde 1950:64).

This fear of childlessness has deep roots in the African religious world-view. Africans believe that the deceased are responsible for the morals of the living. In turn, the living are responsible for the well-being of the deceased. If the living remember the deceased and conduct the proper funerals and other remembrances for their parents, the latter will move happily into a place farther and farther away from being earth-bound, until they eventually are close to God. Should the family not adequately remember a deceased person, that person is likely to become angry and eventually demonic. The fear of not having enough offspring to remember them drives African males to have multiple wives to ensure enough surviving offspring for their eternal salvation (Skinner 1967:368–69).

In biblical times, people also feared childlessness but for a different reason, as we have seen. They needed children to perpetuate their line but not to ensure their well-being in the afterlife.

A second reason for African insistence on polygamy grows out of their cultural division of labor. Wives are responsible for agriculture and, since agriculture can be quite diverse, often one wife is not able to keep up with everything (Reyburn 1967a:73–74). A family may have extensive forest plantings in one place and raise pigs in another. Pigs have to be kept far from the garden, and one wife cannot be in two places at once. So a man will often look for a second wife to take care of part of the women's work (Jongmans and Gutkind 1967:185).

Often the initiative for polygamy comes from the wife, who wants help with the work. In many societies the wife actually stands in for her husband when another woman is being brought into the union. She becomes the legal husband of the additional woman; officially, she is the sociological father of all the children born to that lesser wife. Her husband may sire the children, but the offspring by the lesser wives are hers (Radcliffe-Brown and Forde 1950:4).

Polygamy has, on the whole, been condemned by Christian missionaries. In South America as early as 1530, Catholic missionaries required

---

[1]The technical term for plural wives is actually polygyny. Polygamy itself means multiple mates.

monogamous marriage (Ricard 1966:112). Protestant missionaries usually did the same when they came later.

As a result of such policies in Africa, men who were converted often had to decide which wife or wives to divorce. Frequently, the husband kept a younger wife to ensure ongoing offspring, and abandoned the others, or sold them into prostitution (Barrett 1968:147). Some Cameroonian Christian men were asked what they would do if their older brother or uncle, who was not a Christian, should die and should leave them a number of his wives in a levirate responsibility. Without any hesitation they answered, "We would sell the women as prostitutes and take the money for ourselves" (Reyburn 1967b:259).

Thus, the Christian missionaries' insistence on monogamy in Africa has often led to widespread cultural abuse rather than to greater morality. African independent churches have often broken away from mission churches in part to allow polygamy and keep family morality from disintegrating.

On the other hand, polygamy has been part of the reason for the spread of Islam in Africa. For example, a chief in Mozambique wanted to become a Christian, but the missionary refused to accept him because he was polygamous. Three weeks later the chief accepted Islam, and his whole kingdom became Muslim.

Marriages of Pastoral Peoples

The marriage pattern of the patriarchs, summarized earlier, is typical of peoples who herd animals for their livelihood, as do the Bedouin of the Middle East in modern times (chap. 2). This lifestyle is nomadic because shepherds constantly have to follow the available grass and water with their herds.

The pastoral way of life, found in many parts of the world, has some common characteristics. One is a strong pattern of male dominance. The men herd the flocks, and the women have no economic activity of significant value to balance it out. The main function of the wife is to produce offspring, especially male offspring. The wives also tend to be either close relatives (often cousins) or slaves.

Brideprice

Prevalent in sedentary societies as well as nomadic ones is the brideprice, sometimes also known as dowry, consisting of expensive gifts to the bride and to her family, normally negotiated between the two families before the marriage. The more desirable the bride, the higher the brideprice she commands.

Westerners tend to see a brideprice as buying the woman, a commercial transaction and therefore demeaning. People who practice paying and receiving a brideprice, however, often see it as an honor to the bride and as a significant marriage stabilizer and enhancer.

In areas of Africa where cows are used as the traditional payment of brideprice, for example, the prospective groom must first convince his own family of the validity of the union he is proposing. If they agree, his extended family contributes the twenty or thirty cows required, typically according to rather specific formulas which assign such responsibility. So many animals are provided by the parents and perhaps older siblings, so many by certain uncles and aunts, and so many by other relatives.

Thus, the contributing relatives all have vested interests in the successful continuation of the union and do not look kindly upon efforts to dissolve it on trivial grounds because in trivial cases the cattle are not returned. For them, a divorce would mean supplying another brideprice for the man when he marries again, and they certainly do not want to do that so they pressure the husband to make the marriage work.

On the bride's side, the cows received are likewise spread out among members of the extended family, again according to tribal custom. Should a wife want to get out of the union, all the relatives have to return the cows received from the husband's family, cows which they may have already used to pay brideprice for men in their own family. If even one of the relatives refuses to return his share, the marriage annulment becomes more or less impossible.

Levirate and Other Required or Preferred Marriages

In biblical society, the overriding reason for levirate marriage was primogeniture. The family had to be sure that the family name and lineage were preserved through the firstborn son.

In Africa, however, levirate marriages are quite common for two other reasons. Since a family has already paid the brideprice for a woman, and if she is still of child-bearing age, it is best for a brother of the dead husband to take her rather than to pay an additional brideprice for a different wife. Furthermore, the levirate serves as an insurance policy for the woman's old age. If she has no children of her own to take care of her, the levirate requires a younger brother or other close relative to marry her and provide for her.

Communal Recognition of Marriage

Some community elements described earlier for Hebrew weddings are duplicated in one form or another, from society to society. Family and community involvement in the decision to marry, betrothal, processions of varying length, a ceremony, feasting, and dancing are common around the world.

Cultures differ in the use of writing in connection with marriage arrangements. As in the later Jewish stages, after Old Testament times, some cultures formalize marriage with a written authorization or certificate. Our own society, for example, requires a license—legal permission for a marriage to take place. Once they go through the wedding ceremony of their choice, the couple then receives an official marriage certificate. Should the marriage be dissolved by means of divorce or annulment, the society again gives them certificates to that effect.

Modern Christian Marriage

Christians consider marriage to be a sacred institution. In fact, the Catholic tradition places it among the sacraments.[2] However, nowhere does the Bible explicitly call it so, but rather it uses marriage to symbolize the intimate relationship between God and God's people. It is a metaphor complex upon which many teachings about the Christian church were built.

The Old Testament sometimes speaks of Israel as God's wife.

> Your Creator will be like a husband to you—
> the LORD Almighty is his name (Is 54:5 GNB).

> Then once again [Israel] will call me her husband . . .
> Israel, I will make you my wife;
> I will be true and faithful;
> I will show you constant love and mercy
> and make you mine for ever (Hos 2:16–19 GNB).

Israel's lack of faithfulness to God therefore sometimes came to be spoken of as adultery, and thus sin in general was frequently pictured as marital infidelity. The imagery in the early part of Hosea, for example, is built on this metaphor.

> My children, plead with your mother—though she is no longer a wife to me, and I am no longer her husband. Plead with her to stop her adultery and prostitution. . . . I will not show mercy to her children; they are the children of a shameless prostitute. She herself said, "I will go to my lovers" (Hos 2:2 GNB).

Later, marriage became a metaphor for the relationship of Christ with the church. Paul patterned his words concerning marriage on that metaphor.

> Wives must submit themselves completely to their husbands just as the church submits itself completely to Christ.

---

[2]The Catholic view of marriage as a sacrament rests upon an interpretation of the word "mystery" in Ephesians 5:32 (Coenen, Beyreuther, and Bietenhard 1979:199).

Husbands, love your wives just as Christ loved the church and gave his life for it (Eph 5:24–25 GNB).

In one of Jesus' parables, the end time when Christ will return is spoken of as a marriage feast when the bridegroom comes (Mt 25:1–13).

Theological Implications of Cultural Change

In the West, no longer are marriages arranged by family members. No longer do prospective grooms send for far-away cousins they have never met to be brides. No longer do we pay a brideprice to ensure the family line or keep the couple together. Instead, in our modern Western Christian world our emphasis is based almost exclusively on love between two individuals for each other with relatively little family involvement. Under this arrangement, the marriage bond has become increasingly fragile, and third world societies that are used to arranged marriages find Western marriage to be precarious.

So, are our marriages biblical? Yes, if we are thinking about the biblical emphasis on forming a family. That feature is shared by almost all cultures. But no, if we are thinking about the kind of family, and how it is organized, or how marriage is achieved. Such features depend on local circumstances, local culture, local worldview.

Are our marriages Christian? That depends on whether or not the union blesses God and is blessed by God. It has nothing to do with the form of the ceremony. Western marriage ceremonies, copied all over the world—complete with white gowns which the families cannot afford—do not make the ceremony a Christian one. In fact, foreign marriage patterns, whether Western or biblical, may be profoundly misunderstood as Christians of other cultures adopt them.

Missionaries to the Chulupi in Paraguay once asked me for help to ascertain why husbands and wives who were married and living faithfully together were coming to confess that they were having sexual intercourse. Whenever communion was to be celebrated, about once a quarter, dozens of Christian couples came to the missionaries to confess intercourse between husbands and wives—not infidelity. The missionaries could not understand what was happening.

In contrast to Western society, where we consider the male to be the sexual aggressor, or at least the initiator, in Chulupi society the female took the initiative. Every evening when a nomadic group was not on a march but was resting comfortably at some place, all the unattached men who were interested in sex would start dancing in a large circle in the moonlight. Gradually, one after the other, the unattached women placed themselves behind the men they chose and, as the dancing became more heated, put their hands on the hips of the men with whom they wanted a sexual engagement.

The Chulupi thought they avoided conception if they did not sleep repeatedly with the same individual. Thus, as long as a woman was choosing a different sex partner every night or two, she did not expect to get pregnant. If she did become pregnant anyhow, she put a handful of sand in the baby's mouth to kill it when it was born because it had no sociological father. The Chulupi had strong feelings against bringing bastards into this world.

When a woman began to choose the same man repeatedly for sexual encounters, she was indicating that she was interested in him as a husband. If he was amenable to her approaches, they stayed together and that constituted the first stage in a Chulupi marriage.

Some significant additional steps followed. For example, when the woman gave birth to her first child after the union, the husband had eight days in which to make it a permanent marriage. He did so by finding a nest of wild honey, killing a squirrel, slipping off its skin, filling the skin with honey, and bringing it to the woman who had just given birth. This showed that he was willing to be the baby's sociological father and her permanent husband.

If that was done, the woman had the baby's earlobe pierced on the eighth day. Until then the child had not entered the Chulupi tribal covenant, was not considered a human being, and could be killed. Thereafter, however, any neglect or harm was serious and should the baby die, might be considered murder.

Since the Chulupi were nomadic, a woman often gave birth while the group was traveling. She dropped behind, and gave birth in a squatting position over a hole in the sand. If she did not intend to keep the baby, she waited until the afterbirth had dropped on top of it, and covered it all with sand. If she kept the baby, this indicated to her man that she was interested in a permanent marriage. He then had to make up his mind about performing the squirrel-and-honey ceremony.

After the honey ceremony, the husband could not have intercourse with his wife because she had to dedicate herself to building the infant's soul. The process took from three to five years of lactation, during which the husband satisfied his sexual needs with unattached women who selected him in the nightly dancing around the campfire. After the baby had been weaned, the woman informed her husband, and a festival marked the return of the husband to his wife.

When I was investigating the missionaries' question about the married couples confessing intercourse, I found that I could talk with the men, but Chulupi men and women did not talk about sex with each other. So as a male, I could not possibly get the women's point of view. I had to ask the missionary wife to do the research, suggesting she invite a couple of Chulupi nursing mothers in for a cup of tea. Before she met with them, I spent three evenings discussing sex practices in explicit detail with the missionary husband

and wife, a sort of case hardening to enable her to talk to the Chulupi women about their sexual behavior and understanding.

When the Chulupi women did come, the missionary wife was too nervous to say anything. Even a statement about the weather seemed loaded. So she just sat quiet, serving refreshments. After a short period of silence, one of the Chulupi women opened the conversation and asked the missionary wife, "Does God want us to have more than one baby at the breast?" And from then on the Chulupi women gushed forth with their problems.

They said, "Now that we have become Christians, the men don't go back to the single women because the missionary teaches them to be faithful to their wives. When our husbands stay with us, they eventually want to sleep with us. We fight them off for a while, but finally we let them sleep with us. We then get pregnant again even while we are nursing, so before we have finished building the soul of one child, we are nursing another one. We don't believe that God wants us to be nursing two babies at once. We don't believe that God wants to build only half a soul in each child. We feel that we are going to produce a race of bad people because we have so many children with half-built souls."

Missionaries had tried to teach a form of marriage behavior without understanding or dealing with the worldview of the people they were trying to influence. The new behavior therefore made no sense, and people saw the consequences as disastrous. This new marriage behavior was not "Christian," therefore, because it did not have Christian meaning for the people who were told to do it. Instead, it forced them into what they saw as radical immorality, and gave them no foundation for a new morality.

Culture change through time—as we have seen it in biblical marriage customs—and culture variation all over the world derives from people's presuppositions and is usually expressed in ways that people find fitting. That does not mean that all customs everywhere are equally loving, equally kind, equally appropriate for God's people; but growing in the will of God means that presuppositions must evolve and worldviews must develop, a profound process of culture change, deeper than the behavior changes themselves, important as they may be.

18

The Shifting God(s)
of Western Christianity

Western Christians, especially missionaries from the West, have always declared that they worship and proclaim only one God, the God of the Bible, the God of the whole world. However, in spite of this theological ideal, in actuality Western Christians—including evangelical Christians—commonly indulge in spiritual promiscuity with gods other than the God of the universe. Much like ancient Israel in Canaan, we, too, radically diminish God's place in our worldview and in our lives, substituting various gods from our cultural environment.

Of course, the nearly universal modern awareness of the whole physical world, and even of outer space, has helped Western Christians shake much of the territorial linkage of God which we saw in many world religions and also in early Israel (chaps. 7, 8). Western Christians do believe in a geographically universal God who should be made known to people everywhere. But that is not the whole story.

The Diminution of God

Western culture, with its emphases on science and technology, has for decades been in the process of eliminating God's involvement in ever larger areas of human concern like weather, agriculture, economic well-being, medicine, mental illness, and almost everything else (part 3, introduction). Bonhoeffer spoke of the God of Western religion as a *Deus ex machina*, an artificial element introduced into human thinking to provide quick, superficial solutions. People use this God to provide the answers and explanations beyond the point at which their understanding fails. But such a God is constantly being pushed farther and farther back as our secular knowledge advances.

[According to Julian Huxley] the God hypothesis is no longer of much pragmatic value for our Western interpretation or comprehension of nature and indeed, it often stands in the way of better and truer interpretation. Operationally, "God is beginning to resemble not a ruler but the last fading smile of a cosmic Cheshire Cat" (Robinson 1963:37–38).

A Specialized God of Religion

This diminished God of Western Christianity has become a specialized God, restricted largely to preparing people for the afterlife. This drift seriously troubles most informed third world Christians. In their religious backgrounds, God/gods dealt with all of life, but in the Christianity of the Western missionaries they have been taught to worship a God with a narrow specialization.

I knew a Shona in Zimbabwe (Rhodesia) who was an official in a denominational church, but was increasingly disturbed about his life as a Christian. When he was following his traditional religion, he had lived close to the cave where Mwari 'God' spoke through a woman medium called 'the voice.' People always went there and got specific directions as to which day they should go on a hunt, whether they should go north or south, and whether they should hunt elephant or something else. At planting time they asked Mwari what to plant and when to plant it. The answers were always specific. Christians, on the other hand, have been taught to ask God in prayer, but God did not seem to answer even though they prayed faithfully.

So the troubled Christians had given the missionary a list of things they wanted to know from God, including the questions Mwari had always answered. The missionary, however, had reacted in amazement and said, "You can't expect to get answers from God for these things!" But they needed answers to these questions. Where could they get them? If they could not get them from their Christian God, what was the use of being Christian?

Another time when I was making contact with a translation team, I went out for a walk to think, pray, and see if God would give me direction. Suddenly I became aware that a cluster of Africans was following me. When I walked faster, they walked faster. When I walked more slowly, they walked more slowly. When I turned around and went back to meet them, they stood still.

They asked me if I was the person who had helped an African they knew in another translation project miles from there.

"Yes," I said, "I helped him."

Then they told me their story. One of their daughters was promised in marriage to a bright young man from their village. He got a scholarship and went to a university, after which the government sent him overseas for additional years of training. When the young man came back, he married their daughter, and was given a junior government position in the Ministry of Finance. The young couple then moved into their new home in one of the government highrise apartment buildings in the city.

According to African custom, when relatives visit, the host family feeds and lodges them. In a country village, the hosts draw on their store of food, their garden, their chickens; they also borrow from their extended family and neighbors. What they expend gets roughly balanced out as they visit other people. The city, however, provides attractions which tend to bring relatives for protracted visits in large and disproportionate numbers. The visiting relatives also know, of course, that their hosts get a salary, and therefore seem to be rich. But they know nothing of the expense of living in the city.

As the young couple became established in the capital, dozens of relatives came to spend time with them and to enjoy some of the privileges of having someone famous in the family. They came many at a time and stayed long. The young wife therefore became exceedingly frustrated. She had to provide food, bedding, and room for all these visitors on her husband's inadequate salary, and she despaired because she could not be the good wife her family, her society, and her own sense of propriety demanded of her.

In her depression, she finally took the bus home to her parents, wishing to God that she could get out of this impossible situation. The very next day, her husband got drunk, ran their car into a tree, and killed himself. The moment his wife heard about the accident, she screamed, "I have become a witch! I wished for my husband's death, and now I have killed him!"

The family asked me if I would act as the go-between between them and the missionary. They were all members of the Presbyterian Church, but they did not know whether or not this church had a ritual to dewitch the woman. If it did not, would I then ask for permission for them to go to the African Independent Church, not too far away, which knew how to dewitch? The parents assured me that none of the girl's aunts or grandmothers had been witches, so they were sure that she had just become a witch accidentally, because she had been so distraught. She could be cleansed.

Moved by their sadness, I talked with the missionary, wondering what his personal attitude would be. What would he advise an African family in this predicament to do? Did the Presbyterian Church know how to dewitch an accidental witch?

"No," he said, "the church wouldn't do that!"

Would the mission frown upon such people going to an African Independent Church and having her dewitched? The missionary was convinced that if word ever got out to the African leaders of their church that he had supported such a move, he would be out on his ear, but he said, "Personally, I would quietly encourage them to go to the African Independent Church because our church doesn't have any way of helping them."

Next evening I met the family and told them that they had permission to go to the African Independent Church, but they were not to say anything about it in the Presbyterian church. The specialized God of the Presbyterians was too small, too diminished, to help them.

A Tribal God

In some respects, we give our diminished God many of the characteristics which prophets of ancient Israel and New Testament writers sought for centuries to help the Israelites outgrow. Israel struggled to shake its understanding of Yahweh as a tribal God and to learn to see God as the God of all peoples (chaps. 8, 15). And when Jesus read the Scripture in a Nazareth synagogue, people spoke well of him until he implied that the Messiah was for Gentiles as well as Jews. Then the same people were enraged (Lk 4:22–30).

That struggle to grow out of a tribal God continued in the early Christian church, and Paul's conviction about this matter was sounded with great clarity: "There is no difference between Jews and Gentiles, between slaves and free men, between men and women; you are all one in union with Christ Jesus" (Gal 3:28 GNB). But although we proclaim that God is the God of all peoples worldwide, we shrink God down into our own parochial deity.

Politically, God is the God of our own nation, whichever nation that may be. God is partisan, fighting on our side—the right side! North American Christians fight German Christians, each convinced that their tribal God vindicates them. Christians often are the first to demand a strong military force to protect their country from other peoples and their gods. Our country is "God's country."

Religiously, God is made in the image of our particular biblical interpretation. We see our own understanding of God as biblical; that of other Christians as not. We consider the reflection of God we see dimly in the mirror to be the only true reflection. Those images which others see in the same glass are gods to be destroyed.

I have met Bible translators who considered themselves and their work so close to God and so sacred, that they hesitated to let me look at it, even though they wanted the Bible Society to publish it. In one case, I sat on the doorstep of a mission house for three mornings while the missionaries inside debated about whether I was Christian enough to look at their work. In another I was told outright that they could not put the fruit of their spiritual labors before an "unsanctified" outsider.

How do we identify a tribal God? Kosuke Koyama, a perceptive Eastern theologian, has challenged the Western Christian church with examples of its modern day idolatry, speaking personally and convincingly from his own experience of tribal God worship in Japan (Koyama 1984). He describes how early Japan was polytheistic, but how the nation made a dramatic religious change from polytheism to monotheism toward the end of the nineteenth century. The new monotheism, however, was not a loyalty to a universal God but rather to the tribal God of the Japanese people, a God whose manifestation on earth was the Japanese emperor. When Koyama became a Christian he made a conscious shift from serving that tribal God to serving the God of all the world.

Some of the same symptoms of tribal God worship which he outlines from Japan are conspicuous in Christian groups as well. I have seen them in churches of my own Mennonite Brethren denomination.[1] The evangelical church in America often dismisses any criticism of "Christian" capitalism that comes from socialist countries as lies, not able to see that the church is enmeshed in the overwhelming capitalist machine that helps keep the third world trapped in poverty while the West is living at too high a standard. When less fortunate people say so, they are resented as ungrateful liars. Western Christians have a higher standard of living because the tribal God is blessing the people who are doing God's will.

The tribal God encourages "western movie theology" in which the "good guys" crusade against the "bad guys," as we saw constantly in the Cold War. Western movie theology is also apparent in the current "pro-choice" and "pro-life" debate. Some of the "right to life" people are even willing to engage in violence and killing in order to make their point. After all they are their tribal God's "good guys" doing their tribal God's will.

We Mennonites seldom crusade for the truth with physical aggression, but rather we use fierce verbal attacks, as western movie theology colors our Mennonite Brethren relationship with other Mennonite groups, for example. A long-term feud has been raging between supporters of Grace Bible College (Nebraska) and Bethel College (Kansas) of the Mennonite Church. It began with the tension between the educational philosophies of a Bible institute versus a liberal arts college. But over the years it has grown into a struggle between the fundamentalistic, evangelical, soul-winning outreach type of people and more liberal, or liberal arts college types, who probably have a humanistic tinge.

Within the Mennonite Church of late, furthermore, certain evangelical churches or groups have tended to form clusters of worship apart from the mother church. They have not actually started a separate denomination but nevertheless fellowship only among themselves. Ignoring our traditional

---

[1]My knowledge of the Mennonite situation is partial, and therefore all statements I make about the Mennonite Church and the Mennonite Brethren Church should be considered questions, regardless of whether they are made in the indicative or the interrogative mode. I feel that the indicative statements I make are valid, but I do not presume to know how fully valid they are, nor are all general statements universally valid.

Mennonite emphasis that the lived gospel takes precedence over the professed gospel, these "evangelical" people are claiming that the Mennonite Church has drifted into "works," doing relief work and providing disaster help, but not emphasizing soul-winning enough.

Tension over the Mennonite Central Committee has been raging in all Mennonite branches since it started in the 1920s to aid starving Mennonites in Southern Russia. As fundamentalism has spread in the churches, a segment has suggested that the Mennonite Central Committee fosters the social gospel, since it emphasizes helping over soul-winning.

Fear of the social gospel is certainly no prerogative of Mennonites, of course. It characterizes much of American evangelicalism which has made purity of doctrine more important than purity of life.

The tribal God, furthermore, encourages a "success theology" approach to life. Japan's God helped Japan defeat Russia and Korea, helped the Japanese occupy Manchuria, encouraged them to invade China. Each new victory showed that they were doing God's will, and that God was solidly on their side.

Success theology has also mushroomed in Mennonite circles with increasing affluence. As individual Mennonites accumulate wealth, many interpret their material accumulations to be a direct result of their right relationship with God.

Perhaps the current trend toward building bigger and fancier sanctuaries is a public testimony to success theology. Is the increasing portion of church income which is spent for local church operation an indication of how much higher we rate in our tribal God's eyes than do the poor and the unchurched, or even than do our more numerous fellow Mennonites in the third world?

The tribal God reserves the choicest, if not all the benefits for God's own people. I observed a bitter struggle between the missionaries and the Mennonite colonists who had immigrated to Paraguay. The colonists had been exempted from military service because of their pacifist stance, so the missionaries felt that Paraguayan and tribal converts should be permitted to claim the same military exemption. The colonists, on the other hand, feared that they would jeopardize privileges that were exclusively their own if they shared their exemption with these new Mennonites.

I also remember standing at the train station, about to leave for South America as a missionary, when a mission board member gave me his final words of counsel: *"Aber die Wehrlosigkeit die lass nur zu hause."* 'Now regarding nonresistance, that you had better leave at home.'

In fact, a senior Mennonite Brethren leader recently revealed that the Board of Missions used to struggle bitterly with this issue. Many prominent board members felt that we would endanger our privileges at home and our welcome abroad if we shared with others this unique blessing which God had entrusted to the Mennonite people.

At an international conference between American and third-world churches, leaders from the third world tried to draw the attention of the conference delegates to the affluence of the American church. In reply, they met outrage from the Western church leaders about their ingratitude. Were not Western churches already supplying missionaries, hospitals, schools, and other ministries? And when would the third-world churches be satisfied with what the Western churches were doing for them? Bolstered by the success theology of their tribal God, the Western church leaders did not hear the cry about disparity at all.

Tribal God worship fabricates its own definition of what is holy. For Japan, the emperor was declared so holy that he became unapproachable to ordinary people. And such "homemade holiness," Koyama says, is what the Bible calls graven images or idols.

The general evangelical movement, including large segments of the Mennonite Church, the General Conference Mennonite Church, and the Mennonite Brethren Church, has made the Bible holy in a much more parochial sense than the fact that it is holy because it is God's revelation to people. Homemade tribal-God holiness surrounds the Bible with fences to make it unapproachable except as mediated through tribal theology. It is not holy because God is holy but because it has been declared "inerrant" and "verbally inspired" and is interpreted literally in those passages which appeal to the homemade holiness makers but is spiritualized in the rest.

The "evangelical" Mennonites, including the Mennonite Brethren, have also made themselves "holier than thou" by their emphasis on the Bible, evangelism, and conversion. When I was chair of the Mennonite Colleges Cultural Conference Committee during my Tabor College days, I was frequently ribbed by Mennonites who were not Mennonite Brethren with remarks like "And what do the 'converted' have to say about this?" or "Certainly you Mennonite Brethren ought to be able to find at least one Bible proof for that." In fact, all the larger Mennonite groupings have numerous holier-than-average cliques.

On the more general North American Christian scene, faith missions see themselves as holier than denominational missions. Evangelicals feel themselves holier than the ecumenical wing of the church. The Full Gospel churches feel themselves holier than those who do not have their "full gospel."

The tribal God exempts God's chosen people from criticism because the will of God and the will of God's people always coincide. Because their God doesn't criticize them, no one inside the group may do so, and outgroup criticism can be shrugged off as sour grapes or lies. Christians like Koyama were considered traitors in Imperial Japan. For similar reasons white South Africans shrugged off outside criticism of apartheid and rewarded internal criticism with a generous dose of the "wrath of God."

All Mennonite groups are sensitive to internal criticism, but Mennonite Brethren have been among the most sensitive. Rudy Wiebe's novel *Peace Shall Destroy Many* (Wiebe 1962a) caused intense resentment when it first appeared. He described a fictional Mennonite Brethren Church leader who exerted destructive influence on a fictional church and its young people. At least a dozen church leaders felt that he had written about them and had slandered them personally. Even more communities felt that he had aired their dirty linen in public.

Likewise, Wiebe again aroused anger with his fictitious correspondence between Peter and Petronius (Wiebe 1962b). Peter was a believing member of "God's chosen people," whose mouth dripped piety, and Petronius was an unbelieving Gentile who was incredulous about the situation in which Peter found himself. For example, when Peter insisted that he represented the salt of the earth, Petronius wanted to know why God was interested in having such large piles of Mennonite salt isolated in Winnipeg and in the Fraser Valley of British Columbia. Why didn't God spread out his salt more if God wanted Mennonites to be the salt of the earth?

This God's-people-don't-criticize-God's-people attitude has been highly noticeable among Mennonites who write their own history. I look in vain for really critical internal historical reviews of the Mennonite Brethren denomination. Recently someone read a conference paper realistically depicting problems in the Mennonite colonies in South Russia, but other participants decried the author's negativism and his lack of appreciation for all the good things that had been accomplished.

The tribal God enables "God's people" to rephrase "I don't like you" as "God wants me/us to tell you that God doesn't like you." The Japanese looked down on the Koreans and Chinese, feeling keenly that their tribal God wanted them to remain separate from these barbarians. They justified their cruel treatment and derogatory statements in the press by the belief that God didn't like these people either.

Mennonites look on non-Mennonite immigrants who come into Mennonite areas in much the same way. In 1948 I remember overhearing two elderly gentlemen in the cloakroom of a church talking, and one of them saying, "You know, it is very difficult to go to church nowadays. You have to watch or you find yourself sitting next to one of those garlic-stinking Hungarians." Today an even stronger feeling exists against Asian immigrants from the Indian subcontinent, especially the Sikhs.

Koyama concludes his sobering analysis with a series of questions posed by a Sri Lankan theologian:

> Why is it that after hundreds of thousands of eucharistic celebrations, Christians continue to be as selfish as before? Why have the 'Christian' peoples been the most cruel colonizers of human history? Why is the gap of

income, wealth, knowledge, and power growing in the world today—and that in favor of the 'Christian' peoples? Why is it that persons and people who proclaim eucharistic love and sharing deprive the poor people of the world of food, capital, employment, and even land? Why do they prefer cigarettes and liquor to food and drink for the one-third of humanity that goes hungry to bed each night? Why are cars, cosmetics, pet dogs, horses, and bombs preferred to human children? (Balasuriya 1977:3).

Rivals to the Universal God

We have been discussing the diminution of God into a specialized God of religion, on the one hand, and into a tribal God, on the other. The diminished, specialized, tribal God of modern Western Christianity thus leaves a great deal of room in our lives for other gods to take over. Western Christians therefore happily worship gods which are rivals to the God of the universe. We are idolaters.

Idolatry is the elevation of a preliminary concern to ultimacy. Something essentially conditioned is taken as unconditional, something essentially partial is boosted into universality, and something essentially finite is given infinite significance (Tillich 1953 1:16).

Wealth as God

The Western secular, materialistic and scientific worldview finds the God of the Bible to be largely irrelevant, most blatantly so in the area of economics. When we read the specifics of Old Testament economic law, such as giving back the land to its original owners every fiftieth year (Lev 25:10–13,25–28), charging no interest on money loaned (Lev 25:35–38; Deut 23:19–20; Neh 5:7–10), giving whatever to whoever asks for it (Mt 5:42), and never asking back some item that has been borrowed (Lk 6:30–35), we get the uncomfortable feeling that the God of the Bible knows very little about a viable economic system.

In my younger days, when I was a short-term pastor of a country church, I dropped in on a farmer one Sunday afternoon as he was just beginning his evening chores, with dozens of cows to milk. In mock seriousness I reminded him that God had said that he should work for six days, and that on the seventh he should rest.

"Whoever wrote that knew nothing about cows," he retorted.

However, the issue runs much deeper than that. Third world Christians who have lived in America or who know missionaries well perceive that wealth rather than God is the organizing principle in secularized Western culture, including Western Christianity. The massive economic hole we sense in the universal God leaves a lot of room for an economic idol—for wealth as God.

I was giving a lesson on culture as a structure to some South American Jivaro (Ecuador), and was using the wheel, its hub and its spokes as a model. I had discussed nine areas of human culture as possible hubs and/or spokes in the wheel of culture, and asked if they thought any of these were the hub of the missionary's way of life. Without a moment's hesitation and in one voice they all said, "money." (I had defined economics as how people feel about money, and how they earn and spend it.)

I objected, "But is that what the missionaries talk about?" The people answered, "Of course not, they talk about religion" (defined as how people pray and what they do about God and the spirit world).

To check on whether this reply was accidental, I asked the Jivaro if they had ever heard about communism. Yes, they had. Thirteen tons of Marxist literature had just arrived in their area. Secret classes were being held where they could study it.

Could they venture a guess as to what might be the hub of communism? A little more hesitantly, they said, "Money and chieftainship" (I had defined politics as how people choose a chief and how that chief commands his people). I think few of us could have given a better definition of communism than this characterization as state capitalism (Loewen 1975:xi–xii).

Wealth is not a new God. Jesus recognized wealth as a rival God in his time: "No one can serve two masters. . . . You cannot serve God and wealth" (Mt 6:24; Lk 16:13 NRSV).[2] The apostle Paul also saw the love of money growing in his day, long before capitalism achieved the dominance it has in the West. He pronounced it to be a form of idolatry (Eph 5:5; Col 3:5 GNB). Jesus and Paul did not mention knowledge, physical skill, appearance, family nobility, nationalism, or occupation, all of which can also be gods to us. But wealth and property most quickly act like deities in our lives. They control and direct us.

John White says the twentieth-century church seems to have forgotten to which master she belongs, "painting herself like a hussy in her silly pursuit of Lord Mammon." Or, to use another image, "the church has gone a-whoring after a golden cow."

> Not a calf, if you please, but a cow. I call her a golden cow because her udders are engorged with liquid gold, especially in the West where she grazes in meadows lush with greenbacks. Her priests placate her by slaughtering Godly principles upon whose blood she looks with tranquil satisfaction. Anxious rows of worshipers bow down before their buckets. Although the gold squirts endlessly, the worshipers are trembling lest the supply of sacrificial victims should one day fail to appease her (White 1979:67–68).

---

[2] The god of wealth is called mammon in the KJV. *Mammon* is the Greek word for wealth.

Materialism as God

Despite the cries of those who worship their tribal God, the East/West Cold War was not between the kingdom of God and the "evil empire," but between two kinds of materialism.

> Communist materialism is doctrinaire and oppressive. Capitalist materialism is pragmatic and cancerous. Communist materialism claims that matter is all there is. Western materialism assumes that matter is all that matters. Many people who would never consider themselves to be materialists in the strict sense of the term, nevertheless live as though material things were of supreme importance. . . .
>
> My definition of Western materialism might appear to exclude Christians. No Christian would agree (that is, if the matter were put to him or her as an abstract proposition) that matter is all that matters for our very faith negates the assertion. Yet if our behavior (as distinct from our verbal profession) is examined, many of us who call ourselves Christians begin to look more like materialists. We talk of heaven, but we strive for things.
>
> Yet Christians are rarely happy as materialists. Heaven tugs at us too vigorously. We find ourselves apologizing for our new cars or our larger houses. This tug of war renders most Christians ill at ease and at times ineffective (White 1979:38–39).

Technology as God

Technology, the art of tool-making, is one of the wonderful capacities with which God has endowed human creatures. However, both nations and people can grant technology a life of its own, set it on its own course, and make it their God. People convince themselves that what technology can do, it must do, and do it for them.

Some people demand that we adopt indiscriminately the requirements of modern technology. To them unrestricted technology offers a better life, more luxury, more prosperity and better health, not to mention solutions to the multitude of the world's current problems. Others entrust to unhampered technological development their deepest security needs, believing that superior weapons of technology can save them from the hands of all possible enemies.

For the worshipers of technology it is sacrilegious to think that we should spend less of our resources on technological development and more on human welfare. We need more powerful weapons with which to fight our wars, and we search for technological ways to protect ourselves from the guns on our streets. When we are threatened by an epidemic like AIDS, we turn to technology to find a prevention and cure, but do little to minister to the victims. Our God of technology is not satisfied unless we replace our cars and our computers with more "advanced" ones every five years or less.

The Church as God

For some people, some groups, some denominations, the specialized God of religion has begotten a son, a junior God, the church—my church, my denomination, my community of believers. When the church is God, the community of those who hold common beliefs and practices and who submit to a common rule becomes the ultimate object of trust and loyalty. The church becomes the source of truth. What the church teaches is believed and is believed because it is what the church teaches. The church is trusted to be the judge of what is right and wrong and the guarantor of salvation.

When the church is God, to have faith in God is to have faith in the church. To turn to God is to be converted to the church because the two are identical. The way to God is through the church. The community that once pointed to the faithfulness of God now points to itself as the faithful representative of God. God and the church have become so identified that often the word "God" means the collective representation of the church. God is defined as the one in whom the church believes.

Church history is reinterpreted from the account of the mighty deeds of God in creation, judgment, and redemption, to the story of the church. Church history becomes holy history, an account of the deeds whereby the special community was formed and its rites established. Church rituals, instead of being the dramatic reenactments of what God has done, is doing, and will do for people, become celebrations of the deeds of the church or its functionaries.

The unity of the church, the holiness of the church, and the universality of the church are valued not so much because they reflect the unity, holiness, and universality of one God, but as ends to be sought for the sake of the church. They are virtues to be celebrated because in them the true church makes its appearance. The God to whom reference is made in every act of worship and in every proclamation of the church's message is still acknowledged, but is merged into the church as God (Niebuhr 1943:58–59; Niebuhr 1951:68).

Evangelical Protestants do not hesitate to point to the Roman Catholic church as being the God of Catholics. But especially in evangelical churches which began as small separate movements and continued to be ingrown because of their differences from the world around them, the church has likewise often become God. The small body of fellow believers bonds into a group which gets its life, its sustenance, its identity, from the church. Similarly, larger, more historical churches whose God has been diminished, seek to fill the gap by making the church into a God and thus fall into self-worship.

Mutual Reinforcement of the Gods

We have other gods as well, but those already mentioned illustrate the phenomenon of the shifting gods in the West. As the God of the universe, to whom we still give lip service, has been specialized to religion and particularized to a welter of conflicting interests of nation, denomination, and the individual, three other mutually reinforcing, powerful gods fill the gap left by this diminution.

The God of materialism supplies the motivation. Consumed with the worship of things, goods, belongings, we have turned to technology to provide them for us, and as technology has performed many miracles for us in this century, we worship it also as our God. The God of technology, in turn, rewards some of us with wealth, which makes us comfortable and gives us security, so we worship it, too. The God of wealth, in turn, feeds the God of materialism, making it possible for us to acquire the goods we crave (Goudzwaard 1984:13; Walsh and Middleton 1953:131–39).

So we have a trinity of mutual reinforcement among these three great gods of the gap, three great idols to which we have built our altars, and in whose slavery we live. And that trinity has been co-opted into the service both of our specialized God of religion and of our tribal God. The materialism-technology-wealth trinity of idols nourishes the God of religion and the tribal God, making them more powerful, and us more comfortable in them. The God of the church, spawned by the God of religion, is especially dependent on this trinity of idols and governed by it. And all look to the tribal God for security against other tribal gods and the people who worship them.

The priest in the pulpit, the professor at the lectern, the politician behind the bully pulpit, and the military officers' pronouncements all reverberate in harmony and national unity, and patriotism swells to new heights (Goudzwaard 1984:40). When all these idols cross-fertilize each other and reinforce each other, a strong military procurement can produce enormous economic prosperity and the feeling of national security for all (Goudzwaard 1984:40).

We see our idols more clearly when we examine ourselves in light of other cultures, including biblical cultures. They, too, have their idols, of course, but if we see only their idols and not our own, we do not see much of the truth. Peoples of other cultures sometimes need to see their idols through our eyes, and sometimes we need to see ours through theirs.

19

Looking at Demon Possession
from within Western Categories

Demon possession and exorcism are deeply embedded in the biblical worldview and are equally powerful in the experience of many non-Western Christians (chaps. 11, 12). Yet for a person with a Western worldview they are perhaps the most difficult to understand of all the phenomena discussed in this book. In fact, many Western Christians have a schizophrenic view, believing in the phenomenon when they read about it in the Bible, but not when they hear it suggested in modern life.

I do not believe that such intellectual and spiritual schizophrenia is healthy. In this chapter, therefore, I would like to attempt an understanding of demon possession and exorcism from within a Western perspective.

Two Current Western Approaches to Exorcism

Because of my limited experience in exorcism, I will first summarize and critique two current Western models, a few elements of which I will then use in my proposed model. They are the Wimber-White model, as developed in lectures by John White (1987), and the M. Scott Peck model (1983).

The Wimber-White Model of Exorcism

One of the strongest, most rapidly growing Christian groups which advocate and practice exorcism in North America is the Vineyard Church, until recently led by John Wimber. A prominent member and spokesperson is John White, a psychiatrist. Study of the Wimber-White approach to exorcism is useful here not only for itself but also because it seems to exemplify the current general approach of much North American charismatic Christianity.

It divides reality into two separate domains, the material-natural world and the spiritual-supernatural world, and seeks to blend the spiritual-supernatural worldview of the New Testament with the material-natural worldview of scientifically oriented North American society.

According to the Wimber-White model, mental illness and demon possession—"demonizing" in their terminology—are not the same, and for them the Scriptures themselves clearly make the distinction. Thus, they say, King Saul was obviously demonized (1 Sam 16:23), while David, when he acted out the madman before Achish, the king of Gath (1 Sam 21:10–15), was mimicking ordinary insanity. Rhoda, the maid, is called "mad" when she tells the praying believers that Peter is at the door (Acts 12:15). The man living in the tombs at Gerasa (Lk 8:26–36), however, was clearly demonized (White 1987).

I find this evidence somewhat frivolous. For non-demonic insanity they cite feigned madness in the Old Testament, and a casual incredulous retort in the New. Furthermore, the same word used to describe Rhoda's supposed simple insanity was also used of Jesus by people who said that "he has a demon and is out of his mind" (Jn 10:20 NRSV). Here "out of his mind" and "has a demon" refer to the same phenomenon, expressed in a typical Hebrew doublet.

On the other hand, I agree with White when he chides evangelical churches for limiting the power of the gospel largely to its salvationist dimension, thereby avoiding its therapeutic function. I also agree when he rebukes fundamentalist Christians who see charismatic spiritual manifestations as involving demonic powers. This latter is reminiscent of Jesus' experience when people accused him of operating on Satan's power (Mt 12:22–28; Lk 11:15).

Furthermore, I think that White is right when he says that many cases currently called demonization by charismatics are not really that.[1] He affirms that human sciences are making important advances in their understanding of the way God has designed human beings, and the more we understand this design, he says, the less we have to attribute to demonization.

As a physician and psychiatrist, White asserts that all psychoses probably have physical or chemical causes. For example, a woman officially diagnosed as having paranoid schizophrenia, and with a long history of mental hospital stays, was discovered to have excess fluid in her pericardial sac (the membrane which surrounds the heart), a condition brought on by a thyroid imbalance. When the imbalance was corrected, the excess fluid in the pericardium disappeared, and her symptoms of mental illness also disappeared.

---

[1] In this he is probably in disagreement with Wimber who seems to believe that up to 50% of mental illness cases involve demonization.

In another case, a deluded boy drove his parents from their home at gunpoint and then shot and killed two police officers because he saw them as aliens from outer space "since they had red-glowing eyes." White was able to demonstrate that the boy had a chemical imbalance in the brain. After a week of proper medication, his delusions disappeared, and he was horrified at the evil he had done.

Charismatics accept in theory the existence of nonmaterial spirits, but in the Wimber-White model they relegate them in fact to the ever shrinking residue of what has not been explained by modern science. White's chemical answers to psychosis, which are comforting and satisfying to the average North American, would still leave Africans with the most basic questions which arise from their worldview: Which spirits set these imbalances in motion, and why? They also leave secular Westerners with their logical question which arises out of their worldview: Why not assume that the shrinking residue of supernatural is really material as well? In spite of their profession to the contrary, North American charismatics still operate on the "God of the gap" principle, and not on a truly spirit/spiritual model such as exhibited by Africans or as seen in the New Testament.

The Peck Model of Exorcism

M. Scott Peck is a psychiatrist and lecturer. He grew up in the traditional naturalistic worldview of the North American scene, then dabbled in Buddhist and Islamic mysticism, but finally "made a firm Christian commitment" in 1980 (Peck 1983:11).

Peck points out that the general North American view of reality has no room for the supernatural; 99% of all psychiatrists and the majority of ministers do not believe that a personal devil exists, but all do firmly believe in an evil principle in the world (Peck 1983:182).

Unlike most psychiatrists, however, Peck defines psychotherapy as a form of exorcism—but with the basic difference that exorcism proper involves the use of power which regular psychotherapy seeks to avoid (Peck 1978:185). In fact, he feels that no one individual alone has either enough love or enough power to exorcise demons, but that five or more people are necessary for effective exorcising. He describes two cases of exorcism in which seven and nine people, respectively, cooperated in working for several days from twelve to sixteen hours a day to achieve the exorcism (Peck 1983:189). However, Peck also cautions that the use of power should not violate the victim's self. Power may be employed only with the patient's express permission (Peck 1983:187).

Since demons represent "the spirit of lies and deceit," exorcists must be careful to address either the healthy part of the patient's self or the sick subconscious (the demons), but not both. They should never permit flip-flops, as this is a standard device in what Peck calls the demonic confusion process (1983:195, 209).

Exorcists must provide an accepting, loving, self-expending social context in order for exorcism and healing to take place (Peck 1978:186, 199, 208). This warm but power-charged environment is absolutely essential because loneliness and fear that no one loves them are the principal reasons people let Satan or evil overwhelm them. Thus, the healing context must have enough love, acceptance and strength to permit the demonized person to risk letting go of his "crutch of evil" (Peck 1983:199). The community of love and acceptance must be truly Christian in function, though not necessarily so in name. Thus at the two exorcisms he describes, the participants included self-professed agnostics, nominal Christians, and practicing Christians, but all were people who could truly love, accept, and give themselves on behalf of the suffering victim (Peck 1983:199 fn.). Peck adds that fundamentalist or moralistic Christians are often too judgmental to be able to form a strong, genuinely loving, and accepting community.

However, Peck also says that the love and power of the exorcist(s) do not ultimately exorcise the demon(s), but rather the patient's own choice to be free. In the final stages of the successful exorcisms he describes, the patients grabbed a crucifix and fervently prayed to be free. No sooner had they expressed their choice to be free, and had taken the step of faith, believing that they would be free, than the release came (Peck 1983:197).

Peck says that 95% of what happened in these demon possessions and exorcisms can be explained by known psychiatric dynamics. However, 5% cannot yet be so explained. While he calls it "The Evil Presence" (Martin 1976; Peck 1983:195–96), and hence classifies it as supernatural, he also says that it may only be the patient's own diseased subconscious. Currently, he says, it is "impossible to discern exactly where the human Shadow[2] leaves off and where the Prince of Darkness begins" (Peck 1983:209–10). This Prince of Darkness, which he also calls "the spirit of lies and unreality," finds truth and reality incomprehensible.

People are beginning to see the possibility of the "unification of science and religion," according to Peck (1978:228). In fact, he proceeds along the road toward a scientific model for 95% of the way (1983:195–96), but then suddenly changes the paradigm and begins to speak about the inexplicable 5% residue as the supernatural.

No human beings currently know how to explain everything in terms of the scientific-psychiatric model. In fact, the area of our ignorance may be

---

[2]By "Shadow" Peck means the negative aspect of humanity, what I call the id, or the tendency toward evil.

much bigger than Peck's 5%. But when he switches models, Peck is repeating the traditional fallacy of using the supernatural—God for good, Satan for evil—to explain our ignorance. Once more we are at the God of the gap. Once more, spirit and evil are relegated to the shrinking unknown. This use of the supernatural to "explain away" the areas of human ignorance, it seems to me, is intellectually dishonest.

The universe we inhabit is real and follows laws and patterns that are predictable, but human beings are generally poor observers of nature and of natural processes. They easily succumb to magic, superstition, and prejudice and, as a result, often see what they want to see instead of what is really there (Peck 1978:195). This leads to dogmatism, religious or scientific, which is an ultimate evil (Peck 1978:222–23). We easily fall into the trap of relating two sequential events as being necessarily causally related, seeing miracles where none exist, as when we pray over a swollen joint which later becomes normal (Peck 1978:231).

However, to say "the patient died of a meningococcal infection" is to operate at a superficial level. On a deeper level, patients succumb to meningococcal infection only after their usually reliable natural defense—their immune system—fails (Peck 1978:238–39).

Thus Peck does point us toward the basis for developing models which are solidly anchored in the Western scientific worldview—models both for spirit possession/exorcism and for spiritual growth. He suggests models that could eliminate the current Christian schizophrenia over spiritual phenomena.

The Proposed Model

In this spirit of reducing the distance between science and religion, and of working with categories intelligible to Westerners, I would like now to propose an alternative model of evil spirit possession and exorcism, one based entirely on the Western scientific worldview. Human beings still have many "steps of obedience" to master in the process of bringing the divine image they carry to full fruition (Gen 1:27, 2:15, 19). However, we can learn bit by bit what lies beyond the boundary of our current knowledge.

The model which I am proposing posits God who is Spirit (Jn 4:24) as the First Cause which created, organized, and sustains the world as we know it and the human beings that inhabit it. However, the model does not attempt to define or explain God any further, although God remains the actor and sustainer of it all.

This model is limited in an attempt to account for evil, illness, and demon-possession in terms of the material-mechanical premises of the scientific worldview, but without relegating spirit and evil to the shrinking unknown. I face the same unknown, of course, as do White and Peck, but I treat the unknown with the same assumptions as the scientifically verifiable, thus trying to avoid the fallacy of supernatural residue.

Spirit in Culture-Based Worldviews

1. There is no "literal" way of talking about spirits, not even in the Bible. Earth-bound human beings can speak of them only by analogies, metaphors, or models. The words meaning 'spirit' in Hebrew and Greek—*ruach* and *pneuma* respectively—are themselves not literal but analogies or metaphors. In both languages, the literal meaning is 'wind,' the extended meaning 'breath,' and the figurative meaning 'spirit.' In fact, in Jesus' day conservative Jews like the Sadducees did not believe that such a category as "spirit" even existed (Acts 23:8).

2. Each culture operates within a usually unspoken worldview which functions as a comprehensive model to explain the way the universe is and how human beings operate in it. Worldviews are not reality but functional models of reality; and because humanity still has not mastered all there is to be learned about God's handiwork, all of them are incomplete (chap. 1).

3. Different functional models of the same reality are often held by peoples of different cultures. For example, when a crowded fast-traveling bus suddenly leaves the mountain road and hurtles down the mountain side, killing all its passengers, both Africans and North Americans ask, "What happened?"

When North Americans, who operate on a material-mechanical model of reality, learn that the outside front tire blew out, or that a steering rod broke, they feel confident that they know what caused the accident.

However, such facts do not satisfy Africans, who operate on a spirit model of reality. Mechanical failures are merely symptoms, or the instruments by which the accident was carried out. Africans want to know, "Who caused the tire to blow out or the tie-rod to break, and why?" They therefore consult the spirit world of deceased ancestors to learn the spiritual causes of the accident. They feel satisfied only when the ancestors, via a medium, give them such an answer as that the soul-of-the-dead of the bus driver's great-grandmother was warning the family that some member had committed a major offense which needed to be corrected (chaps. 7, 11).

4. Both demon possession and exorcism are culture-bound, and culture-bound phenomena must be studied in their cultural context to determine their meanings (Songer 1967:232). Comparing any African or Chinese case of evil spirit possession and exorcism directly with any North American case is a misleading enterprise because the cultures operate within different worldviews. Only after we have been able to define the meaning of a symptom, trait, or action within a specific cultural context can we compare it with behavior having a comparable meaning in another culture. Comparing

specific traits—behavior that is superficially similar—apart from their differing cultural meanings is futile.

5. Because behavior which is embedded in radically different worldviews cannot really be compared, the best we can do is "translate" the meanings.[3] Just as the translator of a text seeks to express the meaning of the text in a radically different language, using the words and grammatical categories of that language, so the interpreter of meanings in an alien worldview should seek to express those meanings in the thought and belief categories of her/his own worldview. Translation, whether of text or worldview, is never perfect. There is always loss in the process. But it is the only way we have of profound understanding across worldviews (Smalley, Vang, and Yang 1990:171–81).

That means that if the categories of evil and spirit phenomena are not to shrink to irrelevance before the growth of scientific knowledge, the biblical worldview metaphors, as well as those of Africans, cannot be imported literally into a Western worldview but must be translated into Western scientific categories to the extent of our ability. And when we do not know Western categories into which they can be translated, we look for them in our own naturalistic terms, and do not relegate what we do not understand to a disembodied shrinking residue of biblical worldview.

Western Christians have long since translated the biblical categories of flat earth with firmament dome over it into a globe with atmosphere and outer space, in keeping with our modern worldview. We no longer question the fact that we do so, even though at one time this process seemed unthinkable to Christians (part 2, introduction). It is that continued process of translation that I am seeking in another domain of divine revelation.

Evil, Demon Possession, and Exorcism

1. Human beings are created in the "image of God" (Gen 1:27), which I locate in a person's unconscious (Peck 1978:243–53).

2. Human beings have been ordained by God to have "dominion" in the created universe (Gen 1:28–30). To me, this means that they have been endowed with the capacity necessary to follow God and to understand the design—material or spiritual—which God built into the universe. Therefore, genuine advancement in human understanding of the natural and social sciences is the God-ordained result of our living out the divine image in us, and the fulfillment of our assigned task of mastering the laws underlying the created universe.

---

[3]"Translate" is used here in a metaphoric sense, of course. "Trans-worldview-ate" would be more precise. Bible translators try not to trans-worldview-ate because the worldviews of the Bible are part of the original message. Interpreters and preachers, however, must do so to bring the word of God to a modern world.

3. Good and evil are both produced by human beings making use of divine energy. When disciplined people, obeying God's design, use divine power rightly, they produce good. By the same token, when undisciplined people willfully or carelessly use God's power outside of God's design, they often produce evil.

4. Human beings have been endowed with the capacity of choice and the ability to distinguish between good and evil. Psychologists, following Freud, call the pull toward the good in a person the superego (others, the unconscious), and the pull toward evil they call the id. Thus, every human being has not only a divine image, but also a capacity for self-will and for disobedience to God's design.

5. Human beings are notorious for their unwillingness to "own" their evil deeds, projecting their guilt on others or on circumstances instead. "Not I," says the man to God, "it was the woman you gave me." "Not I," says the woman, "it was the snake you created who deceived me" (Gen 3:12–13). "Not I," says the culprit, "the devil made me do it."

6. Sooner or later, however, people find that the evil they tried to externalize is really still inside them, so they experience it as an alien presence—an "evil spirit." If the presence of the evil becomes intolerable, they may split it off their ego and treat it as a separate personality, resulting in schizophrenia.

7. Similarly, when a young child is sexually abused by an adult whom it trusts, the child may be unable to cope with the evil experience and so splits off a part of its fragile ego, creating a personality other than itself to experience the evil. This produces multiple personalities.

8. Intense awareness of evil within may make people (both the evil-doer and the evil experiencer) feel utterly evil and totally unlovable. They may therefore retreat from human contact and from reality into the realm of "mental illness."

9. Persons suffering extreme cases of alienation and ego fragmentation experience what the Bible calls "demon possession."

10. Because the demon-possessed individuals feel utterly alone and unlovable, the ice-cold core of evil within them needs to be melted down by selfless acceptance and unlimited love exercised by concerned fellow human beings. But few people have developed such a capacity to love the unlovely. A group of concerned people must pool their love in order to provide enough warmth for enough time so that the bound person can risk letting go of his or her evil.

If the love and acceptance of such a healing community of human beings does reach adequate proportions, then the bound individuals may finally be able to risk letting go of their crutch of evil and to experience the love and acceptance of their fellow human beings and of God.

The Unexplained Five Percent

As for the residue of evil which human beings are still unable to explain in terms of science, I think that it is dishonest to sweep it into a shrinking basket of the supernatural, as I have already said. Instead, I assume a naturalistic explanation which has not yet been found. In that vein, I would like to speculate on some miscellaneous new materialistic insights into God and God's working which may turn out to be helpful in developing categories for the phenomena called "spirit" in the Bible.

1. An increasing number of medical thinkers are exploring the possibility that all diseases involve both the psyche and the physical body; that is, that the human psyche (spirit) causes our normal resistance to disease to fail (Peck 1978:239). This "psychic" dimension provides a nonmaterial cause (the African's spirit cause) on the basis of which material agents like microbes and chemical imbalances produce physical and mental illness.

2. In a recent study, some volunteers lived in close, uncomfortable quarters in Antarctica to observe the effects of stress on human beings. The subjects who successfully completed the experiment were found to have developed an abundance of hitherto unknown antibodies. Since there were no known germs in the environment, the researchers suggested that these individuals may have developed antibodies against stress, irritation, frustration, or anger. One individual who did go berserk and had to be removed before the midpoint of the experiment was reached had developed almost no "strange" antibodies (Public Broadcasting Service Series on Antarctic Cold Adaptation Expedition). Can the human body produce antibodies against evil?

3. Certain cancers and AIDS are caused not by microorganisms such as germs but by DNA material containing genetic information. Like evil spirits or Satan, who cannot operate except by taking control of a body (Mt 12:43–45; Lk 8:32–33, 11:24–26; Peck 1983:206), this destructive DNA information cannot function unless it is able to control a human cell. When it does, it can reproduce itself and destroy its environment. The aim of this "body-less invading power" is to put the human body's immune system to "sleep" (or in the case of AIDS to destroy it) so that the evil "alien force" can reproduce and finally enlist the body's own immune system to destroy healthy body cells. Is this viral DNA material equivalent to what the Bible calls evil spirits, namely "intelligent"[4] negative power that has no body?

4. Quarks have been discovered in the course of smashing the atom and studying its smaller component parts (MacCormac 1983:47–70; Lederman

---

[4]"Intelligent" in the restricted sense that DNA bears information which carries out on its own what it is programmed to do, like a computer.

and Teresi 1993:256–410). They are manifestations of energy which apparently has no mass. Is science in the process of discovering spirit-power without a body?

In the Scriptures the "Spirit of God" is often used as a synonym for the "power of God." Compare the Hebraistic doublet "the Holy Spirit will come upon you, and the power of the Most High will overshadow you" (Lk 1:35 NRSV; Loewen 1983a:217–18). Since quarks form one of the most elementary energy sources in atomic structure, are scientists discovering the power which brought the universe into existence and which keeps it functioning even today?

Concluding Plea

I realize that I am playing with fire from the perspective of many Christians, but "the path to holiness calls for questioning everything" (Peck 1978:193). My hesitant effort here may be premature or may be dead wrong, but I want to make an honest statement of faith within the psycho-mechanical model of Western science which forms my worldview. One implication which is disturbing to many is that personal metaphors for spirit, including the Spirit of God, may not be as apt as impersonal ones (chap. 13). We may need some other way of speaking of the Trinity than "three persons." I have not attempted to deal with God, the ultimate Spirit, in this model, but if I had, my worldview would require me to do it in this same way.

But disturbing or not, the fact remains that all worldviews are partial, not fully real (chap. 1). Without translating biblical spirit categories into those of the Western worldview the Bible becomes increasingly irrelevant, just as insisting on a literal flat earth and firmament makes the first chapter of Genesis irrelevant from the perspective of our worldview.

I am not passing judgment on anyone's worldview but my own. From my conversations with native peoples of South America and Africa I know that they have been deeply aware of my spiritual schizophrenia as a Western Christian. They have felt sorry for me because of my "God of the gap" and "devil of the gap" uncertainty.

I want to be able to testify concerning my faith and the content of the Bible to people of a Western scientific worldview, and to do so within categories they can perceive, without compromising either their science or my faith. Such testimony is incomplete and tentative, but it is where I stand now. I want also to avoid trying to operate in our day and in our setting with the New Testament worldview of two thousand years ago, which makes us "double-minded and unstable in every way" because we will be "driven and tossed by the wind" (Jas 1:6–8) of supernaturalism from one side and of naturalism from the other side, to the point where unqualified faith becomes impossible.

In our present state of knowledge, the incompleteness of the Western worldview in its approach to spirit and evil is conspicuous. What I have rejected is the fallacy of sweeping the incompleteness into the diminishing category of "supernatural" and treating it by another system of logic. I insist that both what we know and what we do not know be faced together, and alike.

Does that mean that the supernaturalism of the Bible becomes irrelevant to us? By no means! It becomes more relevant as we learn to translate the Bible's worldviews in ways that make sense. God did not operate in one way in biblical times and another way now, but people saw and interpreted God's operation differently from the way we do now. Their way of seeing must be translated into ours. I have tried to illuminate biblical worldviews in this book precisely to make them more readily translatable. If we can see what God's acts meant to people then, we can better understand their implications for us now.

20

The Bible in My Life

This book has been about discovering more of the message of the Bible through eyes of peoples of different cultures. It is also about some implications of such discoveries which I see for my own North American culture, implications which are sometimes controversial.

In the first chapter I outlined the major stages of my life as established by the several cultural environments in which I have lived, the environments in which my cross-cultural perceptions arose. Now I close the book by recounting the stages in my contact with the Bible through which my knowledge of, concern for, and dependency on the Bible have steadily grown. This is the account of how my life has been marked by progressively richer revelation of God and God's word.

The Bible in My Preparatory Years

I have no clear memories of the Bible in my early childhood in Russia as I was too young. But I do remember vividly how the secret police came every night in Moscow to check our papers and to send as many of us as possible to the Siberian Arctic. Then all the mothers urged us children to pray because God had promised to hear us in our hour of need. Later I discovered that they were referring to "Call upon me in the day of trouble; I will deliver thee" (Ps 50:15 KJV).

After we came to Canada and my parents found employment with a widower in Manitoba, the Bible became an integral part of my life, especially during the long winter evenings. The employer, with whom we lived, owned a large illustrated Bible, and I loved to look at all the pictures. As she mended clothes or darned socks, my mother would quietly tell me the Bible stories, while I looked at the pictures illustrating them. The many times we covered these Bible pictures over three years gave me a solid background in the major stories of the Bible.

In church, the Bible was treated very solemnly as the "word of God." My most active participation was through memorizing verses for each Sunday school class. On some Sunday evenings we also had contests, reciting verses from memory. I participated so faithfully that when my family moved to British Columbia in 1934, my nickname became Schriftgelehrter, 'the learned in the Scriptures.' This was the name given to the scribes of Jesus' time in the German Luther Bible. I am deeply grateful for my childhood church, its Sunday school, and its Bible studies. During the many evening-long Bible discussions in church, I learned how to exegete the word, how to understand its meaning, and how to apply the insights gained to real life situations.

Bible School

Since my parents were too poor to send me to high school, I attended the local Bible school for five successive winters. There I learned how to teach the Bible, preach, and talk with God in prayer. But it was not until much later in life that I learned to listen to God. Then the Quakers taught me about quiet meditation in God's presence.

At Bible school I learned such doctrines as the inspiration of Scripture and divine revelation. The big verse used there was, "All scripture *is* given by inspiration of God, and *is* profitable for doctrine, for reproof, for correction, for instruction in righteousness" (2 Tim 3:16 KJV). My teachers had a mechanical view of inspiration: men of God heard God's voice dictating to them, and they wrote down what God said to them verbatim. To my Bible school teachers, the human authorship of any book of the Bible and its historical and cultural context were not important. We should simply accept what God dictated, because the Spirit of God was the author (Hastings 1902 1:296).

My teachers rejected the view that people reached out to understand God. They held that God revealed the truth to human beings, and God gave humans increasingly more insight. Thus at first, divine revelation was not too specific. For example, right after the original sin, God made the first Messianic promise that something not clearly specified would happen:

> I will make you [the serpent] and the woman hate each other. . . Her
> offspring will crush your head, and you will bite their heel (Gen 3:15 GNB).

Although this reference to redemption was rather veiled, God continued to add more pieces of new information. God said to Abraham, for example, "In thee shall all families of the earth be blessed" (Gen 12:3 KJV), promising that a Savior would come from among the descendants of Abraham. Later, when Jacob blessed Judah, God clarified that this Savior was to be born in the tribe of Judah (Gen 49:10). Before his death, Moses promised the people of Israel that God would raise up another prophet like himself (Deut 18:15).

Another bit of information revealed that Jesus would overcome Sheol, that dark prison of all souls underneath the earth, when it foretold that the Messiah would be resurrected and ascend to heaven (Ps 110:1). Isaiah further clarified that Christ would be born of a virgin, and that his name would be Immanuel (Is 7:14; Mt 1:23 KJV).

My teachers also pointed out that Israel's outlook in the Old Testament was sectarian. The Gentiles, enemies of God, were viewed as excluded from the blessing of this coming Messiah. The psalmist said, "Why are heathen raging against the Lord and against his anointed?" (Num 24:8; Ps 79:6). However, Isaiah indicated that the Savior would also be meaningful to non-Jews, for he called the coming Savior "a light for the Gentiles" (Is 49:6). He foreshadowed Jesus' ministry with

> The Spirit of the Lord GOD *is* upon me; because the LORD hath anointed me to preach good tidings unto the meek; he hath sent me to bind up the brokenhearted, to proclaim liberty to the captives, and the opening of the prison to *them that are* bound; to proclaim the acceptable year of the LORD (Is 61:1–2 KJV; cf. Lk 4:18–19).

The place where the Christ was to be born was reported by Micah (5:2; cf. Mt 2:5–6). We are told that he will ride into Jerusalem upon an ass (Zech 9:9 KJV), and that one of his own will betray him for "thirty pieces of silver" (Zech 11:12 KJV). His forerunner, John the Baptist, was also predicted (Mal 3:1). By means of such passages that I was taught, we got increasingly clearer glimpses of the Savior's coming.

However, my teachers also taught that the prophets saw only the peaks of the coming events, and they had no idea of the valleys that lay between. Occasionally several of these peaks far in the future merged, and so the first and second coming of Christ might be spoken of in the same breath. Thus the Savior's ministry will cause death to be swallowed up in victory, referring to his resurrection at his first coming; but it is followed by "the Lord God will wipe away all tears," referring to his return (Is 25:8 KJV).

My Bible school experience thus greatly increased my knowledge of the content of the Bible, but disregarded the history and culture from which it came. It ignored the fact that the Bible writers were responding to situations in their own time, their own history, their own problems. And, as I learned later, it gave me a canned, inflexible picture of the extraordinarily complex process of revelation, ignoring the possibility of continued revelation to people after Bible times.

The Waunana

Our time with the Waunana dispelled several false notions learned in church and Bible school. I had been taught that the heathen had no contact with the true God and that it was up to me to give them their first glimpse of the truth, but I found that the Waunana already had a lot of truth. Their God Ewandama was also the God of the Bible, and they had known God as long as they had existed—long before we ever came (chap. 1). In fact, their fathers had already told them almost everything we told them in our first message. The big new element we added was that God was now saying, "I want you to let go of the devil's hand and to give me your hand."

We also became aware that the Bible is steeped in culture. We came to realize, for example, that modesty among the Waunana was very different from modesty in our Mennonite background, which Mennonites assumed to be biblical. When the mission board insisted that we should have the Waunana women cover their breasts, the Waunana were horrified and said, "If we cover our breasts then all the men will think that we are prostitutes." A woman who is faithful to her husband always leaves her breasts uncovered.

The University

I think the most important insight about the Bible which I gained when I went on to the university was that my church was largely dealing with canned truth. Because the church had the Bible and the canon was closed, it had all the truth. So people merely had to learn that truth and follow it.

On the other hand, scholars were discovering new truth at the university. I was not tempted to ditch my faith in God, but wondered if I wanted to deal only with canned truth, or whether I should join those who were discovering new truth. When I remembered that "now we see through a glass darkly;... now I know in part" (1 Cor 13:12), I was comforted to realize that in the Scriptures there was room for growth in awareness and knowledge of God.

At the university I began to realize also that new truth, scientific or theological, is generally expressed in metaphor. Thus, Galileo likened the movement of heavenly bodies to a giant machine when he introduced his theories. In the same way, when people discover or become aware of new spiritual truth, they also have to reach for metaphors to describe it—analogies to things already known to them. For example, Peter learned to change his view on Gentiles through a vision in which he was told to eat unclean food (Acts 10:10–28).

Tabor College and the Choco Church

During the years when I was teaching at Tabor College, I spent the vacation months with the Choco church in Panama. There I came to realize that God was trying to speak to me, and that I needed to listen. For example, I had tried to teach Bible reading and prayer in Choco homes, but this was something which God had really asked a tribesperson to do. Then when I, after teaching it, tried to thank God for my wonderful teaching experience, I suddenly felt as if I had been hit over the head with a club. When I told the Choco church about this experience and we identified the man whom God had asked to teach this, they held a prayer meeting on my behalf, praying, "God, we thought that Tiger (my tribal nickname) could not hear your voice at all, but now we realize that he can hear it, and we pray that you will teach him to hear you more often."

I also began to learn that the church can be involved in Scripture translation and that it can experience "the inspiration of translation." When I taught a young man to translate the New Testament into the Waunana language, he was too young to make many decisions alone. So he asked the church to pray, "God, how would you have said this if you had spoken in our language in the first place?" And when God then answered through consensus decision, God's word became a powerful message for them. I realized that not only had God's Spirit been active in the original giving of the word, but is still active in its transmission through translation into other languages.

The Bible in My Bible Society Years

During the years when I worked with the Bible Societies, I had opportunity to enrich my cross-cultural perspective on the Bible enormously because I worked with many translators in many languages. More than that, however, the experience enriched my sense of the ongoing presence and participation of God in the translation and communication process.

Preventing Errors

For one thing, early on I became deeply aware of the many errors in missionary-made Bible translations. As a result, I promised God that I would not only listen to him with my head—with my knowledge of linguistics and anthropology—but also with my heart, to hear what the Spirit was saying. I prayed that God would help me not to let mistakes sneak through. The awareness of inspiration then became real to me when I began to experience God protecting the inspired word against human error.

For example, when we were checking[1] 1 Peter in Northern Lengua (Paraguay), I suddenly developed strong inner discomfort. I told the translators about it, and we went back over all the verses in the passage time and again but did not locate anything. However, my inner discomfort

---

[1]Translation consultants who do not know the language of the translation ask a translator to translate their work literally back into English (or whatever other language they communicate together in). This "back" translation helps the consultant understand how the translators have handled some of the problems they have met.

remained, and I told the translators that I would be coming back again six months later and that we could look at this part of 1 Peter again. When we did so, however, the same discomfort appeared, but again we could not find any problem. The same thing happened on still a third visit.

The missionary translator then told me it was time I accepted the fact that nothing was wrong in these verses. But the mother-tongue translator said, "Please, let me try once more. Every time Jake has felt such discomfort deep down in his innermost, it has meant a problem. I think we should take his discomfort seriously." Then he turned to me and said, "Will you please explain the exegesis of these verses to me again." I did so in Spanish and also in Low German, which he had learned from his Mennonite co-translator.

The Lengua translator then read the passage once more, and exclaimed, "I've found it!" Four verses apart were two negatives, in a language which does not permit double negatives! Four verses apart the message had been essentially negated.

During my Bible Society days I also learned to depend on the guidance of the Spirit when utterly stymied in translation. For example, when we were checking the Gospel of John in the Trio language (Surinam), we came to the words, "and the light was the life of men" (Jn 1:4 KJV). 'To live' or 'life' in this language was a term that was used only of men who had a female consort, and thus it had overtones of sexual cohabitation, like couples "living together" in English.

As I listened to the "back" translation of the Trio rendering, it sounded as if it meant, 'The men's living with women is bright.' But try as I would, I was unable to suggest a better answer. To make matters worse, a consultant from another Bible-translating organization, who also had a Ph.D. in linguistics and who worked in a closely related language, told me in no uncertain terms, "There is no better answer in our language, either. There is no word for 'life'! You can't do any better than this!"

I was somewhat embarrassed and exceedingly frustrated when we halted for lunch, and before my regular after-lunch nap, I committed the problem to the Lord in prayer. When I awoke, a message had arisen from my unconscious saying that many things we consider positive in English are expressed as a negative in this language: fast is unslow, good is unbad, straight is uncrooked. I quickly went to the missionary, and I collected from him twenty some expressions in which the addition of a negative affix 'un' provided a positive quality. Modeled on these constructions, I fabricated a construction of this affix plus 'die' to make the expression 'to undie.' The Trio man roared with laughter when he heard my fabrication and said, "You never say that! But you are right, this is the way to solve our problem." Then he came up with the expression 'undyingness.' This rendered the verse as, 'God's undyingness was like a light that showed people the way.'

Clarifying Categories

I also experienced the Spirit of God's involvement with the Bible when the language of the translation required information which is not specified in the text. The grammars of languages and the meanings of words frequently require translators to include information beyond what is given to us in the wording of Scripture.

The Chulupi language (Paraguay), for example, requires that all nouns and proper names be preceded by a prefix indicating whether or not the item or person being discussed is visible at the time of communication. If not visible, it must be specified whether the referent is only currently invisible or is permanently so. If only currently invisible, it must be further specified whether it was visible only in the myth age, or whether it has never been seen by humans. All in all, there are thirteen possibilities.

When Paul said, "[Jesus] appeared also to me" (1 Cor 15:8 NRSV), the missionary and his tribal co-worker disagreed as to which prefix to use. The missionary, explaining his choice on the basis of his theology and his culture, said, "Paul saw him in a vision"; but the tribal translator, even after listening intently to the missionary's reasoning, said, "We, as a church, asked God how he would have said it in our language and the answer is, 'Paul really saw Jesus!'" The original gives no indication of which prefix to use because the Greek did not require the specification of this information. If the translation in this language is to be as authoritative as the original, it must make explicit the additional required information by new inspiration.

While I was deeply moved by the impact of the newly translated Scriptures in the Waunana setting described earlier, not until I had a similar experience in the Biza-Lala language (Zambia) did I recognize a further important dimension of a truly inspired translation. If a translation is to have authoritative status, the entire church has to be involved in the translation process in order to experience the Spirit's input.

The Biza-Lala already had a poor missionary-made translation. The church was pleading for a new one but because it was a language of only limited use, the Bible Societies could not provide full financing for a translation project, but did make a small sum of money available to the group. The church met and decided that they would give the money to one man who would prepare a first draft. All the other people in the church would participate without pay.

The money was not enough to pay for duplicating the drafts so the translator made five or six copies on his typewriter and sent them out for revision. There were not even enough copies to provide one to each church so several churches had to meet together over each typescript. They, like the Waunana, began to read the translation aloud instead of preaching in their services. They discussed its meaning and, noting the points of special concern marked by the translator, they then prayed: "God, if you had said this in

Biza-Lala in the first place, how would you have said it?"

Biza-Lala has twelve words for basket, whereas Greek has only two, used interchangeably. What Biza-Lala word should be used for basket in the story of the feeding of the five thousand? The translators sent out a letter to all the churches. The individual churches prayed. Then the problem was discussed at regional church meetings, and finally the whole tribe assembled before the paramount chief to discuss and pray together over this matter. Finally they decided which word God would have used for basket in the story of the feeding of the five thousand.

When I returned to the translation some months after this tribal meeting, the translator saw my car coming into the yard and ran to meet me, his face beaming with joy. "Doctor, it has happened!" he said. Then he told me about the tribal meeting, and said, "God has spoken!" Then he confided that he had always suspected that the Bible was white people's God speaking to white people, and that the white people were saying that it was good for Africans also. "But," he said, "now that has all changed because we realize that we Africans have made decisions together with the Spirit of God which no white man could have made. It has truly become God's word to us!"

Ongoing Revelation

When the Bible Societies transferred me to be a translation consultant in Africa, I entered a totally new cultural world. It was much more like the Old Testament than anything I had previously encountered and, as Africans shared their culture with me, I became aware of how many meaningful things in the Bible had escaped me up to this point. In Africa I most fully learned of God's continuing revelation.

Africans made me aware that as a group gets large it develops differing loyalties, and therefore has different genealogies (part 1, introduction). Many cultural idioms now became understandable. When Abraham asked his servant to place his hand between his master's thighs and make a vow (Gen 24:2 GNB), I had not understood what kind of oath was meant. But when Africans enlightened me that the expression was a euphemism for placing his hand on his master's genitals—a very powerful oath because of the taboo involved—the passage gained more meaning for me.

I had to learn that even the difficulties in the original text sometimes are part of God's design. One case was Mark 1:2 where the Greek reads, 'as it is written in the prophet Isaiah,' but a quotation from Malachi follows, with a quotation from Isaiah after that. I had discussed this difficulty with the African translation team, but when all the churches got together to give final approval to the translation of that gospel, a bright individual who had not been one of the translators raised the question, "Say Doctor, what are we going to do about Mark 1:2 where there plainly is a problem?"

I then explained that many people had suggested solutions to this problem. For example, some say that Isaiah also said the same words as Malachi, but that they were not recorded in any of his texts. On the other hand, some translations like the King James Bible cheated, and mistranslated the text, "As it was written in the prophets."

I added that I believed that Mark did not unroll the scroll of Isaiah and check it, but remembered incorrectly when he began quoting these words from Malachi that flow easily into the passage from Isaiah. I didn't know why the Spirit of God did not check him in this instance, but in my experience God's Spirit always has a reason.

When I finished my explanation, the African chair of the meeting told the people, "I think it is time that we praised God." Then for the next forty-five minutes, they praised God that Africans could be first-class Christians. I was totally puzzled, so when an intermission was called, I asked the chairperson privately, "What happened? I don't understand!"

"Oh! Well, you see the missionaries always told us that the prophets in the Bible never made mistakes, but we knew that our own prophets often sneak in some of their own ideas! We have to watch them with hawk's eyes for places where the word of God leaves off and where they begin to put in their own. Since missionaries said the biblical writers never made such mistakes, we thought Africans could never be first-class Christians. But if Mark made such a mistake, then obviously we Africans can be first-class Christians, just like Mark."

I also learned that writing, written records, and the closed canon can be a barrier to ongoing revelation. We are hampered from receiving greater clarity from God as we deal with his word because the canon has been permanently fixed. An African assistant spent time with me every Saturday during which we discussed the work and reached conclusions. I would then dictate a memorandum so that we might both have a record of our decisions. Later on, when questions arose again, I would pull out the original memorandum and look at it. But then my African assistant began to complain, "That is the problem with white people's thinking. Once you have it written down, it becomes fixed. Since we deal with things orally, whenever we meet a problem again, we have to discuss it again and make adjustments because of the new insights that have come." I suddenly realized what a stricture a written record and a closed canon has become for us in the ongoing revelation from God.

The Bible as I Look Back

I had the privilege of studying Hebrew only late in life. It opened many new windows for me, especially on the Old Testament text. I became aware of the tremendous struggle that is waged throughout the Old Testament to have Israel recognize that Yahweh, the tribal God of Israel, really was Elohim, the God of the world (chap.15). Isaiah the prophet saw this truth most clearly, realizing that Yahweh accepted not only his chosen people of Israel, but people from every tribe and nation who were obedient.

I also became aware that the Hebrew text has a cultural bias toward the Israelite version of things. Since the Hebrews were monotheistic, they disdained all polytheists and referred to their gods as 'idols' (Ps 96:5 KJV), or called them 'devils' (Lev 17:7 KJV).

In the New Testament, also, the synoptic gospels carry strong anti-Gentile sentiment. Jesus instructed the disciples to go only to the people of Israel, not to the Gentiles (Mt 10:5–6; 15:24). Salvation comes only from the Jews (Jn 4:22). The writers of these gospels even seem to have put such words into Jesus' mouth, as when he says to the Syrophoenician woman, "It isn't right to take the children's food and throw it to the dogs" (Mk 7:27 GNB), meaning, take food intended for Jews and give it to Gentiles.

Throughout Acts and the Pauline epistles, the gospel is for the Jew first and only then for the Gentile (Acts 13:46; Rom 1:16; 2:9). The apostle Peter was amazed to experience God's Spirit coming down on the household of gentile Cornelius and came to realize that God treats everyone on the same basis (Acts 10:34–35).

A reverse kind of prejudice is apparent in the Gospel of John, probably the last gospel written (about AD 100) (Bratcher 1975). There we find strong sentiment against the Jews as a class, ignoring the fact that Jesus and his disciples were Jews, and that it was only certain Jewish leaders who acted against Jesus. "Jews" are shown as persecuting Jesus (Jn 5:16); as trying to stone him (Jn 10:31–32); as trying to kill him (Jn 7:1; 11:53). They also persecute Jesus' disciples (Jn 15:20). This anti-Jewish phrasing has influenced some Christians through the centuries to think of Jews as "Christ killers" (Bratcher 1975).

Many people also detect an anti-feminine bias in some of the epistles. Women are not to be in authority over men (1 Tim 2:11–14). Women are told to keep silent in the church (1 Cor 14:34–35). They are to be subject to their husbands (1 Pet 3:1,5). Thank God, other passages indicate that God is impartial (Job 34:18–19). "[God] sendeth rain on the just and the unjust" (Mt 5:45). "There is no difference between Jew and Gentile, male or female" (Rom 10:12; Gal 3:28).

All that leads me back to the marvel and mystery of the trajectory of divine purpose. God chose human beings, limited as they are, to be the divine messengers of God's word. God accepted the limitations their cultures placed on them and worked with them within those strictures. Of course, God was always trying to reduce the barriers that a people's culture put in the way, as when the Jewish attitude against the Gentiles was modified in Peter's life (Acts 10:9–16,34–35).

Individual human prejudices can severely limit God's work, but God does still work with prejudiced individuals (Mk 6:5). When Nathanael was called to become Jesus' disciple, his prejudice showed through when he said, "What good can come from Nazareth?" He was just told to "come and see" (Jn 1:46). Jesus recognized that having been raised in Nazareth, he would not be accepted as a prophet in his home country (Lk 4:24), and that some people would look down on his carpenter past (Mk 6:3). It seems to me that God tries to reveal the truth to people in spite of their culture, prejudice, and ignorance, and comes as close as circumstances allow.

I also learned to see the trajectory in the long range. Israel's move to Egypt was not just an effort to escape the famine, but also God's way of changing Israel's limited view of the afterlife through the elaborate afterlife of the Egyptians (chaps. 2, 4). In Egypt, God also made a single people out of the fractious twelve tribes. In redeeming them from Egypt and ending their slavery, God gave them a model of the redemption that was to come through Jesus Christ (Ex 3:7–10; Hos 11:1). In Egypt, God also gave them an educated leader in Moses (Acts 7:22).

When God had the people removed from Palestine to captivity in Assyria, Zoroastrianism was sweeping that part of the world. In captivity the Jews came into touch with the God of light and the God of darkness, and their own view of evil was refined dramatically. Their view of afterlife also shifted so that they became aware of punishment for the wicked at the end times. Their view of heaven and hell was greatly enlarged (chaps. 2, 3).

Over the years, I have come to appreciate God more deeply and also to appreciate God's Word more deeply. I marvel at divine wisdom, at how much truth God was able to get across in the books of the Bible to culturally bound and prejudiced individuals. I am amazed at God's infinite patience with people who have such limited views. I am grateful that God's Spirit, which inspired the Scriptures centuries ago, is still with us, helping us translate it into other languages. I am confident that God will continue to speak and also confident that God's Word endures forever (1 Pet 1:23,25).

Appendix A

Abbreviations

Translations Cited

ASV   1901. *The Holy Bible*. American Standard Version. New York: Thomas Nelson and Sons.

BJ   1978. *La Bible de Jérusalem*. Paris: Les Éditions du Cerf.

CEV   1991. *Contemporary English Version*. Common language version. New York: American Bible Society.

FC   1982. *La Bible en Français courant*. Common language version. Paris: Alliance Biblique Universelle.

GN   1982. *Die Bibel in heutigem Deutsch*. Common language version. Stuttgart: Deutsche Bibelgesellschaft.

GNB   1976. *Good News Bible*. Today's English Version. Common language version. New York: American Bible Society.

KJV   1934. *Thompson's Chain Reference Bible*. Authorized Version (King James). Indianapolis: B. B. Kirkbridge Bible Co.

L   1951. *Die Bibel*. Luther Version. Stuttgart: Wuerttembergische Bibelanstalt.

LXX   1935. *Septuaginta*. Septuagint Version. Stuttgart: Deutsche Bibelstiftung.

NC   1976. *Sagrada Biblia*. Nacar-Colunga Version. Madrid: Biblioteca de Autores Cristianos.

NRSV   1989. *The Holy Bible*. New Revised Standard Version. New York: American Bible Society.

ReV   1898. *The Holy Bible*. Revised Version. Oxford: The University Press.

RV   1960. *La Santa Biblia*. Reina-Valera Version. Mexico: Sociedades Bíblicas en América Latina.

RSV   1977. *The Holy Bible*. Revised Standard Version. London: William Collins for the Bible Societies.

SEG   1979. *La Sainte Bible*. Segond Version. Paris: La Société Biblique.

VP   1979. *Dios Habla Hoy: La Biblia Versión Popular*. Common Language Version. New York: Sociedad Biblica Americana.

Ancient Documents Cited

Acts	Acts	Jub	Jubilees
Amos	Amos	Jude	Jude
ApAb	Apocalypse of Abraham	Judg	Judges
ApAdam	Apocalypse of Adam	1 Kgs	1 Kings
ApEl	Apocalypse of Elijah	2 Kgs	2 Kings
ApocEzek	Apocryphon of Ezekiel	LAE	Life of Adam and Eve
ApMos	Apocalypse of Moses	LeAris	Letter of Aristeas
AsMos	Assumption of Moses	Lam	Lamentations
2 Bar	2 (Syrian Apocalypse of) Baruch	Lev	Leviticus
		LivPro	Lives of the Prophets
3 Bar	3 (Greek Apocalypse of) Baruch	Lk	Luke
		2 Mac	2 Maccabees
Col	Colossians	3 Mac	3 Maccabees
1 Chr	1 Chronicles	Mal	Malachi
2 Chr	2 Chronicles	MartIs	Martyrdom and Ascension of Isaiah
1 Cor	1 Corinthians		
2 Cor	2 Corinthians	Mic	Micah
Dan	Daniel	Mk	Mark
Deut	Deuteronomy	Mt	Matthew
Ecc	Ecclesiastes	Nah	Nahum
1 En	1 (Ethiopic Apocalypse of) Enoch	Neh	Nehemiah
		Num	Numbers
2 En	2 (Slavonic Apocalypse of) Enoch	Obad	Obadiah
		OdesSol	Odes of Solomon
3 En	3 (Hebrew Apocalypse of) Enoch	1 Pet	1 Peter
		2 Pet	2 Peter
Eph	Ephesians	Phil	Philippians
Esth	Esther	Prov	Proverbs
Ex	Exodus	Ps	Psalms
Ezek	Ezekiel	Ps-Phoc	Pseudo-Phocylides
4 Ezra	4 Ezra	PssSol	Psalms of Solomon
Gal	Galatians	QuesEzra	Questions of Ezra
Gen	Genesis	Rev	Revelation
GkApEzra	Greek Apocalypse of Ezra	RevEzra	Revelation of Ezra
Hab	Habakkuk	Rom	Romans
Heb	Hebrews	Ruth	Ruth
Hos	Hosea	1 Sam	1 Samuel
Is	Isaiah	2 Sam	2 Samuel
Jas	James	Song	Song of Songs
Jer	Jeremiah	T12P	Testaments of the Twelve Patriarchs
Jn	John		
1 Jn	1 John	TAb	Testament of Abraham
Job	Job	TAdam	Testament of Adam
Joel	Joel	1 Thes	1 Thessalonians
Jon	Jonah	2 Thes	2 Thessalonians
Josh	Joshua	1 Tim	1 Timothy

2 Tim	2 Timothy		(Testament of theTwelve
TJob	Testament of Job		Patriarchs)
Levi	Testament of Levi	TSol	Testament of Solomon
	(Testament of the	VisEzra	Vision of Ezra
	Twelve Patriarchs)	Zech	Zechariah
TReu	Testament of Reuben		

Appendix B

Pseudepigrapha

Since the pseudepigraphic books of the ancient Jews and early Christians are neither well known nor usually easily accessible to modern Christians, here follow descriptions of the ones to which reference has been made in this book. Since precise dates are not known, those given below suggest the approximate span during which each book was likely written. The entries are alphabetized by the abbreviations used for the books (see app. A). This appendix does not include books of the Old or New Testaments or deuterocanonical books (the Apocrypha).

ApAb   Apocalypse of Abraham

Date: first or second century AD. Original language: probably Hebrew. Language of existing manuscripts: Slavonic. Israel's election as God's people and their covenant with God. Unique division of the world into two parts, earth and garden of Eden (Rubinkiewicz 1983).

ApAdam   Apocalypse of Adam

Date: first to fourth century AD. Language of existing manuscripts: Coptic. Gnostic document containing secret revelations about the apocalypse, communicated by Adam to Seth. Unique in drawing sharp distinction between creator God of Genesis and supreme God, of whom creator God eventually becomes an enemy (Macrae 1983b).

ApEl   Apocalypse of Elijah

Date: first to fourth century AD. Original language: probably Greek. Languages of existing manuscripts: Greek, Sahidic (Coptic). Composite work containing discussions of prayer and fasting, prophetic description of events preceding antichrist, description of antichrist, account of three martyrdoms, and oracle concerning judgment to occur "on that day." Dualism between good and evil. Righteous led to the heavenly city by angels (Wintermute 1983).

ApocEzek   Apocryphon of Ezekiel

Date: first century BC to first century AD. Languages of existing manuscripts (fragments): Hebrew, Greek. Includes eloquent statement on resurrection and final judgment. Body and soul will be reunited in future judgment (Mueller and Robinson 1983).

ApMos   Apocalypse of Moses
See: Life of Adam and Eve (LAE).

AsMos   Assumption of Moses
Date: first century AD. Original language: probably Greek. Possibly fragment of Testament of Moses (below). Contains account of dispute between Michael and Satan over body of Moses, referred to in Jude 9. The Council of Nicea reportedly quoted this book (Priest 1983).

2 Bar   2 Baruch
Full title: Syriac Apocalypse of Baruch. Date: probably second century AD. Original language: probably Syriac, perhaps Greek. Languages of existing manuscripts: Syriac, Arabic. Speaks of destruction of Jerusalem, 587 BC (Klijn 1983).

3 Bar   3 Baruch
Full title: Greek Apocalypse of Baruch. Date: first to third centuries AD. Original language: probably Greek. Language of existing manuscript: Slavonic. Baruch, scribe of Jeremiah, laments destruction of Jerusalem. Angel comforts and guides Baruch through heavens and their mysteries. Five-heaven cosmology is distinctive. Contains information about angels; describes how Satanael had name changed to Satan (Gaylord 1983).

1 En   1 Enoch
Full title: Ethiopic Apocalypse of Enoch. Date: second century BC to first century AD. Original language: Hebrew or Aramaic. Language of existing manuscripts: Ethiopic; partial manuscripts in Aramaic, Greek, and Latin. Textual variants called recensions A and B. Attributed to Enoch, descendent of Adam (Gen 5:21–24), authorship probably composite. Recounts old traditions concerning Enoch as knowing mysteries of universe and future world. Expounds on sons of God having intercourse with women (Gen 6:1–4). Quoted in Jude 14, 15 (Isaac 1983).

2 En   2 Enoch
Full title: Slavonic Apocalypse of Enoch. Date: late first century AD. Original language: probably Greek. Languages of present manuscripts: Old Slavonic. Versions: longer recension called A, shorter one J. Amplifies events pertaining to Enoch, followed by some descendants (Gen 5:21–32). Includes visits to paradise and place of torment, with statement of seven-heavens cosmology. Discusses angels and calendar system arising from study of creation (Anderson 1983).

3 En   3 Enoch

Full title: Hebrew Apocalypse of Enoch. Date: fifth or sixth century AD. Original language: Hebrew. Account of Rabbi Ishmael journeying into heaven and seeing God's throne and chariot. Revelations from archangel Metatron (Alexander 1983).

4 Ezra   4 Ezra

Full title: Fourth Book of Ezra, also 4 Esdras in Latin Vulgate. Date: late first century AD. Characterizes Hades as having chambers like wombs (*sic*) for souls of dead (4 Ezra 4:42) (Metzger 1983).

GkApEzra   The Greek Apocalypse of Ezra

Date: second to ninth century AD. Original language: probably Greek. Contains visions, together with long discussions of angels and archangels, final judgment of all people, and images of heaven and earth in final conflagration (Stone 1983a).

Jub   Jubilees

Date: probably second century BC. Original language: Hebrew. Languages of existing manuscripts: Hebrew, Greek, Syriac, Latin, Ethiopic. Somewhat longer restatement of Genesis and early parts of Exodus, reporting matters revealed to Moses during forty days on Mount Sinai (Ex 24:18). Introduces angels and demons, chief of whom is Mastema, equivalent to Satan. Considered canonical by Ethiopian Coptic Church (Wintermute 1983).

LAE   The Life of Adam and Eve

Also called: Apocalypse of Moses. Date: first century AD. Original language: possibly Hebrew. Languages of existing manuscripts: Greek, Latin. Describes burial of Adam and Eve in earthly paradise. Talks about paradise in third heaven (Johnson 1985).

LivPro   The Lives of the Prophets

Date: first century AD. Original language: probably Hebrew. Treats three major prophets and twelve minor ones, plus seven non-literary prophets. Includes theological discussion of guilt, punishment, and expiation. Assumes resurrection. Usual name for devil is Beliar. Sheds light on veneration of saints in parts of Christian church (Hare 1985).

3 Mac   3 Maccabees

Date: before 70 AD. Original language: probably Greek. Reports a crisis faced by Alexandrian Jews when Egypt was made a Roman province in 24 BC (Anderson, H. 1985).

MartIs   Martyrdom and Ascension of Isaiah

Probably consists of two different works, Martyrdom of Isaiah and Vision of Isaiah. Date: second century BC to fourth century AD. Authorship: multiple. Original language of martyrdom section: Hebrew. Recounts what Isaiah suffered at the hands of Jewish king Manasseh. Vision of Isaiah is Christian. Demonology of combined work important, speaking of Sammael, Beliar, and Satan (Knibb 1985).

OdesSol   Odes of Solomon

Date: late first to early second centuries AD. Original language: Greek or Hebrew. Portrays God as having breasts from which milk of salvation flows. Gentiles treated negatively. God gracious and merciful. Messiah exalted. Some odes foreshadow Gospel of John (Charlesworth 1985a).

PssSol   Psalms of Solomon

Date: first century BC. Original language: Hebrew. Existing manuscripts: Greek and Syriac. Eighteen psalms reacting to capture of Jerusalem, invasion, destruction of society. No distinction in eschatological hope between individual and nation (Wright 1985).

QuesEzra   Questions of Ezra

Date: unknown. Two versions: A and B. Dialogue between prophet and angel of the Lord, with description of seven heavens, lower ones negative and upper ones positive. Hell located in third heaven. Contains clear contrast between angels and demons, righteous and sinners. References to intermediate state like purgatory (Stone 1983b).

RevEzra   Revelation of Ezra

Date: before ninth century AD. Original language: probably Latin. Contains calendrical information for foretelling future (Fiensy 1983).

T12P   Testament of the Twelve Patriarchs

Date: probably second century BC. Original language: Aramaic or Hebrew. Languages of existing manuscripts: Greek, Armenian, Slavonic, Hebrew, Aramaic. Greek manuscripts in two varieties, A and B, both with Christian interpolations. Modelled on last utterances of Jacob (Gen 49). Universe has three heavens, different from original Hebrew ones. Manifests strong dualism between spirits of truth and error. The head of spirits of error is Beliar, also called Satan. Women inherently evil and entice men. Misled the watcher-angels (Gen 6:1–4; TReu 5:6). Affirms resurrection of the faithful. Included here: Testament of Levi. Other books with similar titles below do not belong to this group (Kee 1983).

TAb   Testament of Abraham

Date: first or second century AD. Languages of existing manuscripts: longer form (recension A) in Rumanian, shorter form (recension B) in Greek. Concept of salvation for all peoples, with no distinction between Jew and Gentile, but strong emphasis on judgment according to deeds (Sanders 1983b).

TAdam   Testament of Adam

Date: between second and fifth centuries AD. Languages of existing manuscripts: Syriac (three versions), Greek, Aramaic, Ethiopic, Old Georgian, Armenian. God's intent was eventually to make Adam god. Angels described as forming a hierarchy (Robinson 1983).

TIsaac   Testament of Isaac

Date: second century AD. Languages of existing manuscripts: Coptic, Ethiopic, and Arabic. Important in Coptic church, fixing day which commemorates Isaac. Archangel Michael sent by God to warn Isaac of his death. Ends saying that Jesus is Messiah, the son of virgin Mary, and incarnation of God (Stinespring 1983).

TJob   Testament of Job

Date: probably first century BC to first century AD. Original language: probably Hebrew, perhaps Greek. Theological outlook of hellenistic Judaism, with highly developed doctrine of Satan and angels, and considerable interest in angelic glossolalia (Spittler 1983).

TLevi   Testament of Levi

See: Testament of the Twelve Patriarchs (T12P).

TMos   Testament of Moses

Date: first century AD. Original language: probably Greek. Repeats Deuteronomy 31–34. Contains farewell exhortation by Moses to Joshua before his death. Includes story of dispute between Michael and Satan over body of Moses, which exists also separately as the Assumption of Moses (above). Influence shown in some New Testament passages (e.g. Jude 9,12–13,16; 2 Pet 2:13; Acts 7:16–43; Mt 24:19–21). Manuscript ends with unfinished sentence indicating part has been lost (Priest 1983).

TReu   Testament of Reuben

See Testament of the Twelve Patriarchs (T12P).

TSol   Testament of Solomon

Date: first to third centuries AD. Original language: similar to New Testament Koine Greek. Contains folktales about Solomon building temple in Jerusalem, with special attention to nuisance demon Ornias, with whose help Solomon captures Beelzebul, prince of demons. Many syncretistic beliefs about astrology, demonology, angelology, magic, and medicine (Duling 1983).

VisEzra   ″   Vision of Ezra

Date: fourth to seventh centuries AD. Original language: probably Greek. Language of existing manuscripts: Latin. Closely parallels some New Testament apocrypha, and thoroughly Christian, with motifs like value of confession, penitence, almsgiving, and Christians going into their eternal rest (Mueller and Robbins 1983).

Appendix C

God's Names in European Translations

This appendix is a supplement to chapter 16, illustrating how the various Hebrew names for God in the Old Testament have been translated into some major European languages. The listing is accompanied by notes which call attention both to the general principles employed in the translations and, occasionally, to unique features.

Since a number of the names function differently in different contexts, each function is listed separately under numbered headings, followed by representative examples, a, b, c. In some instances, where a comparative listing reveals little or no new information, only a summarizing note to that effect is given.

The listings are coded in various ways:

(a) Parentheses within a biblical quotation make explicit noncontiguous information necessary to specify the context. For example, (he called the altar) '*el* the *elohim* of Israel' (example 2b).

(b) Parentheses within a comparative listing of the translations make explicit the antecedent of a pronoun found in the text. For example, (God) the one who (example 1b GNB).

(c) Parentheses after a biblical reference indicate that the verse is numbered differently in some translations. For example, Ps 68:20 (21) (example 2a).

(d) An asterisk (as in *god or *lord) indicates that the language in question uses either only lower case letters (like Greek) or only initial capital letters (like German), and so the god/God or lord/Lord distinction does not apply (example 1a LXX).

(e) The symbol # in a comparative listing marks a significant absence, such as that a name present in the original has been left implicit in the translation, usually because it is clear from the context (example 2b LXX).

(f) Single quotes are sometimes used to show the meaning of a Hebrew word. For example, I am *el* of Beth-*el* 'house of *el*' (example 1d).

(g) The letter "o" is used in comparative listings to mark vocative-instances where God is being addressed. For example, (David prayed, saying) o *adonai*, o *yahweh* (example 26e).

(h) The translations listed include both traditional, formal correspondence (literal) type translations (FoC) and modern dynamic equivalent ones, usually called common

267

language versions (CL). The *Bible de Jérusalem* is neither. The translations are grouped by language. The ones quoted, with their respective abbreviations, are:

LXX	Greek FoC	Septuagint version
KJV	English FoC	King James (Authorized) version
GNB	English CL	Good News Bible/Today's English Version
L	German FoC	Luther version
GN	German CL	Die Gute Nachricht
SEG	French FoC	Segond version
BJ	French	Bible de Jérusalem
FC	French CL	Français Courant version
NC	Spanish FoC	Nacar-Colunga version
VP	Spanish CL	Versión Popular/Dios Llega al Hombre

Forms of *el*

1. *el* used as a class noun referring to the supreme God.

1a. Is 45:22: look to me...all the ends of the earth, for I am *el*, and there is no one else. *el* is translated as "God" in all versions. GNB highlights God's uniqueness, as stressed in the context, with "only."

LXX	the *god	KJV	God	GNB the only God
L	*God	GN	*God	
SEG	God	BJ	God	FC God
NC	God	VP	God	

1b. Deut 32:18: forgotten the *el* that formed you. All translations render *el* as "God."

LXX	*god	KJV	God	GNB (God) the one who
L	*God	GN	the *God who	
SEG	the God who	BJ	the God who	FC the God
NC	God	VP	the God who	

1c. Hos 11:9: I am *el*, and not a man. The usage in this verse suggests contrast between deity and humanity (see section 8, below). All translations use "God."

1d. Gen 31:13: I am *el* of Beth-*el* 'house of *el*'. *el* specifies the particular God who is associated with a specific place. Only LXX translates *el* in the place name. KJV, L and GN draw attention to *el* in the transliterated name by separating it with a hyphen. All others treat the second *el* merely as a part of the place name.

LXX	the *god...in *god's place		
KJV	the God of Beth-el	GNB	God who appeared to you at Bethel
L	*God...Beth-El	GN	*God who resides in Bet-El
SEG	God...Bethel	BJ	God...Bethel
FC	the God who appeared to you at Bethel		
NC	God...Betel	VP	the God who appeared to you at Bethel

2. *el* as a proper name for the God of Israel. (There are one or two examples in this listing which could possibly also be read as the proper name of the supreme God.)

2a. Ps 68:20 (21): *el* is to us the *el* of salvation. KJV, GNB, NC, and VP mark one *el* with the possessive pronoun, LXX with the definite article, thus avoiding the proper name issue and redundancy. L and GN avoid the issue by using a relative pronoun for the second *el*.

LXX	the *god...god	KJV	our God...a God	GNB	our God...a God
L	a *God who	GN	a *God who		
SEG	God...the God	BJ	the God...a God	FC	God...a God
NC	God...our God	VP	our God...a God		

2b. Gen 33:20: (he called the altar) *el* the *elohim* of Israel. KJV, SEG, NC, and VP transliterate the entire expression as a single proper name, though NC gives part of its meaning in parentheses; GNB, BJ, and FC do not blur the distinction and treat *el* as a proper name and *elohim* as a class noun; L interprets *el* as the qualifier "mighty," GN repeats God twice, and LXX drops the *el* entirely.

LXX	#...the *god of Israel			
KJV	El-elohe-Israel		GNB	El, the God of Israel
L	the mighty *God of Israel		GN	*God is the God of Israel
SEG	El-elohe-Israel		BJ	El, God of Israel
FC	El-God of Israel			
NC	El Elohe Israel (the God of Israel)			
VP	El-Elohe-Israel			

2c. Gen 46:3: I am *el* the *elohim* of your father. Only NC conserves *el* as a proper name, LXX and GN drop it entirely, the rest translate both as "God/god" and use the name redundantly.

LXX	#...the *god	KJV	God, the God	GNB	God, the God
L	*God, the God	GN	#...the *God		
SEG	the God, the God	BJ	God, the God	FC	God, the God
NC	El, the God	VP	God, the God		

2d. Ps 50:7: I am *el* your *elohim*. None of the translations treat *el* as a proper name. All except GN use "God/god" twice; L, GN, BJ, FC, and VP introduce "I," the first-person pronoun; GN uses the reflexive, emphatic pronoun, the rest use *el* as an appositive to I; KJV and VP introduce emphasis—KJV with "even," VP by making two short sentences.

LXX	the *god your god			
KJV	God, even your God		GNB	God, your God
L	I, *God, am your *God		GN	I myself am your *God
SEG	God, your God		BJ	I, God, your God
FC	I, God, your God			
NC	God, your God		VP	I am God, I am your God

3. *el* as a proper name, functioning as an alternative or substitute for *yahweh*.

3a. Num 23:8: how can I curse whom *el* has not cursed; how can I defy whom *yahweh* has not defied? LXX inverts the order but like all the others follows its usual rendering.

LXX	*lord...god			
KJV	God...the LORD		GNB	God...the LORD
L	*God...the Lord		GN	*God the Lord...he

SEG	Godthe Eternal One	BJ	GodYahve
FC	Godthe Lord		
NC	GodYave	VP	Godthe Lord

3b. Ps 78:19: (speaking about *yahweh*) they spoke against *elohim* saying, can *el* furnish (water)? All render both as "God/god," GN and VP each use the corresponding pronoun once.

| GN | (God) him...*God | VP | (God) him...God |

4. *el* as the proper name of a Canaanite deity.

4a. Ezek 28:2: (in a prophetic oracle against Tyre and its king who says) I am *el* in the seat of *elohim* I sit. No translation treats *el* as a proper name. LXX, KJV, L, and SEG equate it with the Supreme God; KJV, L, SEG, and NC treat *elohim* as the Supreme God; GNB, GN, FC, and VP treat both *el* and *elohim* as class nouns, NC and BJ treat only *el* as a class noun; BJ uses the adjective 'divine' to translate *elohim*; LXX and VP treat *elohim* as a plural.

LXX	*god...gods	KJV	God...God	GNB a god...a god
L	*God...God	GN	a *God...a God	
SEG	God...God	BJ	a god...divine	FC a god...a god
NC	a god...God	VP	a god...gods	

5. *el* as a class noun (appellative) referring to a pagan deity.

5a. Judg 9:46: the house of *el berith*. LXX, GNB, and FC mark it as an idol, possibly on the basis of Judges 8:33 where a *baal* by that name is mentioned; BJ, NC, and VP treat it as a composite name and transliterate both words; KJV, SEG, and possibly L treat it as a pagan deity, but GN is ambiguous with the compound noun "Covenant-god," which could, in fact, refer to *yahweh*.

LXX	Baal of the covenant		
KJV	the god Berith	GNB	Baal-of-the-Covenant
L	the *God Berith	GN	their *Covenant-god
SEG	god Berith	BJ	El-Berit
FC	Baal-Berith		
NC	El-Berit	VP	El-berit

5b. Deut 32:12: there was no strange *el* with him. All translations see *el* as referring to a pagan deity. GNB translates as "foreign god," all others as "God/god."

5c. Is 44:10: who formed an *el* or melted a graven image. All translations treat *el* as a pagan deity; GNB and VP invert the order and make it a comparison "as a god"; they also make explicit that it was for worshiping.

LXX	*god...unprofitable engraving		
KJV	god...image	GNB	a metal image to worship as god
L	*God...idol	GN	*God...idol picture
SEG	god...idol	BJ	God...statue
FC	god...idol		
NC	god...idol	VP	a statue for worship as a god

5d. 2 Kgs 5:18: to the house of *rimmon. el/elohim*, the noun classifier, is left implicit in the original and a proper name in conjunction with a house poses a potential ambiguity. LXX, KJV, L, and SEG leave it ambiguous; the rest resolve the ambiguity either by marking it as a temple rather than house, or by identifying Rimmon as "god," see GNB, GN, and FC.

LXX	house of Rimmon		
KJV	house of Rimmon	GNB	temple of Rimmon, the god of
L	Rimmon's house	GN	temple of his *God Rimmon
SEG	house of Rimmon	BJ	temple of Rimmon
FC	temple of his god		
NC	temple of Rimmon	VP	temple of Rimmon

6. *el* referring to multiple gods.

6a. Dan 11:36: magnify himself above every *el*. All translations use or imply plural gods.

KJV	every god	GNB	any god	L	everything divine
all others	all gods				

7. *elim* (regular plural of *el*) rendered as "gods" or "strong men."

7a. Ex 15:11: who among the *elim* (*o yahweh* is like you)? All interpret *elim* as 'gods'; only VP translates the rhetorical question with an implied 'no one' answer as a statement: "no god is like you." All others translate as "gods."

7b. Job 41:25: (when he rises up) the *elim* are afraid. Only VP renders it as "gods"; GNB, BJ, and FC give gods as an alternative in a footnote; KJV, GNB, L, GN, and SEG render it "strong ones," "the strongest," "the most valiant"; but LXX, BJ, and NC give it entirely different readings—LXX with "quadrupeds" and BJ and NC with "waves."

LXX	four-footed animals		
KJV	the mighty	GNB	even the strongest (fn: gods)
L	the Strong ones	GN	even the strongest
SEG	the most valiant ones	BJ	the waves (fn: gods)
FC	the chiefs (fn: gods)		
NC	the waves	VP	the gods

7c. Dan 11:36: speak against/is greater than the *el elim*. LXX, KJV, L, SEG, BJ, and FC read the Hebrew as a possessive, and render it "god/God of gods"; GNB, GN and VP treat the *el* as "supreme" or "true God."

LXX	against all the *gods and the god of gods		
KJV	the God of gods		
GNB	any god, superior even to the Supreme God		
L	*God of all Gods		
GN	mightier than all *Gods, even than the highest God		
SEG	the God of gods	BJ	the God of gods
FC	the God of gods		
NC	all the gods and the God of gods		
VP	all the gods...the true God		

7d. Ezek 32:21: the *ele* 'possessive form of *elim*' *gibborim* 'mighty ones' shall speak from Sheol. In this case none of the translations render *elim* as "gods"; all use some term suggesting 'powerful' or 'strong'; only KJV tries to duplicate the possessive form, all others render it as an attribute.

LXX	the giants		
KJV	the strong among the mighty	GNB	the greatest heroes
L	the strong heroes	GN	the mighty warriors
SEG	powerful heroes	BJ	the most powerful heroes
FC	the most valiant warriors		
NC	the strong among the strong	VP	the most powerful leaders

8. *elohim* as a generic class noun (appellative) that could be translated "deity."

8a. Ps 14:1: (the fool has said) not there is *elohim*. All translations use "God"; GN makes explicit God's power over men, FC negates God's power, not his existence.

LXX	not there is *god		
KJV	no God	GNB	no God
L	no *God		
GN	a *God with whom one must reckon does not exist		
SEG	definitely there is no God	BJ	God is no more
FC	God is without power (fn: God doesn't exist)		
NC	not there is God	VP	God doesn't exist

8b. 2 Kgs 5:15: there is no *elohim* in all the earth, except in Israel. All translations render it "god/God," only GNB uses both a lower case "god" and a first letter capital "God."

LXX	no *god, but that one		
GNB	no god, but the God	GN	only in Israel is there a *God
FC	no other God, but the one	All others	no God

9. *elohim* referring to the God of the universe.

9a. Gen 6:12: then saw *elohim*. All translations except LXX have "God," LXX has "lord the god"; FC uses the corresponding pronoun to refer to "God."

LXX	*lord the god	FC (God) he	All others	God

9b. 1 Kgs 18:24: the *elohim* who answers by fire, he is *elohim*. All translations except GN and FC repeat the word god, but KJV and NC have both in capitals; GNB, SEG, BJ, and VP have only the second *elohim* beginning with a capital; GN, FC, and VP make the quality 'true' explicit.

LXX	*god...god	KJV	God...God	GNB	god...God
L	*God...God	GN	which of the two is the true *God		
SEG	god...God	BJ	the god...God		
FC	he who...is the true *God				
NC	the God...God	VP	god...the true God		

9c. Dan 2:47: (King Nebuchadnezzar says to Daniel:) your *elohim* truly is *elohim* of *elohim*. Only in the third instance do all translations agree with the plural lower case "gods," with GNB, GN, FC, and VP making explicit "all"; KJV, SEG, and NC capitalize the first two, GNB, FC, and VP capitalize the first and use "the greatest" for the second; GN has "truly lord/master" for the second.

LXX	*god...god...gods		
KJV	God...God...gods	GNB	God...the greatest...all gods
L	*God...God...Gods	GN	God...is truly *Lord...of all Gods

SEG	God...God...gods	BJ	god...God...gods
FC	God...truly the greatest ...all the gods
NC	God...God...gods	VP	God...the biggest...all the gods

10. *elohim* referring to multiple gods (with plural verbs or plural modifiers).

10a. Ex 12:12: I will execute judgment on all the *elohim* of Egypt. All translations use the plural "gods."

10b. 2 Chr 13:9: a priest for not *elohim*. Only SEG and BJ use the singular capital "God"; all others use the plural lower case "gods"; GNB calls them "so-called" and VP uses "gods" twice.

LXX	*gods	KJV	gods	GNB	so-called gods
L	*Gods	GN	*Gods		
SEG	God	BJ	God	FC	gods
NC	gods	VP	gods who are not gods		

10c. Is 42:17: you (pl) are our *elohim*. All translations use the plural lower case "gods" to agree with the plural pronoun; only GNB says "call images their God."
GNB   call images their God

10d. 2 Kgs 19:18: you have put their *elohim* into the fire for they were not *elohim*. All translations use "gods" in both cases, but the four CL translations bring out "not real gods" in various ways.

| GNB | gods...no gods at all | GN | *Gods...no Gods at all |
| FC | no true gods | VP | gods...in reality were no gods |

10e. 1 Sam 4:8: the *elohim* who struck (plural verb) the Egyptians. GN, BJ, FC, and VP ignore the plural verb and use the singular "God"; KJV uses a plural capital "Gods"; several use the corresponding singular or plural pronoun.

LXX	*gods	KJV	Gods	GNB	gods
L	*Gods	GN	*God		
SEG	gods	BJ	(God) he	FC	this God
NC	(powerful gods) these who				
VP	(this powerful God) who				

11. *elohim* referring to specific pagan male deity.

11a. Judg 8:33: made *baal-berith* their *elohim*. All translations use lower case singular "god"; GNB and GN translate *berith* as "covenant"; LXX both transliterates *berith* and translates it, creating an ambiguity that suggests 'covenant god' which would be *yahweh*. Possibly it is being used facetiously here.

LXX	Baalberith into covenant...into *god
GNB	Baal-of-the-Covenant their god
GN	the covenant-Baal...their *God
All others	god

12. *elohim* referring to a specific female deity.

12a. 1 Kgs 11:5: Solomon went after Ashtoreth, the *elohim* of the Sidonians. Only LXX uses a derogatory "abomination" instead of "goddess"; SEG and BJ use the sexually undifferentiated "divinity"; all others use "goddess."
LXX   the abomination   SEG   divinity   BJ   divinity

13. *elohim* referring to polytheism treated negatively.

13a. Is 21:9: he smashed to earth all the graven images of their *elohim*. LXX uses the derogatory "handmade images/idols"; this is followed by GNB "idols they worshiped," GN and SEG "idol images"; all others retain plural lower case "gods."
LXX   handmade images/idols

13b. 2 Sam 7:23: (you redeemed your people) from the nations and from their *elohim*. LXX uses the (derogatory) "temples"; NC makes no reference to the gods of the nations; all the others have the lower case plural "gods."
LXX   temples   NC   #

13c. Ps 96:5: the *elohim* of all nations are idols. A number of translations emphasize idols; LXX calls the gods "demons," GNB "only idols," GN "only dead idols," NC "vain idols," and BJ and FC emphasize their "nothingness."

LXX	*gods...demons		
KJV	gods...idols	GNB	gods...only idols
L	*Gods...idols	GN	*Gods...only dead idols
SEG	gods...idols	BJ	gods...nonexistent
FC	gods...nonentities		
NC	god...vain idols	VP	gods...nothing

14. *elohim* in ambiguous contexts.

14a. Gen 3:5: you shall be as *elohim* knowing good and evil. LXX, KJV, SEG, and BJ render it as plural, all the others read it as singular referring to the supreme God, GN makes it emphatic with "exactly like God."

LXX	*gods	KJV	gods	GNB	God
L	*God	GN	exactly like *God		
SEG	gods	BJ	gods	FC	(God) him
NC	God	VP	God		

14b. 1 Kgs 12:28: behold your *elohim* which brought you out of Egypt. LXX, KJV, GNB, L, and VP read it as plural "gods," all others read it as "God."

14c. Ps 8:5: thou hast made him a little less than *elohim*. LXX renders it "angels," this is followed by KJV and FC; BJ and VP render it as "a god," all the others read it as referring to God himself. Several provide alternative readings in notes. This example could also belong to the next category.

LXX	angels		
KJV	angels (fn: God)	GNB	yourself (fn: gods or angels)
L	*God	GN	(*God) you
SEG	God	BJ	a god
FC	angels (fn: celestial beings)		
NC	God	VP	a god

15. *elohim* used with restricted meanings such as 'supernatural beings, ghost, big, great.'

15a. Gen 6:2: the sons of *elohim* saw the daughters of men. GNB and FC treat it as referring to supernatural beings, all the others render it literally as "god."

15b. Ex 21:6: his master shall bring him (the slave) to *ha-elohim*. LXX and KJV read it as "the religious authorities who are God's representatives among men"; GNB,

GN, and FC see it more as the place where God will be the witness; SEG, BJ, NC and VP render it "God," and only L as "Gods."

LXX	to the tribunal of *god		
KJV	to the judges	GNB	to the place of worship
L	the *Gods	GN	in the presence of *God
SEG	God	BJ	God
FC	make God his witness		
NC	God	VP	God

15c. 1 Sam 28:13: *elohim* I have seen coming out of the earth. GNB and GN render it as "a spirit"; BJ and FC as "a ghost"; SEG, NC, and VP read it as lower case singular "god"; all the others say "gods."

LXX	*gods	KJV	gods	GNB	a spirit
L	*Gods	GN	a *Spirit		
SEG	a god	BJ	specter (fn: supernatural being)		
FC	some kind of phantom/ghost				
NC	a god	VP	a god		

15d. Jon 3:3: Nineveh, a vastly *elohim* city. All translations render it "great," but KJV, GN and VP try to match the Hebrew emphasis in some way.

KJV	exceeding great	GN	great world-famous
VP	so great		

15e. Gen 1:2: the *ruach* 'wind/breath/spirit' of *elohim* moved above the waters. Only LXX can match the Hebrew *ruach*'s area of meaning, all other translations chose one or the other of the three possible meanings. All translations leave "god/God" in the text, but many give the alternatives "strong" or "mighty" in a footnote. BJ stands out in negating the possibility of the "spirit of God" reading in this context.

LXX	wind/spirit of *god		
KJV	spirit of God		
GNB	power of God (fn: spirit of God, wind of God or awesome wind)		
L	spirit of *God	GN	spirit of *God (fn: a mighty wind)
SEG	spirit of God	BJ	a wind of God (fn: not 'spirit of God' here)
FC	the breath of God (fn: spirit of God or terrible wind)		
NC	spirit of God	VP	spirit of God

15f. 1 Kgs 3:28: saw the wisdom of *elohim* in him. NC and BJ stand out with "divine," all others use "god/God"; the four CL versions make explicit a verb.

LXX	mind of *god		
KJV	wisdom of God	GNB	God had given him wisdom
L	wisdom of *God	GN	*God had given him wisdom
SEG	wisdom of God	BJ	divine wisdom
FC	God himself had filled him with wisdom		
NC	divine wisdom	VP	God had given him wisdom

For additional uses of *elohim* as a qualifier see 'garden of God' probably meaning 'beautiful' (Ezek 28:13); 'mountain of God' probably meaning 'holy' or 'massive' (Ps 68:16); 'fire of God' probably meaning 'fierce' (Job 1:16).

16. *el* and *elohim* in contrast.

16a. Josh 22:22: the *el* of *elohim* (is) *yahweh*; the *el* of *elohim* (is) *yahweh*. GN and FC have no repeat; GNB, NC, L, and GN translate *el* as "mighty/almighty"; FC uses "supreme"; KJV and FC transpose *yahweh*, KJV actually making it "LORD God," like a composite name; KJV and BJ treat *elohim* as "gods"; LXX and SEG just repeat "God"; all translations render *yahweh* in their usual way.

LXX	the *god god...lord (repeat)
KJV	the LORD God of gods (repeat)
GNB	the Mighty one is God! He is LORD! (repeat)
L	the strong *God, the Lord (repeat)
GN	the Almighty God (no repeat)
SEG	God, God, the eternal one (repeat)
BJ	the God of gods, Yahve (repeat)
FC	the Lord is God Supreme (repeat)
NC	the all-powerful God, Yave (repeat)
VP	the Lord and God of all the gods (no repeat)

17. *eloah* as a singular referring to the supreme God.

17a. Deut 32:15: he abandoned the *eloah* who made him. All translations render it "god/God," NC, VP, GNB, SEG, and FC have "God, the Creator," thus making a praise name out of it.

17b. Ps 50:22: you who forget *eloah*. All render it "god/God," but GNB, GN, and FC, who have God speaking, use the corresponding pronoun "me."

17c. Job 3:4: let not *eloah* look, from above. All translations except LXX render it "God," KJV attempts a praise name with "God above"; LXX uses "lord."

17d. Ezra 5:1: the name of the *elah* of Israel was over them. All translations render it "god/God."

17e. Dan 2:20: the name of *elah* be blessed forever. All translations use "god/God."

18. *elah* as a plural referring to other gods.

18a. Jer 10:11: the *elah* who have not made the heavens and the earth. All translations render it plural "gods."

18b. Dan 2:11: (no one knows except) the *elah* whose dwelling is not with men. All translations render it plural "gods."

19. *eloah* referring to a pagan deity.

19a. Dan 11:38: *eloah* of fortresses he will honor. All translations except KJV treat *eloah* as referring to a "god" not "God."
KJV   the God

19b. 2 Chr 32:15: no *eloah* of any nation. All translations treat it as referring to a "god."

Forms of *yahweh*

20. *yahweh* as the universal God's personal name (very rare and somewhat doubtful;

usually it is the personal name of God of the Hebrews).

20a. Ps 83:18 (17 or 19): (God) whose name alone is *yahweh*. All translations except KJV follow their standard rendering for *yahweh*; KJV transliterates it as JEHOVAH; FC adds "only" with "God."

LXX	*lord	KJV	JEHOVAH	GNB	LORD
L	*Lord	GN	*Lord		
SEG	the Eternal One	BJ	Yahve		
FC	you are lord, the only God				
NC	Yave	VP	Lord		

21. *yahweh* as the personal name of the tribal God of the Hebrews.

21a. Ex 15:3: *yahweh* is his name. In this verse the translations follow what could be considered their normal way of rendering *yahweh*. BJ and NC transliterate it; SEG translates it by its meaning; the rest all render it "Lord"—KJV and GNB with all capital letters, FC and VP with only the first letter capital; GN introduces the emphatic "the only."

LXX	*lord (fn)	KJV	LORD	GNB	LORD
L	*Lord	GN	the only *Lord		
SEG	the Eternal One	BJ	Yahve	FC	the Lord
NC	Yave	VP	The Lord		

21b. Ex 6:3: unto Jacob, by my name *el shaddai*, but by my name *yahweh* was I not known unto them. All translations except KJV follow their normal rendering of *yahweh*, KJV again transliterates the name in all capitals; this all capital letters usage is followed by FC and VP; GNB and VP make explicit qualifiers, possibly to mark it as the "ineffable name."

LXX	*lord		
KJV	JEHOVAH	GNB	my holy name, the LORD
L	*Lord	GN	*Lord
SEG	the Eternal One	BJ	Yahve
FC	"LE SEIGNEUR" 'the lord'		
NC	Yave	VP	my true name: EL SEÑOR 'the lord'

21c. Ex 3:18: *yahweh elohim* of the Hebrews has met us...that we may sacrifice to *yahweh* our *elohim*. All translations except LXX follow their normal renderings; LXX drops the *yahweh/elohim* distinction; FC piles up all the names as appositives in the first instance and uses only the pronoun "him" in the second; GNB likewise uses only the pronoun in the second instance, both also blur the distinction, at least in part.

LXX	the *god...our god
KJV	LORD God...LORD our God
GNB	the LORD, our God...the LORD, our God
L	the *Lord, the Hebrews' God
GN	the *Lord the God...him
SEG	the Eternal One, the God...the Eternal One, our God
BJ	Yahve, our God
FC	the Lord, the God of the Hebrews, our God...him
NC	Yave, the God...Yave, our God

VP   the Lord, the God...the Lord, our God

21d. Deut 6:4: hear, O Israel, *yahweh* our *elohim* is one *yahweh*. All translations follow their usual renderings, but GNB and FC reorder the construction to express emphasis by putting "God" into final position.

LXX   *lord the god of us...lord
KJV   LORD, our God...LORD
GNB   the LORD—and the LORD alone—is our God
L   the *Lord our God...Lord
GN   the *Lord is our God the Lord
SEG   the Eternal One, our God...the Eternal One
BJ   Yahve our God...Yahve
FC   the Lord, the Lord only is our God
NC   Yave, our God...Yave
VP   the Lord our God is the only Lord

22. *yahweh* functioning as a substitute for *elohim*.

22a. Gen 6:5: *yahweh* saw. LXX renders it by the combined name "lord the god," KJV as GOD (all capitals), the rest follow their usual rendering.

22b. Gen 17:1: appeared *yahweh*. All follow their normal rendering.

22c. Gen 30:24: *yahweh* shall add to me a son. Only LXX renders it "god," but GN and VP with "he" have "God" as the antecedent; the rest follow their usual rendering.

LXX   *god   GN   (*God) he   VP   (God) he

23. *yah* the shortened form of *yahweh* occurring alone.

23a. Ps 68:4 (5): by *yah*, his name. All translations except KJV follow their usual rendering for *yahweh*; KJV transliterates the name "Jah" here.

23b. Ex 17:16: a hand is on the throne of *yah*; war with Amelek from generation to generation is *yahweh*. All translations follow their usual rendering for *yahweh* except LXX which leaves *yah* implicit.

LXX   #...*lord
KJV   LORD...LORD   GNB LORD...LORD
L   *Lord...Lord   GN   *Lord...between him
SEG   the Eternal One...the Eternal One
BJ   Yahve...Yahve   FC   Lord...Lord
NC   Yave...Yave   VP   Lord...Lord

Forms of *adonai*

24. *adonai* functioning as a substitute for 'God.'

24a. Dan 9:7: o *adonai*, righteousness belongs to you. All translations render it "lord/Lord," their usual pattern.

LXX   *lord   KJV O Lord   GNB you, Lord
L   you *Lord   GN   you *Lord
SEG   Lord   BJ   to you, Lord FC   Lord
NC   Lord   VP   you, Lord

24b. Gen 20:4: O my *adonai*, are you going to kill. All translations follow their usual pattern.

24c. Lam 2:1: how *adonai* has clouded over the daughter of Zion. All translations follow their normal pattern, only VP uses a pronoun whose antecedent is "Lord."

25. *adon* more or less unmarked, referring to God (relatively infrequent).

25a. Mal 3:1: the *adon* whom you seek shall suddenly come. All translations render it "lord/Lord" as usual; only GN has "I, the Lord."

25b. Ps 147:5: great is our *adon* and of great power. The two Spanish versions differ—NC substitutes "Yave" and VP uses "God," possibly because Lord was felt to be ambiguous; all others follow their usual rendering.

26. *adon* marked as referring to God, often by other divine names.

26a. Josh 3:11: the ark of the covenant of *adon* of all the earth. L and NC depart from their usual patterns, using "ruler" and "owner" respectively.

26b. Josh 3:13: the ark of *yahweh*, *adon* of all the earth. LXX, NC, and GN substitute "covenant" for *yahweh* and so use only "lord/Lord"; in GNB and VP one occurrence of "Lord" does double duty; FC replaces both with the adjective "sacred"; the rest follow their usual renderings.

LXX	of the covenant of the *lord of all the earth		
KJV	LORD, the Lord	GNB	#...LORD of all the earth
L	*Lord, ruler	GN	#...of the *Lord of all the earth
SEG	the Eternal One, the Lord		
BJ	Yahve, Lord	FC	sacred box
NC	#...of the owner of all the earth		
VP	#...of the Lord of all the earth		

26c. Is 1:24: therefore says *ha* 'the' *adon*, *yahweh sabaoth* 'armies.' KJV, L, SEG, BJ, and NC treat *adon* and *yahweh* as usual, but LXX, BJ, and NC transliterate *sabaoth*, while KJV and SEG translate it literally; GNB and VP compress the whole expression into "Lord Almighty"; FC renders *adon* "supreme master" and *yahweh sabaoth* as "Lord of the universe"; LXX translates *adon* with "absolute master," but transliterates *sabaoth*; GN handles *adon* as usual, but *yahweh sabaoth* appears as "sovereign of the whole world."

LXX	absolute master, *lord sabaoth
KJV	Lord, the LORD of hosts
GNB	the LORD Almighty, Israel's powerful God
L	*Lord, Lord Zebaoth
GN	the *Lord, the sovereign of the whole world
SEG	the Lord, the Eternal One of the armies
BJ	Lord Yahve Sabaot
FC	the supreme master, Lord of the universe
NC	the Lord, Yave Sebaot	VP	the Lord almighty

26d. Ex 4:10: said Moses to *yahweh*, o my *adonai*. GN and VP reduce the two to one "Lord." The others treat both as usual.

26e. 2 Sam 7:19: (David prayed saying) o *adonai*, o *yahweh*. Only LXX retains two vocatives; all the others reduce them to one, but KJV, GN, BJ, FC, and NC put a second name as an appositive; GNB, SEG, and VP reduce the two to a single name; GNB and SEG convert one of the names into a qualifier.

LXX	*lord...lord		
KJV	LORD...Lord	GNB	#, no LORD
L	*Lord...Lord	GN	#...*Lord
SEG	Eternal One...Lord		
BJ	Yahve...Lord	FC	Lord...Lord
NC	Yave...Lord	VP	#, Lord

27. *yahweh* and *adon* in contrast.

27a. Ps 110:1: *yahweh* said to my *adon*. KJV, GNB, SEG, BJ, and NC indicate that *yahweh* is speaking; GNB and GN specify that this Lord means "God"; only GNB, GN, and FC indicate that the second "Lord" refers to the king; the rest remain ambiguous.

LXX	the *lord...my lord		
KJV	the LORD...my Lord	GNB	the LORD...my lord, the king
L	the *Lord...my Lord	GN	*God, the Lord...my Lord and king
SEG	The Eternal One...my Lord		
BJ	Yahve...my Lord	FC	the Lord God...my Lord the king
NC	Yave to my Lord	VP	Lord to my lord

28. *yahweh* and *elohim* in contrast.

28a. Gen 28:20–21: if *elohim* will be with me...*yahweh* will be to me *elohim*. LXX obscures the distinction by using "Lord God"; GNB, GN, and FC seem to follow this lead at least in part.

LXX	*lord the god...lord...god		
KJV	God...LORD...God	GNB	you (LORD)...you...God
L	*God...Lord...God	GN	the *Lord...he alone...God
SEG	God...the Eternal One...God		
BJ	God...Yahve...God	FC	Lord...Lord...God
NC	Yave...Yave...God	VP	God...Lord...God

28b. Hos 13:4: I am *yahweh* your *elohim*...you shall have no *elohim* but me. There is considerable variation between capital and lower case "God/god"; see KJV, GNB, NC, VP, SEG, BJ, and FC.

LXX	*lord...god...god		
KJV	LORD...God...god	GNB	LORD...God...God
L	*Lord...God...God	GN	*Lord...God...God
SEG	the Eternal One...God...God		
BJ	Yahve...God...God	FC	Lord...God...God
NC	Yave...God...god	VP	Lord...God...God

28c. Josh 24:14: turn from the *elohim* your fathers served, and serve *yahweh*. All translations render *elohim* as plural, even though there is no plural marker; *yahweh* is treated in each one's usual manner.

LXX	*gods...the lord		
KJV	gods...the LORD	GNB	gods...only the LORD
L	*God...the Lord	GN	*Gods...the Lord
SEG	gods...the Eternal One		

BJ	gods...Yahve	FC	gods...the Lord
NC	gods...Yave	VP	gods...the Lord

29. *yah* or *yahweh* reduplicated.

29a. Is 12:2: for *yah yahweh* is my strength and my song. LXX, BJ, NC, and VP reduce it to a single "Lord" or "Yahve"; GNB, GN, and FC render it "lord" plus "he"; SEG repeats "Eternal One"; KJV uses LORD JEHOVAH translating one and transliterating the other; L says "God the Lord" making "Lord" an appositive.

LXX	*lord		
KJV	the LORD JEHOVAH	GNB	the LORD, he
L	*God the Lord	GN	the *Lord, he
SEG	the Eternal One, the Eternal One		
BJ	Yahve	FC	the Lord, he
NC	Yave	VP	the Lord

29b. Is 38:11: I shall not see *yah yah* in the land of the living. LXX, BJ, NC, and VP keep it as one sentence and so translate only one *yah*; all the others translate it in two clauses, though GNB, GN, and FC elide the pronoun in the second clause.

LXX	the salvation of *god		
KJV	LORD...LORD	GNB	LORD...#
L	*Lord...Lord	GN	*Lord...#
SEG	the Eternal One...the Eternal One		
BJ	Yahve	FC	Lord...#
NC	Yave	VP	Lord

29c. Is 26:4: (trust) for *yah yahweh* is a rock forever. LXX translates one as "god" and treats the other as a qualifier; L translates it "God" but uses "Lord" as an appositive; GN reverses it and treats "God" as the appositive; GNB and VP reduce it to one name, and VP uses a pronoun; FC creates an emphatic expression; KJV again renders one "LORD" and transliterates the other; SEG merely repeats the name; BJ and NC make two clauses and repeat their transliteration.

LXX	the *god the great the eternal one		
KJV	LORD JEHOVAH	GNB	the LORD
L	*God the Lord	GN	the *Lord, our God
SEG	the Eternal One, the Eternal One		
BJ	Yahve, for Yahve	FC	the Lord, yes, the Lord
NC	Yave, for Yave	VP	(Lord) he

30. Composite *adon yahweh*.

30a. Ex 23:17: all males shall appear before *adon yahweh*. LXX renders the combined form as "*lord the god," this is followed by KJV, GNB, FC, and NC; GNB and FC with the first person "me" actually treat the composite as an appositive; only GN and VP reduce it to a single "Lord."

LXX	*lord the god		
KJV	Lord GOD	GNB	me, the LORD your God
L	the *Lord, the Ruler	GN	the *Lord
SEG	the Lord, the Eternal One		
BJ	the Lord Yahve	FC	me, the Lord your God
NC	Yave, your God	VP	the Lord

30b. Jer 46:10: this is the day of *adon yahweh sabaoth*. LXX, GN, and VP reduce *adon yahweh* to one "Lord"; GNB changes the *adon* into "sovereign"; the rest follow their usual rendering; *sabaoth* is transliterated by LXX, L, and BJ; KJV and NC translate it literally as "hosts/armies," while the four CL translations try to render its meaning as "almighty" or "of the world."

LXX	*lord sabaoth		
KJV	Lord GOD of hosts	GNB	Sovereign LORD Almighty
L	*Lord Lord Zebaoth	GN	the *Lord of the world
SEG	the Lord, the Eternal One		
BJ	the Lord Yahve Sabaot	FC	the Lord, the God of the universe
NC	Yave, God of the armies	VP	the Lord almighty

31. Composite *adonai yahweh*.

31a. Is 25:8: *adonai yahweh* will wipe away all tears. LXX reduces it to "god" only, NC and VP to "Lord" only; FC and KJV render it "Lord God/ GOD"; GNB has "Sovereign LORD" as antecedent, and GN the "Lord of the world."

LXX	the *god		
KJV	the Lord GOD	GNB	(the Sovereign LORD) he
L	the *Lord Lord	GN	(the *Lord of the world) he
SEG	the Lord, the Eternal One		
BJ	The Lord, Yahve	FC	the Lord God
NC	the Lord	VP	(the Lord) he

31b. Gen 15:2: Abraham said, '*adonai yahweh*, what do you give to me?' Only LXX reduces it to one name; GN, BJ, and FC translate the "my" of *adonai*, but GN and FC attach it to "God"; VP joins two names with "and."

LXX	absolute master		
KJV	Lord GOD	GNB	Sovereign LORD
L	*Lord Lord	GN	*Lord, my God
SEG	Lord, the Eternal One		
BJ	my Lord Yahve	FC	Lord my God
NC	Lord, Yave	VP	Lord and God

31c. 2 Sam 7:28: now, o *adonai yahweh*, you are the *elohim* himself. LXX translates both with "lord"; only LXX and NC translate the "my" of *adonai*. GN strengthens the *elohim* with "true."

LXX	*lord, my lord...the god		
KJV	o Lord GOD...that God	GNB	Sovereign LORD...God
L	*Lord, Lord...God	GN	you *Lord are the true God
SEG	Lord Eternal...God	BJ	Lord Yahve...God
FC	Lord God...God		
NC	my Lord, Yave...God	VP	you, Lord...God

32. Composite *yahweh adon*.

32a. Hab 3:19: *yahweh adon* is my might. LXX, KJV, FC, and NC render it "Lord God" with variations; GN and VP reduce it to a single "Lord."

LXX	*lord the god		
KJV	LORD God	GNB	Sovereign LORD

L	*Lord Lord	GN	the *Lord who
SEG	The Eternal One, the Lord		
BJ	Yahve, my Lord	FC	the Lord God
NC	Yave, my God	VP	the Lord

33. Composite *yahweh adonai.*

33a. Ps 68:20 (21): to *yahweh adonai* are the issues of death. GNB departs from its usual pattern with "LORD, our Lord"; FC and VP use "God" as the antecedent; GN, NC, and VP reduce it to one name.

LXX	the *lord lord		
KJV	GOD the Lord	GNB	the LORD, our Lord
L	*Lord Lord	GN	(*Lord) he is our *Lord who
SEG	the Eternal One, the Lord		
BJ	Lord Yahve	FC	(God) he, the Lord
NC	Yave who	VP	(God) he

34. Composite *yahweh elohim.*

34a. Jon 4:6: and *yahweh elohim* ordained a plant. Most translations follow their standard pattern; GN reduces the composite name to "God," VP inverts the order and makes *yahweh* the appositive.

LXX	*lord the god	KJV	the LORD God
GNB	the LORD God		
L	*God the Lord	GN	*God
SEG	the Eternal One	BJ	Yahve God
FC	the Lord God	VP	God the Lord
NC	Yave, God		

34b. Gen 2:4b-7: (v.4b) in the day that *yahweh elohim* was creating... (v.5)...for *yahweh elohim* had not sent rain... (v.7) and *yahweh elohim* formed man. Most translations follow their standard pattern, but LXX blurs the transition by using only "God"; GN introduces "God, the Lord" in verse 4 but reverts to "God" only; GNB uses only "he" in verse 5.

	Verse 4	Verse 5	Verse 7
LXX	the *god	the god	the god
KJV	the LORD God	the LORD God	the LORD God
GNB	the LORD God	he	the LORD God
L	*God the Lord	God the Lord	God the Lord
GN	*God, the Lord	God	God
SEG	the Eternal God	the Eternal God	the Eternal God
BJ	Yahve God	Yahve God	Yahve God
FC	the Lord God	the Lord God	the Lord God
NC	Yave God	Yave God	Yave God
VP	God, the Lord	God, the Lord	God, the Lord

34c. Ps 72:18: blessed be *yahweh elohim*, the *elohim* of Israel. SEG renders the whole name in capitals; GNB, GN, FC, BJ, and NC reduce *yahweh elohim* to one name *yahweh* which they treat in their standard way; VP uses "God" in the first instance and transposes "Lord" to the appositive position; L renders both, but transposes them.

LXX	*lord the god, the god		
KJV	the LORD God, the God	GNB	the LORD, the God
L	*God the Lord, the God	GN	the *Lord, the God
SEG	THE ETERNAL GOD, THE GOD		
BJ	Yahve, the God	FC	Lord, the God
NC	Yave, God	VP	God, Lord and God

34d. Ex 3:18: say to him, *yahweh elohim* of the Hebrews met us. Only LXX, KJV, and BJ treat it as a composite name, all the others structure it as an appositive, LXX in addition leaves out *yahweh*.

LXX	# the *god		
KJV	the LORD God	GNB	the LORD, the God
L	the *Lord, the Hebrews' God	GN	the *Lord, the God
SEG	the Eternal One, the God	BJ	Yahve God
FC	the Lord, the God	NC	Yave, the God
VP	the Lord, the God		

34e. Jer 30:2 (1; LXX 37:2): thus says *yahweh elohim* of Israel. Only LXX, L, and FC treat it as a composite name, but FC has it as an appositive to "I."

LXX	*lord the god		
KJV	LORD God	GNB	the LORD, the God
L	the *Lord, the God	GN	the *Lord, the God
SEG	the Eternal One, the God	BJ	Yahve, the God
FC	it is I, the Lord God	NC	Yave, God
VP	the Lord, the God		

35. Composite *yah elohim*.

35a. Ps 68:18: to dwell among the rebellious, o *yah elohim*. LXX, KJV, GNB, SEG, FC, and NC all treat it as a composite name; BJ and VP leave out *elohim*.

LXX	*lord the god	KJV	the LORD God
GNB	the LORD God		
L	*God the Lord	GN	the *Lord, our God
SEG	the Eternal God	BJ	Yahve #
FC	Lord God		
NC	o Yave God	VP	you, Lord #

36. Composite *yahweh el*.

36a. Ps 94:1: o *el* of vengeance, o *yahweh el* of vengeance show yourself. KJV and L transpose the composite name into first position; GNB, GN, and VP do not repeat the expression; NC uses "Yave, God" in both expressions.

LXX	the *god...lord, the god		
KJV	o LORD God...o God	GNB	LORD, you are a God
L	*Lord God...God	GN	*God...Lord
SEG	God...Eternal God	BJ	God...Yahve God
FC	God...Lord God		
NC	Yave, God...Yave, God	VP	Lord, God

36b. Ex 34:6: (*yahweh*) passed before his face and said, *yahweh, yahweh* is merciful. LXX leaves out the first *yahweh*; L, BJ, NC, and VP treat it as sort of a name chant; GNB, GN, and FC all change it to first person; GN has "God" as the antecedent to "I," and it expands the expression into several short sentences.

LXX	# *lord the god		
KJV	the LORD, the LORD God	GNB	(LORD) I, the LORD am a God
L	the *Lord, Lord, God		
GN	(God) I am the *Lord, Lord is my name. I am a God...		
SEG	the Eternal One, the Eternal God		
BJ	Yahve, Yahve God		
FC	(Lord) I am the Lord. I am a God		
NC	Yave, Yave, God	VP	The LORD! The Lord! God

37. Doublet *el elohim* versus *yahweh elohim*.

37a. Num 16:22: saying, o *el elohe* of the spirits of all flesh. LXX, KJV, SEG, BJ, and NC simply repeat the name "God"; GNB, L, GN, FC, and VP switch to second person and thus "you" translates one of the original names.

LXX	*god god	KJV	o God, the God	GNB	o God, you are
L	o *God, you who are a God				
GN	life comes from you *God, you				
SEG	o God, God	BJ	o God, God	FC	o God, you who
NC	o God, God	VP	o God, you who		

37b. Num 27:16: let *yahweh elohe* of the spirits of all flesh. Only GN, FC, and VP put it into the second person; VP treats them as two names joined by "and"; only LXX and FC treat it as a composite name, all the others as an appositive.

LXX	*lord the god		
KJV	the LORD, the God	GNB	LORD, God, source of
L	the *Lord, the God	GN	*Lord, you God
SEG	may the Eternal One, the God		
BJ	may Yahve, God	FC	Lord God, you
NC	may Yave, the God	VP	God and Lord, you who

Comparative Listing of Praise Names Based on *el/elohim*

38. *elohim amen* 'so be it, truth.'

38a. Is 65:16: shall bless himself in *elohe amen*. LXX, L, and FC read it as the "real God," KJV, SEG, and BJ as "God of truth," and GNB, GN, NC, and VP as "faithful God."

LXX	the real/genuine *god		
KJV	the God of truth	GNB	the faithful God
L·	the genuine *God	GN	"with the faithful *God"
SEG	the God of truth	BJ	the God of truth
FC	the only true God		
NC	the faithful God	VP	the faithful God

39. *el elyon* 'the most high God.'

39a. Gen 14:18: (Melchizedek) the priest of *el elyon*. The translations are very similar with variations only in capital versus lower case letters.

LXX	the *god the most high

KJV	the most high God	GNB	the Most High God
L	*God the Highest	GN	the highest *God
SEG	the God Most-High	BJ	the God Most High
FC	the God Most-High		
NC	The God Most High	VP	the God most high

40. *elohim elyon* 'the most high God.'

40a. Ps 57:2 (3): I will cry unto *elohim elyon*. Only GNB, L, GN, and BJ treat *elyon* as an appositive.

LXX	the *god the most high		
KJV	God most high	GNB	God, the Most High
L	*God, the most high (Very Highest)		
GN	*God, the Highest		
SEG	God Most-High	BJ	God the Most-High
FC	God Most-High		
NC	The God Most High	VP	the God most high

40b. Ps 78:56: provoked the *elohim elyon*. KJV inverts the order; GNB uses "Almighty"; GN uses only "the Highest" but in a parallel construction with "God" in the next line.

LXX	the *god most high		
KJV	the most high God	GNB	the Almighty God
L	*God the Highest	GN	the *Highest
SEG	the God Most-High	BJ	God the Most-High
FC	the God Most-High		
NC	the God Most High	VP	the God most high

41. *elyon* 'the most high' alone.

41a. Deut 32:8: *elyon* divided. Only GN and FC make explicit the implicit class noun "god."

LXX	*the most high		
KJV	the Most High	GNB	the Most High
L	the *Very Highest	GN	the highest *God
SEG	the Most-High	BJ	the Most-High
FC	the God Most-High		
NC	the Most High	VP	the Most High

41b. 2 Sam 22:14: *elyon* gave forth. Only GNB, GN, and FC make the class noun explicit, VP achieves something similar with its appositive to "Lord" left over from a reduced parallelism.

LXX	*the most high	KJV	the most High
GNB	Almighty God		
L	the *Highest	GN	the highest *God
SEG	the Most-High	BJ	the Most High
FC	God Most-High		
NC	the Most High	VP	the Lord, the Most High

41c. Lam 3:38: out of the mouth of *elyon*. Only GNB differs with "his command," with "LORD" as the antecedent to the pronoun; all others have "God."

41d. Dan 7:22: saints of the *elyon*. Only GNB differs with "Supreme God"; all others have "God."

42. *elah illai* 'God the most high' (probably of Chaldean origin).

42a. Dan 3:26: servants of *elah illai*. GNB, SEG, and NC use "supreme" as the modifier.

LXX	the *god the most high		
KJV	the most high God	GNB	the Supreme God
L	*God the Highest	GN	the highest God
SEG	supreme God	BJ	God Most-High
FC	God Most-High		
NC	the supreme God	VP	the most high God

42b. Dan 5:21: (Nebuchadnezzar) knew that *elah illai* ruled. NC leaves out the classifier "God"; GN makes explicit "alone."

LXX	the *god the most high		
KJV	the Most High God	GNB	the Supreme God
L	*God the Highest	GN	the highest *God alone
SEG	the supreme God	BJ	the God Most High
FC	the God Most-High		
NC	the Most High	VP	the most high God

43. *illai* 'the most high' alone.

43a. Dan 4:25 (22): the *illai* rules in the kingdom of men. Only the CL translations make explicit the class noun "god."

LXX	*the most high		
KJV	the most High	GNB	the Supreme God
L	the *Highest	GN	the highest *God alone
SEG	the Most-High	BJ	the Most High
FC	the God Most High		
NC	the Most High	VP	the most high God

43b. Dan 4:34: my understanding returned and I blessed *illai*. Only the CL translations make explicit the class noun "god"; GN has it as the antecedent, and uses direct address.

LXX	*the most high		
KJV	the most High	GNB	the Supreme God
L	the *Highest	GN	(you, the highest *God) I praise you
SEG	the Most-High	BJ	the Most High
FC	the God Most-High		
NC	the Most High	VP	the most high God

44. *el olam* 'eternal, everlasting God.'

44a. Gen 21:33: called on the name of *yahweh*, the *el olam*. All translations render *olam* "eternal" or "everlasting"; only FC inverts the order and changes the focus.

LXX	name of the *lord god eternal
KJV	the LORD, the everlasting God
GNB	the LORD, the Everlasting God
L	the *Lord, the everlasting God

GN	the *Lord, the eternal God
SEG	the Eternal One, God of eternity
BJ	Yahve, God of eternity
FC	the eternal God, calling him Lord
NC	Yave, the eternal God
VP	the Lord, the eternal God

45. *elohim olam* 'eternal, everlasting God.'

45a. Is 40:28: not heard that *elohim olam yahweh* the creator. GN and FC have restatements for "eternal/everlasting."

LXX	*god eternal the god
KJV	the everlasting God, the LORD
GNB	the LORD, the everlasting God
L	the *Lord, the eternal God
GN	the *Lord, our God...for all times
SEG	the God of Eternity, the Eternal One
BJ	Yahve is an eternal God
FC	the Lord is God from age to age
NC	Yave is an eternal God
VP	the Lord, the eternal God

46. *elohim qedem* 'God the refuge.'

46a. Deut 33:27: the *elohe qedem* is your refuge. Most translations read *qedem* as forming one expression with *elohim*, but GNB and FC read it as belonging with the predicate.

LXX	*god (from) the beginning		
KJV	eternal God		
GNB	God has always been your defense		
L	the ancient *God	GN	the eternal *God
SEG	the God of eternity	BJ	the God of ancient times
FC	(God) since the beginning, he (is your refuge)		
NC	the eternal God	VP	the eternal God

47. *el roi* 'God the seeing one.'

47a. Gen 16:13: she called the name of *yahweh*, the one speaking to her, you *el roi*. The three French translations SEG, BJ, FC, and also NC all transliterate the name, FC has both the transliteration and its meaning.

LXX	you the *god the one seeing me		
KJV	thou God seest me	GNB	"A God who sees"
L	you *God see me	GN	the *God who looks at me
SEG	El-roi	BJ	you are El-Roi
FC	you are El-Roi, the God who sees me		
NC	Atta-El-Roi 'God of the vision'		
VP	"the God who sees"		

48. *el shaddai* 'God almighty.'

48a. Gen 17:1: I am *el shaddai*. LXX leaves out *shaddai*; BJ and NC transliterate the name; GN gives a restatement of "almighty."

LXX	the *god of you		
KJV	the Almighty God	GNB	Almighty God
L	the almighty *God	GN	the *God who possesses all power
SEG	the almighty God	BJ	El Shaddai
FC	the almighty God		
NC	El Sadai	VP	the almighty God

48b. Ex 6:3: I appeared to Abraham by the name of *el shaddai*. All translations follow their regular pattern, only FC uses all capitals in this instance.

LXX	his *god		
KJV	God Almighty	GNB	Almighty God
L	the almighty *God	GN	the *God who possesses all power
SEG	the almighty God	BJ	El-Shaddai
FC	ALMIGHTY GOD		
NC	El-Sadai	VP	almighty God

48c. Ezek 10:5: the voice of *el shaddai*. LXX transliterates *shaddai* here, while NC translates it as "omnipotent."

LXX	*god saddai		
KJV	Almighty God	GNB	Almighty God
L	the almighty *God	GN	the almighty *God
SEG	almighty God	BJ	almighty God
FC	almighty God		
NC	omnipotent God	VP	the almighty God

49. *shaddai* 'almighty' alone.

49a. Ruth 1:20: *shaddai* has dealt bitterly with me. LXX and NC translate it, but BJ transliterates it; the CL translations make explicit a class noun.

LXX	*the sufficient one	KJV	the Almighty
GNB	the LORD Almighty ("LORD" transposed from the next clause)		
L	the *Almighty	GN	the *Lord who possesses all power
SEG	the Almighty	BJ	Shaddai
FC	the almighty God		
NC	the Omnipotent	VP	the almighty God

49b. Job 22:23: if you return to *shaddai*. NC again translates it; LXX replaces it with "lord"; GNB and GN use "God," and BJ again transliterates the name.

LXX	the *lord	KJV	the Almight	GNB	God
L	the *Almighty	GN	(*God) him		
SEG	the Almighty	BJ	Shaddai	FC	the Almighty
NC	the Omnipotent	VP	the Almighty		

Comparative Listing of Praise Names Based on *yahweh*

50. *yahweh elyon* 'God most high.'

50a. Ps 7:17 (18): praise the name of *yahweh elyon*. GN and FC substitute "God" for *yahweh*; some treat it as a combined name, others as an appositive.

LXX	*lord the most high		
KJV	the LORD most high	GNB	the LORD, the Most High
L	the *Lord, the Very Highest	GN	the highest *God

SEG	of the Eternal One of the Most-High		
BJ	of the Most-High	FC	God Most-High
NC	the Lord Most High	VP	the Lord...the Most High

51. *yahweh nissi* 'God the refuge.'

51a. Ex 17:15: built an altar and called the name of it *yahweh nissi*. Only LXX translates nissi as "refuge"; KJV, BJ, and NC transliterate the whole name, but NC also gives the meaning in parentheses.

LXX	Lord my refuge		
KJV	Jehovah-nissi	GNB	"The LORD is my Banner"
L	the *Lord is my banner	GN	"our standard is the *Lord"
SEG	the Eternal One is my banner		
BJ	Yahve-Nissi	FC	"the Lord is my standard"
NC	Yave nissi (Yave is my banner)		
VP	"The Lord is my banner"		

52. *yahweh raah* 'God the shepherd.'

52a. Ps 23:1: *yahweh raah*. Only LXX renders it as a verb, "shepherds," all the rest render it by the noun "shepherd."

LXX	Lord shepherds me		
KJV	the LORD is my shepherd	GNB	the LORD is my shepherd
L	the *Lord is my shepherd	GN	you, *Lord, are my shepherd
SEG	the Eternal One is my shepherd		
BJ	Yahve is my shepherd	FC	the Lord is my shepherd
NC	Yave is my shepherd	VP	the Lord is my shepherd

53. *yahweh rapha* 'God the healer.'

53a. Ex 15:26: I am *yahweh rapha*. All follow their normal rendering of *yahweh* and all translate *rapha* by its meaning, with some small differences.

LXX	*lord the healer of you		
KJV	the LORD that healeth thee		
GNB	the LORD, the one who heals you		
L	the *Lord, your doctor	GN	I, the *Lord, am your doctor
SEG	the Eternal One who heals you		
BJ	it is I, Yahve, who give you back your health		
FC	I am the Lord, the one who heals you		
NC	Yave, your healer	VP	the Lord, who heals you

54. *yahweh sebaoth/sabaoth* 'God the army/armies, host/hosts.'

54a. 1 Sam 1:3: *yahweh sebaoth* is victorious. BJ and NC transliterate the composite name, LXX and L only *sabaoth*; LXX, GN, and FC introduce "god"; KJV and SEG translate *sabaoth* literally; GN and FC merge it with another phrase in the verse; GNB and VP translate *sabaoth* as "almighty."

LXX	the *lord god sabaoth		
KJV	the LORD of hosts	GNB	the LORD Almighty
L	the *Lord Zebaoth	GN	the *Lord, the God of Israel
SEG	the Eternal One of the armies		
BJ	Yahve Sabaot	FC	the Lord God of Israel
NC	Yave Sabaot	VP	the Lord Almighty

54b. Zech 7:4: the word of *yahweh sabaoth* came. LXX introduces a new rendering "the mighty," others follow their normal rendering.

LXX	*lord the mighty		
KJV	the LORD of hosts	GNB	the LORD
L	*Lord Zebaoth	GN	the *Lord of the whole world
SEG	the Eternal One of the armies		
BJ	Yahve Sabaot	FC	the Lord of the universe
NC	Yave Sebaot	VP	the Lord almighty

54c. Is 3:15: saith *adonai yahweh sebaoth*. Only VP leaves out *adonai*, all others translate it "Lord"; most handle *yahweh sebaoth* as in the earlier examples, but LXX translates it "armies," while GN and FC use "God of the universe."

LXX	*lord lord of the armies	VP	the Lord Almighty
KJV	Lord GOD of hosts		
GNB	I, the Sovereign LORD Almighty		
L	the *Lord Lord Zebaoth		
GN	(Lord) the God of the entire world		
SEG	the Lord, the Eternal One of the armies		
BJ	Lord Yahve Sabaot		
FC	the Lord, the God of the universe		
NC	the Lord Yave Sebaot		

55. *yahweh elohim sebaoth/sabaoth* 'God the God of the army/armies, host/hosts.'

55a. Jer 38:17 (LXX 45:17): thus says *yahweh elohim sebaoth*, the *elohim* of Israel. LXX reduces the whole expression to "lord"; GNB and VP leave out *elohim*; others follow their standard renderings.

LXX	*lord # #
KJV	the LORD, the God of hosts, the God of Israel
GNB	the LORD # Almighty, the God of Israel
L	the *Lord, the God Zebaoth, the God of Israel
GN	the *God of Israel, the Lord of the world
SEG	the Eternal One, the God of the armies, the God of Israel
BJ	Yahve, the God Sabaoth, the God of Israel
FC	the Lord, God of the universe and God of Israel
NC	Yave Sebaot, the God of Israel
VP	the Lord # Almighty, the God of Israel

55b. Amos 5:14: *yahweh elohim sebaoth* be with you. LXX with "ruler of all" introduces a new way of translating *sebaoth*; GN returns to the "God of Israel" rendering here.

LXX	*lord the god the ruler of all VP the Lord, the God Almighty
KJV	the LORD, the God of hosts
GNB	the LORD God Almighty
L	*Lord, God Zebaoth
GN	Come to the *Lord...then the God of Israel will be with you
SEG	the Eternal One, the God of the armies
BJ	Yahve, God Sabaot
FC	the Lord, the God of the universe
NC	Yave Sebaot (v. 15: Yave, God Sebaot)

56. *yahweh shalom* 'God of peace.'

56a. Judg 6:24: called it *yahweh shalom*. LXX translates both but inverts the order; KJV and NC transliterate the composite name, while BJ transliterates only *yahweh*; FC stands out by making explicit the verb "give."

LXX	peace of the Lord		
KJV	Jehovah-shalom	GNB	"The LORD is Peace"
L	the *Lord is peace	GN	"the *Lord is peace"
SEG	the Eternal One peace		
BJ	Yahve-Peace	FC	"the Lord gives peace"
NC	Yave salom	VP	"The Lord is peace"

57. *yahweh shammah* 'God here/there (a specific place).'

57a. Ezek 48:35: the name of the city/place will be *yahweh shammah*. Translations differ in usage of "here" or "there"; LXX uses only a pronoun whose antecedent is "*lord god"; GNB transcribes the name in all capitals; GN uses "God" and follows a slightly different exegesis; only NC transliterates the whole name but it gives the meaning in parentheses.

LXX	(*lord god) his name is there		
KJV	the LORD is there	GNB	"The LORD-IS-HERE!"
L	the *Lord is here	GN	"the city of God"
SEG	the Eternal One is here		
BJ	"Yahve is there"	FC	"The Lord-is-there"
NC	Yave Samma (Yave is there)	VP	"The Lord is here"

58. *yahweh tsidkenu* 'righteous, righteousness.'

58a. Jer 23:6: call its name *yahweh tsidkenu*. LXX transliterates; translations vary greatly in their renderings: "righteousness," "salvation," "victory," "vindication," "justice."

LXX	*lord iosedek		
KJV	THE LORD IS OUR RIGHTEOUSNESS		
GNB	"the LORD Our Salvation"		
L	the *Lord our righteousness	GN	"The *Lord is our Salvation"
SEG	the Eternal One our justice	BJ	"Yahve-our-justice"
FC	the Lord is our vindicating judge		
NC	"yave Zidquenu": Yave our righteousness		
VP	'the Lord is our victory'		

59. *yahweh yireh* 'God sees, watches, provides.'

59a. Gen 22:14: called the name of the place *yahweh yireh*. KJV and SEG transliterate the whole name, BJ and NC only *yahweh*; LXX and L render *yireh* "sees," FC "watches," and all the others render it "provide." (VP, with "gives what is necessary," gives the meaning of provide.)

LXX	the Lord sees		
KJV	Jehovah-jireh	GNB	"the LORD Provides"
L	the *Lord sees	GN	"the *Lord provides"
SEG	Jehova-Jire	BJ	'Yahve provides'

FC	the Lord watches here/there
NC	Yave will provide
VP	'the Lord gives what is necessary'

Other Praise Names

60. *al* 'up, upwards.'

60a. Hos 7:16: they turn/return, but not to the *al*. There are some textual problems here, and at least two exegeses: that 'not upwards' means (1) to Baal or to vain idols, (2) to the Most High. LXX, NC, BJ, and VP follow the first exegesis; KJV, GN, SEG and FC follow the second; GNB tries to give both, while L focuses on an improper conversion change.

LXX	they turn to that which is nothing		
KJV	to the most High		
GNB	turning away from me to a god that is powerless		
L	they "convert" but not truly	GN	(the *Lord) not to me
SEG	to the Most-High	BJ	to Baal
FC	(the Lord) but not to me		
NC	to those who worship/serve nothing		
VP	to their idols (fn: textual problems)		

60b. Hos 11:7: to *al* they call. The Hebrew text is unclear as shown by the variant translations. Only KJV and SEG render it "Most High."

LXX	does not exalt him
KJV	to the Most High
GNB	because of the yoke that is on them (fn: Hebrew unclear)
L	no one lifts himself up
GN	because the yoke presses them (fn: upwards)
SEG	to the Most-High
BJ	one calls them from above
FC	one calls them to get up/arise
NC	the eyes of those who rise to them
VP	upwards

61. *kodesh* 'the most high'.

61a. Deut 32:8: when *kodesh* divided. Only GN and FC make explicit the implicit "God."

LXX	the *most high		
KJV	the Most High	GNB	the Most High
L	the Very *Highest	GN	the highest *God
SEG	the Most-High	BJ	the Most High
FC	the God Most-High		
NC	the Most High	VP	the Most High

61b. 2 Sam 22:14: *kodesh* uttered. Only the CL translations make the class noun explicit, VP by means of reducing a parallelism.

LXX	the *most high		
KJV	the most High	GNB	Almighty God
L	the *Highest	GN	the voice of the highest God

SEG	the Most-High	BJ	the Most High
FC	the God Most-High		
NC	the Most High	VP	the Lord, the Most High

Bibliography

Alexander, P. 1983. 3 (Hebrew Apocalypse of) Enoch. In Charlesworth, ed. 1983:223–316.

Alfrink, B. 1959. L'idée de résurrection d'après Daniel XII, 1–2. *Biblica* 40:369.

Anderson, F. I. 1983. 2 (Slavonic Apocalypse of) Enoch. In Charlesworth, ed. 1983:91–222.

Anderson, H. 1985. 3 Maccabees. In Charlesworth, ed. 1985: 509–723.

Ascham, John B. 1918. *The Religion of Israel*. New York: The Abingdon Press.

—. 1920. *The Religion of Judah*. New York: The Abingdon Press.

Ausubel, Nathan. 1964. *The Book of Jewish Knowledge*. New York: Crown Publishers.

Aytoun, R. A. 1923. *God in the Old Testament*. New York: George H. Doran.

Barrett, David B. 1968. *Schism and Renewal in Africa*. London: Oxford University Press.

Balasuriya, Tissa. 1977. *Eucharist and Human Liberation*. Colombo: Centre for Society and Religion Publications.

Berquist, Jon L. 1995. *Judaism in Persia's Shadow*. Minneapolis: Fortress Press.

Boorstin, Daniel J. 1983. *The Discoverers*. New York: Vintage Books.

Bousset, D. Wilhelm. 1926. *Die Religion des Judentums im Späthellenistischen Zeitalter*. Tübingen: Verlag von J. V. B. Mohr (Paul Stiebeck).

Boyce, M. 1975. *A History of Zoroastrianism*. Vol. 1: *The Early Period*. Leiden: Brill.

—. 1979. *Zoroastrians*. London: Routledge and Kegan Paul.

—. 1982. *A History of Zoroastrianism*. Vol. 2: *Under the Achæmenids*. Leiden: Brill.

—. 1984. Persian Religion in the Achæmenid Age. In Davies and Finkelstein, eds. 1984:279–307.

Bratcher, Robert G. 1975. "The Jews" in the Gospel of John. *The Bible Translator* 26.4:401–409.

Brown, F. R., S. R. Driver, and C. A. Briggs. 1978. *Hebrew and English Lexicon of the Old Testament*. London: Clarendon Press.

Bunknowske, Eugene. 1983. Personal communication.

Cardinall, A. W. 1970. *Tales Told in Togoland*. Westport: Negro Universities Press.

Charlesworth, J. H. 1983a. Editor's Preface. In Charlesworth, ed. 1983: xv–xvii.

—. 1983b. Introduction for the General Reader. In Charlesworth, ed. 1983:xxi–xxxiv.

—. 1985a. Odes of Solomon. In Charlesworth, ed. 1985:725–74.

—. 1985b. History of the Rechabites. In Charlesworth, ed. 1985:443–62.

—, ed. 1983. *The Old Testament Pseudepigrapha*. Vol. 1. New York: Doubleday.

—, ed. 1985. *The Old Testament Pseudepigrapha*. Vol. 2. New York: Doubleday.

Cleland, James T. 1983. Foreword for Christians. In Charlesworth, ed.1983:x–xi.

Codrington, R. H. 1965. Mana. In Lessa and Vogt 1965:255–57.

Coenen, Lothar, Erich Beyreuther, and Hans Bietenhard, eds. 1979. *Theologisches Begriffslexikon zum Neuen Testament*. 2 vols. Wuppertal, Germany: Theologischer Verlag R. Brockhaus.

Craigie, Peter C. 1978. *The Problem of War in the Old Testament*. Grand Rapids: W. B. Eerdmans.

Daneel, M. L. 1970. *The God of the Matopo Hills: An Essay on the Mwari Cult in Rhodesia*. The Hague: Mouton.

Daught, Gary F. 1993. Contradictions Do Not Make the Bible a House of Cards. *Mennonite Reporter* 23 (Nov 15):7.

Davies, John. 1971. *Moses and the Gods of Egypt*. Winona Lake, IN.: BMH Books.

Davies, W. D., and Louis Finkelstein, eds. 1984. *The Cambridge History of Judaism*. Vol. 1: *The Persian Period*. Cambridge: Cambridge University Press.

de Rosny, Eric. 1985. *Healers in the Night*. Maryknoll, NY.: Orbis Books.

Douglas, J. D., ed. 1974. *The New Bible Dictionary*. London: Intervarsity Press.

Douglas, Mary. 1985 [1966]. *Purity and Danger: An Analysis of the Concepts of Pollution and Taboo*. London: Ark Paperbacks.

Duling, D. C. 1983. Testament of Solomon. In Charlesworth, ed. 1983: 935–88.

Eichrodt, Walther. 1961. *Theology of the Old Testament*. 2 vols., 4th ed. Philadelphia: The Westminster Press.

Eliade, Mircea. 1978. *From the Stone Age to the Eleusinian Mysteries. A History of Religious Ideas*. Vol. 1. Chicago: University of Chicago Press.

—. 1982. *From Gautama Buddha to the Triumph of Christianity. A History of Religious Ideas*. Vol. 2. Chicago: University of Chicago Press.

Ellis, Alfred Burdon. 1966 [1890]. *The Ewe-speaking People of West Africa*. Oosterhout, Netherlands: Anthropological Publications.

Ellis, William. 1965. Tabu. In Lessa and Vogt, 1965:262–65.

Evans-Pritchard, E. E. 1967. Some Features of Nuer Religion. In Middleton, ed. 1967:133–58.

Fawcett, Thomas. 1971. *The Symbolic Language of Religion*. Minneapolis: Augsburg Publishing House.

Ferm, Vergilius. 1945. *An Encyclopedia of Religion*. New York: Philosophical Society.

Ferré, Frederick. 1983. Organizing Images and Scientific Ideals: Dual Sources for Contemporary Religious World Models. In van Noppen, ed. 1983:71–90.

Fiensy, D. A. 1983. Revelation of Ezra. In Charlesworth, ed. 1983:601–604.

Fosdick, Harry Emerson. 1941 [1924]. *The Modern Use of the Bible*. New York: The Macmillan Company.

Gaylord, H. E., Jr. 1983. 3 (Greek Apocalypse of) Baruch. In Charlesworth, ed. 1983:653–80.

Gottwald, Norman K. 1985a [1926]. *The Tribes of Yahweh*. Maryknoll, NY.: Orbis Books.

—.1985b. *The Hebrew Biblez: A Socio-literary Introduction*. Philadelphia: Fortress Press.

Goudzwaard, Bob. 1984. *Idols of Our Time*. Downer's Grove, IL.: Intervarsity Press.

Green, Jay, ed. 1976. *The Interlinear Hebrew-Greek-English Bible*. 4 vols. Wilmington: Associated Publishers and Authors.

Hammer, R. 1976. *The Book of Daniel*. London: Cambridge University Press.

Handy, E. C. S. 1965. Mana in Polynesia. In Lessa and Vogt 1965:257–62.

Hanson, Paul D. 1978. *Dynamic Transcendence*. Philadelphia: Fortress Press.

—.1986. *The People Called: The Growth of Community in the Bible*. New York: Harper Row.

Hare, D. R. A. 1985. The Lives of the Prophets. In Charlesworth, ed. 1985:379-400.

Hastings, James, ed. 1901–1907. *A Dictionary of the Bible*. 5 vols. New York: Charles Scribner's Sons.

Henning, W. B. 1951. *Zoroaster: Politician or Witch Doctor?* London: Oxford University Press.

Herskovitz, M. J. 1937. African Gods and Catholic Saints in New World Religious Belief. *American Anthropologist* 39:635–43.

Hinnells, J. R. 1969. Zoroastrian Saviour Imagery and Its Influence on the New Testament. *Numen* 16:164.

—.1973. *Persian Mythology*. London: Hamlyn.

—.1976. Zoroastrian Influence on the Judaeo-Christian Tradition. *Journal of the K. R. Cama Oriental Institute* 45:15.

—. 1981. *Zoroastrianism and the Parsis*. London: Ward Lock Educational.

Hultgård, A. 1979. *Das Judentum in der hellenistisch-römischen Zeit und die iranische Religion–ein religionsgeschichtliches Problem*. In Temporini and Hasse, eds. 1979 II.19.1:512–90.

Isaac, E. 1983. 1 (Ethiopic Apocalypse of) Enoch. In Charlesworth, ed. 1983:3–4.

Johnson, N. D. 1985. Life of Adam and Eve. In Charlesworth, ed. 1985: 249–96.

Jongmans, D. G., and P. C. W. Gutkind. 1967. *Anthropologists in the Field*. New York: Humanities Press.

Josephus, Flavius. N.d. *The Works of Flavius Josephus*. Philadelphia: David McKay, Publishers.

Kaiser, Walter C., Jr. 1978. *Toward an Old Testament Theology*. Grand Rapids, MI.: Zondervan Publishing House.

—.1987. *Toward Rediscovering the Old Testament*. Grand Rapids, MI.: Zondervan Publishing House.

Kaufman, Yehezkel. 1960. *The Religion of Israel: From Its Beginning to the Babylonian Exile*. New York: Schucken Books.

Kee, H. C. 1983. Testaments of the Twelve Patriarchs. In Charlesworth, ed. 1983:775–828.

Klijn, A. F. J. 1983. 2 (Syriac Apocalypse of) Baruch. In Charlesworth, ed. 1983:615–52.

Knibb, M. A. 1985. Martyrdom and Ascension of Isaiah. In Charlesworth, ed. 1985:143–76.

Knight, Douglas A. and Gene M. Tucker, eds. 1985. *The Hebrew Bible and Its Modern Interpreters*. Philadelphia: Fortress Press and Chico, CA.: Scholars Press.

Koyama, Kosuke. 1982. Tribal Gods or Universal God. *Missionalia* 10.3:106–12.

—.1984. *Mount Fuji and Mount Sinai*. London: SCM Press Ltd.

Kraybill, D. B. 1978. *The Upside-down Kingdom*. Scottdale: Herald Press.

Lanternari, Vittorio. 1963. *The Religions of the Oppressed: A Study of Modern Messianic Cults*. New York: The New American Library of World Literature.

Lederman, Leon, and Dick Teresi. 1993. *The God Particle: If the Universe is the Answer, What Is the Question?* New York: Bantam Doubleday Dell Publishing Group.

Lessa, W. A., and E. Z. Vogt, eds. 1965. *Reader in Comparative Religion*. 2nd ed. New York: Harper and Row Publishers.

Lewis, C. S. 1946. *The Great Divorce*. New York: The Macmillan Co.

Loewen, Jacob A. 1961. Good News for the Waunana. *Practical Anthropology* 8:275–78.

—.1962. A Choco Indian in Hillsboro, Kansas. *Practical Anthropology* 9:129–33.

—.1964a. Culture, Meaning and Translation. *The Bible Translator* 15:189–94.

—.1964b. Reciprocity in Identification. *Practical Anthropology* 11:145–60.

—.1965a. Mennonites, Chaco Indians, and the Lengua Spirit World. *Mennonite Quarterly Review* (October):280–306.

—.965b. Mennonite Encounter with the "Innermost" of the Lengua Indians. *Mennonite Quarterly Review* 39:40–67.

—.1967. *The Christian Encounter with Culture*. Monrovia, CA.: World Vision International.

—.1969. Myth and Mission: Should a Missionary Study Tribal Myths? *Practical Anthropology* 16:147–85.

—.1975. *Culture and Human Values: Christian Intervention in Anthropological Perspective*. Pasadena, CA.: William Carey Press.

—.1976. Mission Churches, Independent Churches, and Felt Need in Africa. *Missiology* 4:405–25.

—.1981. *The Practice of Translating*. New York: United Bible Societies.

—.1983a. The Function of Metaphors in Religious Communication. Unpublished.

—.1983b. Clean Air or Bad Breath? *The Bible Translator* 34:213–19.

—.1984. The Names of God. *The Bible Translator* 35:201–11.

—.1985a. Translating the Names of God: How to Choose the Right Name in the Target Language. *The Bible Translator* 36:201–207.

—.1985b. Translating the Names of God: How European Languages Translated Them. *The Bible Translator* 36:401–11.

—.1986a. The German Language, Culture and the Faith. Paper presented at the Mennonite Brethren Study Conference, Winnipeg, November 13–14.

—.1986b. Which God do Missionaries Preach? *Missiology* 14:3–19.

—.1988. Demon Possession and Exorcism in Africa, in the New Testament Context and in North America. In Swartley, ed. 1988:118–45.

—.1995. The Hopi "Old Testament": A First-Person Essay. *Missiology* 23.2: 145–54.

Loewen, Jacob A., Albert Buchwalter, and James Kratz. 1965. Shamanism, Illness, and Power in Toba Church Life. *Practical Anthropology* 12: 250–80.

Loewen, Jacob A., and Wesley J. Prieb. I.p. *Only the Sword of the Spirit!* Fresno, CA.: Mennonite Brethren Historical Society.

MacCormac, Earl R. 1983. Religious Metaphors: Linguistic Expressions of Cognitive Processes. In van Noppen, ed. 1983:47–70.

MacRae, George W. 1983a. Foreword. In Charlesworth, ed. 1983:ix–x.

—.1983b. Apocalypse of Adam. In Charlesworth, ed. 1983:707–709.

Madsen, William. 1957. *Christo-Paganism: A Study of Mexican Religious Syncretism.* New Orleans: Middle American Research Institute.

Martin, Malachi. 1976. *Hostage to the Devil.* New York: Reader's Digest Press.

Mayer, R. 1956. *Die Biblische Vorstellung vom Welten Brand.* Bonn: Orientalisches Seminar der Universität Bonn.

Metzger, B. M. 1983. The Fourth Book of Ezra. In Charlesworth, ed. 1983:517–60.

Middleton, John, ed. 1967. *Gods and Rituals.* Garden City, NY.: The Natural History Press.

Milingo, E. 1984. *The World in Between.* Maryknoll, NY.: Orbis Books.

Moberly, R. W. L. 1992. *The Old Testament of the Old Testament.* Minneapolis: Fortress Press.

Moltmann, J. 1977. *The Church in the Power of the Spirit: A Contribution to Messianic Ecclesiology.* New York: Harper and Row.

Mueller, J. R., and G. A. Robbins. 1983. Vision of Ezra. In Charlesworth, ed. 1983:581–90.

Mueller, J. R., and S. E. Robinson. 1983. Apocryphon of Ezekiel. In Charlesworth, ed. 1983:487–96.

Murdock, George Peter. 1934. *Our Primitive Contemporaries.* New York: The Macmillan Company.

Naroll, Raoul. 1983. *The Moral Order.* Beverly Hills: Sage Publications.

Nicklesburg, G. W. E. 1972. *Resurrection, Immortality, and Eternal Life in Intertestamental Judaism.* Cambridge, MA.: Harvard University Press.

Nida, Eugene A. 1961. *Bible Translating.* London: United Bible Societies.

—. 1964. *Toward a Science of Translating.* Leiden: E. J. Brill.

—. 1968. *Religion Across Cultures.* New York: Harper and Row.

Nida, Eugene A., and Charles R. Taber. 1969. *The Theory and Practice of Translation.* Leiden: E. J. Brill for the United Bible Societies.

Nidich, Susan. 1985. Legends of Wise Heroes and Heroines. In Knight and Tucker, eds., 1985:445–64.

Niebuhr, H. R. 1943. *Radical Monotheism and Western Culture.* New York: Harper Torchbooks.

—. 1951. *Christ and Culture.* New York: Harper and Brothers.

Peck, M. Scott. 1978. *The Road Less Traveled.* New York: Simon and Schuster.

—. 1983. *People of the Lie.* New York: Simon and Schuster.

Phillips, J. B. 1952. *Your God Is Too Small*. London: Epworth Press.

Pobee, John S. 1979. *Toward an African Theology*. Nashville: Abingdon Press.

Priestly, J. 1983. Testament of Moses. In Charlesworth, ed. 1983:919–34.

Radcliffe-Brown, A. R., and Daryll Forde. 1950. *African Systems of Kinship and Marriage*. London: Oxford University Press.

Reyburn, William D. 1958. The Missionary and Cultural Diffusion. Part 1. *Practical Anthropology* 5:141.

—. 1967a. Polygamy, Economy, and Christianity in the Eastern Cameroun. In Smalley, ed. 1967:65–83.

—. 1967b. The Missionary and the Evaluation of Culture. In Smalley, ed. 1967:258–61.

Ricard, Robert. 1966. *The Spiritual Conquest of Mexico*. Berkeley, Los Angeles: University of California Press.

Ringgren, Helmer. 1980. *Israelite Religion*. Philadelphia: Fortress Press.

Robinson, John A. T. 1963. *Honest to God*. Philadelphia: The Westminster Press.

Robinson, S. E. 1983. Testament of Adam. In Charlesworth, ed. 1983:989–95.

Rosenberg, David, and Harold Bloom. 1990. *The Book of J*. New York: Grove Weidenfeld.

Rosin, Hellmut. 1956. *The Lord Is God*. Amsterdam: Nederlandsch Bijbelgenootschap.

Rubinkiewicz, R. 1983. Apocalypse of Abraham. In Charlesworth, ed. 1983: 681–706.

Russell, Bertrand. 1961. *Religion and Science*. New York: Oxford University Press.

Sanders, E. P. 1983a. Testaments of the Three Patriarchs. In Charlesworth, ed. 1983:869–70.

—. 1983b. Testament of Abraham. In Charlesworth, ed. 1983:871–902.

Sandmel, Samuel. 1983. Foreword for Jews. In Charlesworth, ed. 1983:xi–xiii.

Sanneh, Lamin. 1989. *Translating the Message: The Missionary Impact on Culture*. Maryknoll, NY.: Orbis Books.

Schmidt, Wilhelm. 1965. The Nature, Attributes and Worship of the Primitive High God. In Lessa and Vogt, eds. 1965:21–33.

Setiloane, G. M. 1976. *The Image of God Among the Sotho-Tswana*. Rotterdam: A. A. Balkema.

Shaked, S. 1984. *Iranian Influence on Judaism*. In Davies and Finkelstein, eds. 1984:308–25.

Shutt, R. J. H. 1985. Letter of Aristeas. In Charlesworth, ed. 1985:5–6, 7–34.

Skinner, Elliott P. 1967. Christianity and Islam Among the Mossi. In Middleton 1967:353–76.

Skinner, John. 1963. *A Critical and Exegetical Commentary on Genesis*. Edinburgh: T. and T. Clark.

Smalley, William A. 1994. *Linguistic Diversity and National Unity: Language Ecology in Thailand*. Chicago: University of Chicago Press.

—, ed. 1978. *Readings in Missionary Anthropology II*. Pasadena, CA.: William Carey Library.

Smalley, William A., Chia Koua Vang, and Gnia Yee Yang. 1990. *Mother of*

Writing: The Origin and Development of a Hmong Messianic Script. Chicago: University of Chicago Press.

Songer, H. 1967. Demonic Possession and Mental Illness. *Religion in Life* 36:119–27.

Spittler, R. P. 1983. Testament of Job. In Charlesworth, ed. 1983:829–68.

Stinespring, W. F. 1983. Testament of Isaac. In Charlesworth, ed. 1983:913–18.

Stone, M. E. 1983a. Greek Apocalypse of Ezra. In Charlesworth, ed. 1983:561–80.

—. 1983b. Questions of Ezra. In Charlesworth, ed. 1983:591–600.

Swartley, Willard M., ed. 1988. *Essays on Spiritual Bondage and Deliverance.* Occasional Papers of the Institute of Mennonite Studies 11.

Temporini, Hildegard, and Wolfgang Hasse, eds. 1979. *Aufstieg und Niedergang der Römischen Welt.* Berlin: Walter de Gruyter.

Tillich, Paul. 1953 [1951]. *Systematic Theology.* London: James Nisbet.

Titiev, Mischa. 1963. *The Science of Man.* Revised and enlarged ed. New York: Holt, Rinehart and Winston.

Tucker, Gene M. 1985. Prophesy and the Prophetic Literature. In Knight and Tucker, eds. 1985:325–68.

van der Horst, P. W. 1983. Pseudo-Phocylides. In Charlesworth, ed. 1985:565–82.

van Noppen, J. P., ed. 1983. *Metaphor and Religion: Theolinguistics 2.* Brussels: Wettelijk Depot.

Venberg, Rodney. 1971. The Problem of a Female Deity in Translation. *The Bible Translator* 22:68–70.

von Rad, Gerhard. 1962a. *Genesis.* Philadelphia: The Westminster Press.

—. 1962b. *Old Testament Theology.* Vol. 1. London: Oliver and Boyd.

—. 1965. *Old Testament Theology.* Vol. 2. London: Oliver and Boyd.

Walsh, Brian J., and J. Richard Middleton. 1953. *The Transforming Vision: Shaping a Christian World View.* Downers Grove, IL.: InterVarsity Press.

Ward, Keith. 1974. *The Concept of God.* New York: Collins Fountain Paperbacks.

White, John. 1979. *The Golden Cow.* Downers Grove, IL.: InterVarsity Press.

—. 1987. Spiritual Oppression, Mental Illness and the Christian Response. Four lectures presented in the Brighouse United Church, Richmond, British Columbia, January 30–31.

Wiebe, Rudy. 1962a. *Peace Shall Destroy Many.* Aylesbury, England: Watson and Viney.

—. 1962b. Petronius and His Pew Pals. *Mennonite Brethren Herald* 1.1 (Jan 19):2.

—. 1962c. Peter's Corner. *Mennonite Brethren Herald* 1.14 (Apr 19):2; 1.15 (Apr 27):2.

Wink, Walter. 1984. *Naming the Powers: The Language of Power in the New Testament.* Philadelphia: Fortress Press.

—. 1986. *Unmasking the Powers: The Invisible Forces that Determine Human Experience.* Philadelphia: Fortress Press.

—. 1992. *Engaging the Powers: Discernment and Resistance in a World of Domination.* Minneapolis: Fortress Press.

Winston, David. 1966. The Iranian Component in the Bible, Apocrypha, and Qumran: A Review of the Evidence. *History of Religion* 5:180–213.

Wintermute, O. S. 1983. Apocalypse of Elijah. In Charlesworth, ed. 1983: 721–54.

—. 1985. Jubilees. In Charlesworth, ed. 1985:35–142.

Wright, Michael A. 1978. Some Observations on Thai Animism. In Smalley, ed. 1978:115–21.

Wright, R. B. 1985. Psalms of Solomon. In Charlesworth, ed. 1985:639–70.

Yamauchi, Edwin M. 1990. *Persia and the Bible*. Grand Rapids: Baker Book House.

Yarshatere, Ehsan, ed. 1983. *The Cambridge History of Iran*. Vol. 3. *The Seleucid, Parthian and Sisernian Period*. Cambridge: Cambridge University Press.

—, ed. 1985. *The Cambridge History of Iran*. Vol. 2. *The Median and Achæmenian Periods*. Cambridge: Cambridge University Press.

Zervos, G. T. 1983. Apocalypse of Daniel. In Charlesworth, ed. 1983:755–72.

Index of References
to Ancient Documents

Index of Subjects

The once fiercely independent Tiger—nickname for Jake by the Choco Indians—reduced to a wheelchair and dependency, first by a stroke in 1993 and in 1999 by a broken hip. He considers this book as his last testament to all his missionary colleagues. With him his ever-loving wife, Anne.

Biography

Jacob Loewen's journey in missions began pretty well at his birth in Russia in 1922. His mother, widowed one month after Jake was born, dedicated him to missionary service when he was a tiny sickly infant. Afterwards the family immigrated to Canada in 1930. Although he did not formally finish high school, due to the financial straits of his family, he was able to attend a Bible school and earned a high school equivalency certificate. He attended the Missionary Medical Institute in Toronto, Canada, in 1942–1943 to learn missionary medicine. He also attended the Summer Institute of Linguistics (Wycliffe Bible Translators) in Briercrest, Saskatchewan. In 1945 Loewen was married to Anne Enns. They began married life at Tabor College in Hillsboro, Kansas. He received a Bachelor of Arts degree in humanities in 1947, and in December of that year he and Anne were sent to Colombia, South America, as Mennonite Brethren missionaries.

The Loewens served in Colombia until 1957 with a two-year furlough to the States in 1953–1955, during which time Jake studied anthropology at the University of Washington. Because of the severe religious persecution in Colombia, they were recalled to the States in 1957. Loewen finished his Ph.D. at the University of Washington and was then appointed a professor of anthropology and modern languages at Tabor College. During the summers, he worked among the Waunan in Panama.

In 1964 Loewen began working with the American Bible Society in South America. He trained translators, consulted on translation problems, and supervised Bible translation quality throughout the continent. In this role he experimented with training mother-tongue speakers as translators, with the consent of his supervisor, Eugene Nida. When he reported on this process at a workshop in Spain in 1969, Third World representatives urged that mother-tongue translation become a worldwide Bible Society policy.

In the summer of 1970 Loewen taught at the Muslim University of Mashad, Iran. That September, the United Bible Societies (the world fellowship of national Bible societies) decided that Africa was ready for mother-tongue translators. Loewen was made responsible for Central Africa: Angola, Zambia, Malawi, Zimbabwe, and Mozambique, with

333

some advisory responsibility in South Africa. Finally, in 1979–1984 he served as translation consultant in West Africa, responsible for Ghana, Benin, Niger, Burkina Faso, and Togo. By the time Loewen retired in 1984 he had worked with several hundred different languages.

Since his retirement he has served in a number of short-term overseas assignments, such as facilitating reconciliation after a church split in India, helping Mennonite workers with the Kekchi Indians in Guatemala, and doing a survey of the Hopi mission situation in Arizona. In spite of a stroke in 1993, he is able to write with his left hand and employs a part-time secretary to help him continue his research.

From all his missionary experiences Loewen learned that God was at work in the various cultures of the world long before the first missionary came and would still be working after the last missionary left.